THE JEZEBEL VIRUS

FINDING FREEDOM FROM SPIRITUAL ABUSE

TIM HOWARD

Scriptures marked NIV are taken from the NEW INTERNATIONAL VERSION (NIV): Scripture taken from THE HOLY BIBLE, NEW INTERNATIONAL VERSION ®. Copyright© 1973, 1978, 1984, 2011 by Biblica, Inc.™. Used by permission of Zondervan

The Jezebel Virus: Finding Freedom from Spiritual Abuse
Copyright © 2019 Tim Howard

Interior and Cover design by: Pine Hill Graphics

Published by ACW Press
PO Box 110390
Nashville, Tennessee 37222
www.acwpress.com

The views expressed or implied in this work do not necessarily reflect those of ACW Press. Ultimate design, content, and editorial accuracy of this work is the responsibility of the author(s).

All rights reserved. No part of this publication may be reproduced, stored in a retrieval system, or transmitted in any form or by any means—electronic, mechanical, photocopy, recording or any other—except for brief quotations in printed reviews, without the prior written permission of the authors.

Printed in the United States of America.

Every leader needs to read this book. And especially every Senior Pastor. I promise if you do, your staff will thank you. It has already changed not just how I lead, but it has actually changed my team because I have learned how to listen to them and to now recognize the Jezebel spirit. I can't thank Tim Howard enough for writing this! It has been a game changer for me!

        Kirk Proctor, Senior Pastor, Faith Church, Lansing, MI

Tim Howard's take on *The Jezebel Virus* is an eye-opening exposé of a deadly virus plaguing leaders in our culture. To have someone call this has been rare through the years. The leader influenced by the Jezebel Virus slowly weaves a web of manipulation and slowly the destruction begins. Tim's exposure of this spirit will encourage those who have found themselves in situations being led by a *Jezebel* leader or help bring correction to those who have led in this manner. *The Jezebel Virus* is a "cannot-put-down" book that will encourage you.

        Rod Querry, Executive Leadership Coach, The Arcue Group

With a pastor's heart and a warrior's cry, Tim Howard exposes our enemy and his tactics to "steal, kill and destroy" the church. With full reliance on the life-giving power of the gospel, and God's unfailing grace, Tim's heart and story is on full display. May this book strengthen and encourage you, as it has for me, and our church.

        Chad Rush, Director of Healing Ministries, Watermark Church

So enlightening, so practical and so biblical! This book has brought added freedom to me personally, as well as our entire Wellsprings team.

        Larry Johnson, Pastor to the Seniors, Central Wesleyan Church

The spirit of Jezebel is plaguing our churches. This book gives us an accurate guide for detecting and navigating abusive leadership. A must read for church leaders at all levels.

            Dan Shows, President, Shows Coaching

Some subjects are so difficult to approach that we tend to sweep them under a rug and act as if nothing is wrong. But if you are in ministry leadership long enough, you will encounter the mysterious dimensions of unhealthy power and control. This book brings light, not only to the spiritual dynamics of "control and manipulation", but also provides excellent practical information about how to break free from its grip.

         Dwayne Brothers, Senior pastor, The GatheringQC Church

With in-depth spiritual knowledge and the heart of a familiar friend, Tim Howard delivers the most comprehensive guide to the *Jezebel Virus* that is overtaking churches, ministries, and non-profit organizations across the world. This must-read book exposes the controlling, intimidating, and destructive patterns of Jezebel-led leaders and provides a strategic cure for breaking the chains of Jezebel's control.

       Bryan Todd Savage, Senior Pastor, Greenville Community Church

Acknowledgements

The concepts for this book are the result of years of observation, leading freedom sessions, conversations with wounded leaders, and research. My travels to hundreds of churches in the United States and all across the world have given me the unique perspective to write this book, and I am grateful to God for the privilege of helping set captives free. I also am grateful to the many who have stood by my side in this journey.

Especially I would like to thank my wife, Gracie, for her patience with me, and her support of me. There were countless nights where my mind was in a state of deep reflection, and not as present with her as I should have been. I love you and am deeply grateful for your understanding.

I also would like to thank my good friend, David, who spent many hours with me discussing the concepts of this book. His input kept me balanced and on target. He also spent hours and hours reading and rereading the content to help me stay focused and on mission.

I wish to thank the many who contributed to this project and for their immeasurable assistance in writing this book. I am so very blessed to work with the amazing staff at Wellsprings of Freedom, who on countless occasions have prayed over me, encouraged me, and cheered me on to finish this project. To our president, Rev. Brian Burke, thank you for nearly fifteen years of friendship and support.

I am also grateful for the multitudes of wounded brothers and sisters in Christ who willingly stepped forward to share their painful interactions with Jezebel-led individuals and environments. Though their stories may not be in this book, their combined experiences gave me the insight I needed to see behavioral patterns and tendencies associated with the Jezebel spirit. And last, but not least, I am grateful to all of our Wellsprings team members scattered throughout the world, who regularly tell me that they are upholding me in prayer. This book is a result of your prayers. I deeply appreciate all of you.

Table of Contents

Foreword 9
Introduction. 11
1. The Jezebel Virus. 15
2. What Are the Symptoms of the Jezebel Virus? 31
3. Jezebel—Under the Spiritual Microscope 57
4. The Tenacity of Jezebel 79
5. How Jezebel Affects the Team 95
6. Understanding and Interacting with Jezebel's Host 111
7. Ahab 135
8. How Jezebel Destroys the Organization 155
9. Hope for the Jezebel Host 175
10. Protection Against the Jezebel Virus 207
11. Answering the "Why" Questions 223
12. You're Not Crazy 245

    Bibliography. 271

Foreword

Over the last few years, I have watched numerous well-known pastors in the United States fall from grace and lose their credibility as church leaders. Gifted leaders and dynamic communicators who once led large, thriving congregations and organizations were suddenly exposed and forced to resign. Allegations of spiritual abuse, control, intimidation, financial mismanagement, and abuse of power have been brought to light and made public. Independent investigations have been commissioned to confirm these grievous accusations. In the process, thousands of "wounded warriors" have left their beloved churches as spiritual casualties of war.

For most Christians living in North America, there are *natural* explanations for such tragedies in the church and non-profit world. We blame things such as lack of accountability, insufficient organizational guidelines and policies, and/or a "corporate culture." While all of these things may in fact be true, I believe there is an additional component at work behind the scenes in the unseen realm – a *supernatural* explanation for why anointed pastors, board members, non-profit leaders, and accomplished businesspeople and managers become so abusive toward those under their authority. I call it the "Jezebel" influence.

In this book, *The Jezebel Virus*, Pastor Tim Howard does a masterful job at exposing the Jezebel spirit and painting a picture of how this destructive and divisive evil spirit infects relationships and entire organizations. These leadership insights aren't written by an inexperienced by-stander, but by a seasoned business manager, pastor, and non-profit leader who has lived and seen firsthand the damaging effects of what a Jezebel-led leader can do to those around them. This is a book written "from the trenches," designed to better equip leaders with the tools necessary to put an end to the cycles of abuse that sabotage organizations.

It is important to note that this book is not intended to indict any one particular individual, leader, church, or group. The author has gone to great lengths to protect the identity and privacy of any employer or organization whom he has observed or encountered throughout his lifetime. The sole intent of *The Jezebel Virus* is to help readers understand how the Jezebel spirit enters in, takes root, and slowly begins to wrap its controlling tentacles around an entire church or organization.

Rev. Brian S. Burke
President
Wellsprings of Freedom International
Fall, 2019

Introduction

This book is about the spiritual abuse many of us have experienced at the hand of a person or persons controlled by a Jezebel spirit. I have focused mostly on how this spirit attacks churches and nonprofits, but I'm fully aware of how this spirit also wreaks havoc on marriages and other relationships. Because the church is where people go for hope and healing, it makes sense that the enemy would want to infiltrate and undermine our beloved institutions. When the very place we go to for help is in fact a place where deep wounds are inflicted, our wounds are compounded and a foreboding emptiness settles into our heart. Slowly, those wounded by controlling and manipulating church leaders begin to drift away. Some find their way into another church where they may attend, but the wounds of mistrust keep them from serving. Others just disappear into an isolationist faith that believes in God from the safety and comfort of their own home. In both cases, highly gifted people who were created to bless the body of Christ are rendered useless for years, or perhaps the rest of their lives.

My intention for writing this book is to expose the Jezebel spirit and awaken the body of Christ to its destructive behaviors. Jezebel's influence is not limited to just clergy; it can also be found in board members, staff members, spouses, employees, friends, denominational leaders, mentors, parents, small group leaders, and financial partners. Wherever a new or successful work of God is underway, you can expect a spirit of Jezebel to attempt to infiltrate the organization. Abusive patterns of behavior are not necessarily always from the leadership down; they can be found at all levels. Pastors have been secretly sabotaged by board members or influential church members. Employees within departments can be manipulated and controlled by other employees. Mid-level staff members can try to take down the leader or are abusive to those under their supervision. Certainly, top level leaders are influenced by Jezebel to abuse others, or are controlled by a Jezebel-led person to cause damage to people and organizations.

All scenarios where Jezebel exists cause harm and destruction. I'm convinced if we know what to look for, if we can recognize the destructive patterns of Jezebel, we can thwart most of Jezebel's diabolical schemes. However, Jezebel is a slippery deceiving spirit that either manipulates or dominates people into submission. It knows how to survive even when it is under scrutiny, and typically escapes all blame for bad behavior. Unfortunately, those who are being abused, or those trying to point out the abuse, are the ones usually forced out of the organization—thus, allowing the abusive behavior to continue and even escalate to higher levels.

Because of the confusion that swirls around most Jezebel-influenced environments, things can become very chaotic. It can seem almost impossible to navigate a path through the uncharted waters of dysfunction. I hope that by uncovering the tactics used by Jezebel, all involved will find some level of assistance from this book. I have tried to provide helpful options for those being abused, those wanting to stop the abuse, those supporting the abusive person, and even a way out for the Jezebel-led abuser. Environments controlled by Jezebel are difficult to manage even when you know what is happening. Trying to do so without any understanding will make you think you are losing your sanity. This book will provide compass-like insight and wisdom to guide you on your journey. It cannot, however, guarantee smooth passage. The freewill decisions of those around you will partially impact the outcome of your immediate journey. But your own freewill decisions give you ultimate control of your future.

Writing a book of this nature certainly has its challenges. Sometimes in order to get a clearer picture of how the spirit of Jezebel operates, God positions you to see things, or experience things firsthand. Throughout my life, I have either personally experienced the hurt and pain of this spirit, or have been placed next to others who are enduring their own version of an abusive Jezebel environment. Experiencing it up close and personal is no picnic; it is a painful journey. But I believe it was necessary. It allowed me to zoom in and gather insights that I would have otherwise missed. I suspect those who read this book and are living in a Jezebel-controlled environment will find a version of their story in the book. On the other hand, those who are abusively controlling others will dislike the book, and will hold on to their excuses for why it is appropriate to control other people. It usually falls along the line of everything is permissible as long as the cause of Christ is advanced. In other words, it is mission over character. Seldom are they able to see how their control is wounding people and slowly destroying the organization. They typically cannot see that the cause of Christ is not attained through the spiritual abuse of other believers. I pray their eyes will be opened.

There is a common misconception about the spirit of Jezebel. It is the notion that because Jezebel in the Bible is a woman, this spirit is limited to attacking women. That is not true. The Jezebel spirit attacks both men and women and uses them for its destructive purposes. Being an ordained minister in The Wesleyan Church, I wholeheartedly agree with our denominational viewpoint that fully promotes women in ministry. As you read this book, you may find similarities with a current person in your life, or be reminded of different individuals from the past who have harmfully manipulated and controlled you. Both men and women are capable of such behavior. When you read the name Jezebel, or Jezebel-led person, I am referring to a demonic spirit, and/or the man or woman it uses to accomplish its mission to destroy. I urge you to not associate this spirit with women only.

This book is the accumulation of nearly twenty years of observation and research. There are no concepts presented in this book that stem from one single event or institution. Each Jezebel characteristic and behavioral pattern presented had to have corroborating examples from other books and/or testimonies from multiple individuals and varying locations before being placed in the book. Because of the nature of our ministry at Wellsprings of Freedom, we get numerous calls every week from churches all around the world who are seeking advice on how to deal with the Jezebel spirit. Each situation is different, but the demonic spirit of Jezebel operates the same way no matter the language or setting. For whatever reason, the Jezebel spirit seems to be spreading at an alarming rate. As you read the many testimonies and stories presented in this book, you will see they each come from a wide range of settings, some secular and some church related. It was the growing number of inquiries about the Jezebel spirit that led to our decision to write a book.

Chapter 1

The Jezebel Virus

Definition: A virus is a small infectious agent that can only replicate itself inside the cells of another organism.

It can happen anywhere. An infectious viral agent is introduced into a body of people and nearly the entire group can become infected. Our first thought might be to think the communicable agent to be some sort of disease or cold virus being spread from person to person. It's easy for us to think that way because most of us have been exposed to viruses that have affected us physically. However, there is another form of viral agent that becomes planted within organizations, and this one attacks us in a totally different way. It is an agent that, once it is fully released within an organization, has the potential to cause unimaginable destruction. In fact, its sole purpose is to destroy. This silent agent is rarely uncovered until it has unleashed its fury upon a whole group of unsuspecting and innocent people. Churches, nonprofits, businesses, professional agencies, hospitals, factories, offices, and departments of all sizes can be affected. Professional staff, administrative staff, creative teams, and high performing teams can all become negatively touched or influenced by this agent of destruction. Though no one single person or organization is immune, churches, church organizations, nonprofits, mission agencies, mission fields, and para church organizations largely seem to be the target.

The silent agent infecting our churches and ministries is called the Jezebel spirit. The existence of this spirit is probably not an entirely new concept to many of you. Yet, churches and ministries all over the world continue to be controlled, hindered, held captive, divided, and destroyed by this spirit. As I have been studying and observing the effects of this spirit for over twenty years, I have found that it has a way of tainting or infecting nearly everything it touches in one way or another. It truly is like a virus being released within our midst, and that is why I have entitled this book *The Jezebel Virus*.

Just as the easy-to-recognize symptoms of a cold virus spreads from one person to another, so do the symptoms of the Jezebel virus within an organization. With a cold, people experience fevers, headaches, chills, runny noses, coughing, sneezing, sore throats, and several other unpleasant side effects. With the Jezebel virus, the symptoms are not as much physical as they are mental. Some of the classic signs of the Jezebel virus in your organization may include feelings of heaviness, frustration, hopelessness, and manipulation. You may feel controlled, bullied, unheard, devalued, pushed out, unimportant, fearful, and unappreciated. In addition, it is not uncommon to feel like you are losing your mind, but you can't quite put your finger on why. Chaos, busyness, and an unshakable inability to ever be or feel good enough, are normal parts of your daily routine. Those who are infected by the Jezebel virus will become very unhappy with their jobs, even though they love the work they are doing. It isn't the actual job itself that brings despair, it's the atmosphere and surroundings of your work environment.

Sadly, for many, there was a time when you loved your job and your work environment. It wasn't until someone got a promotion, transferred into the department, or was just hired that things began to change. Within weeks or months, the whole atmosphere slowly changed into something almost unrecognizable. The job you used to love and looked forward to going to each day somehow turned into a pit of despair. It is possible your department was already struggling with these things before you were hired, but you didn't know that until you started working there.

The truth is that almost anywhere there is a Jezebel spirit, and a person who is highly influenced by a Jezebel spirit, relationships and organizations around that individual will begin to crumble. It may not happen right away, but over the course of time things just begin to come unraveled. Not every problem found within an organization is caused by a Jezebel spirit. There are many reasons why organizations fail. But there are some recognizable patterns that may indicate a Jezebel spirit is at work trying to lead your department or organization into a destructive tailspin. Phone calls and conversations with people from all across our country confirm this to be true. This is why the Jezebel spirit works very hard to invade churches and ministries. Its goal or mission is to destroy and take out whatever it can! Even if it is only a single department, it will do so. If it can take out a small group, or a Bible study, it will not hesitate. Because it is a demonic spirit, or a fallen angel who works for Satan, it is more than capable of scheming and devising plans to do great harm. It is well aware that by attacking the organization at the highest levels it can achieve the greatest amount of destruction. So, Jezebel will do its best to set its sights on the uppermost leadership team.

I'm convinced that if a church or an organization can learn in advance what the symptoms of a Jezebel virus look like, they can protect themselves before things get too far out of hand. In Ephesians 6:12, we are told that our struggle is not against flesh and blood, but against the rulers, authorities, and powers of this dark world. Unfortunately, trying to deal with this force of evil after the fact is very challenging and difficult. Jezebel is capable of unbelievable deception, destruction, division, discouragement, and disunity. All too often the damage wrought by this spirit cannot be easily undone. It typically attaches itself to a human being and works through that individual to accomplish its mission. Only by knowing how it works and catching it as early as possible will you be able to minimize the damage. The longer a Jezebel spirit is able to entrench itself into a body of people, the greater its ability to negatively influence people and protect itself from being removed. It's not that much different with a cold virus or another type of virus, and the best-case scenario is to keep the virus away, period.

Common Characteristics of Jezebel

Before we go much further, I think it will be helpful for us to have a basic idea of what the Jezebel spirit looks like. Later in this book we will take a much deeper look at many of the things a Jezebel spirit does within an organization. However, to help us get better acquainted with Jezebel and its tendencies, and to know if it is present in our organization, here is a list of the most common characteristics. These characteristics are often displayed by the person the Jezebel spirit is using to bring destruction. Jezebel attaches to humans and every human is different. No two people being influenced by this spirit will act exactly the same way. There will be some who will exhibit many of the characteristics listed, while others only a few. And the characteristics can vary between men and women. It is important to not assume that a person harboring one of the characteristics is controlled by Jezebel. We should expect a Jezebel-led person to demonstrate a pattern of exhibiting several of the following characteristics:

- Controlling
- Dictatorial
- Creates an atmosphere of chaos and confusion
- Defensive
- Refuses to submit to any authority
- Manipulating—tears, anger, guilt, flattery, fear, favors
- Demands respect with no intention of earning it
- Always right—never wrong
- False prophetic voice—but think their gift is higher than anyone else's
- Will blatantly lie to protect their image, position, or mission
- Highly critical of others—but they themselves cannot receive correction
- Impossible to please
- Creates division through deception
- No remorse for how they treat people
- False humility
- Emotional outbursts and temper tantrums
- Prideful
- Can seldom say "I'm sorry" and mean it
- Forms unhealthy alliances—builds an inner circle of people who submit only to them
- Works hard for the leader to win over their trust
- Calculating and strategic in its effort to gain control and power
- Revengeful—those who try to highlight their abusive behaviors, quickly become their enemies
- Selfish—it's always about them
- Always seeking more power
- Strives to befriend and control the leader
- Unsympathetic
- Seldom take responsibility for their mistakes

- Intimidation that causes others to fear
- Appears to be highly religious
- Seeks to control finances
- Targets gifted and anointed staff and volunteers for removal
- Will not hire leaders, only people who will blindly follow
- Plays the victim in order to get sympathy and manipulate people into an alliance

The Jezebel Spirit

Jezebel is a spirit of evil. It is a demon that seeks to operate through people. This particular spirit exhibits high levels of control. Because it is a spirit of evil, it is able to affect our lives and organizations in an unseen manner. It uses people to accomplish most of its mission to destroy, but is more than capable of functioning in a supernatural way. By attacking the minds and emotions of others in the organization, it is able to do even greater damage. It attaches itself to specific individuals in order to gain access into organizations or relationships. But it is able to do even more harm operating as a spirit of evil over an organization or a territory. Much like the demonic spirit referred to in Daniel 10, who was prince of the Persian kingdom and resisted an angel of the Lord for twenty-one days. One individual can bring this spirit into your organization, but once that has happened, it will try to claim your organization as its territory. Because its goal is to destroy, it will attempt to infect everyone in your ministry.

It is able to place a cloud of hopelessness and doom over groups of people. It can intensify the emotions of fear and anxiety in humans. It works in and alongside of the person it has chosen to complete its targeted assignment of destruction. For the sake of this book, let's call those people Jezebel-led individuals. Picture if you will, a Jezebel-led person causing harm within an organization through domination, manipulation, or control.

While at the same time a spirit of Jezebel is working as a supernatural accomplice to intensify levels of fear and anxiety in those the Jezebel-led person is controlling. A truer picture of what is really going on would be just the opposite. Jezebel is the destructive force using the Jezebel-led person to be its accomplice. Most Jezebel-led people don't even know this is happening, nor do they realize they are being controlled by a spirit of evil.

Jezebel is capable of doing many things in and through a Jezebel-led individual, but it doesn't stop there. If we limit our attention to the Jezebel-led person, we will miss the unseen warfare that is happening in our midst. The Jezebel spirit controls the Jezebel-led person to do harmful things, while at the same time playing mind games on those in the organization. Feelings of depression, heaviness, fear, chaos, and confusion will often be placed over the people in the organization. The Jezebel spirit will blind the leadership team to the harmful practices of the Jezebel-led person to protect its chosen one from being removed. For those who may try to remove a Jezebel-led person from the team, always remember there is a spirit of evil that will actively be protecting the Jezebel-led person. We must be mindful of how each play a role in destroying our organizations.

The Jezebel spirit is arrogant, entitled, and demanding, and expects to always have its way. When it doesn't get its way, it becomes filled with vengeance, and will retaliate using any means necessary. It will show no mercy! Very often these traits will manifest in the Jezebel-led person it uses to achieve its dark purposes. Jezebel acts as a puppet master who shrewdly controls the actions of the Jezebel-led person.

Jezebel vs Jezebel-led

Perhaps the most confusing aspect of writing a book on a specific demonic spirit and explaining how it works is trying to separate out the work of the demonic spirit from the person the spirit is attached to and uses to accomplish its mission. Unfortunately, it all blends together. Yes, there is a demonic spirit behind the scenes manipulating individuals in many of our institutions. That causes us to want to extend grace to these individuals, which Jezebel usually uses to its advantage. Grace should be offered, but not in the fashion you might think. Grace typically offered to a Jezebel-led individual almost always allows them to remain in control. Letting a Jezebel-led individual remain in a position of power and control is like offering a drink to an alcoholic.

We must strive to extend love and compassion to all individuals led by a Jezebel spirit. However, we must also understand they have free will and have chosen to act in controlling ways. This is why it all gets complicated for us in the church. Who do we blame for the problems—a spirit or a person? The answer is both. It is important that we understand the demonic connection between a spirit of evil and an individual. In Chapter 6 of Charles Kraft's book, *The Rules of Engagement,* he makes these observations:

> *There are certain limitations to what God and Satan can do in the human realm. These limitations are related to the cooperation God and Satan receive from humans.*
>
> *Neither God nor Satan can get their way all the time. The issue of the free will of the individual is always the deciding factor. Both God and Satan seek our allegiance directly and work in and through circumstances and other people to influence us in our choices.*

It is interesting to note that not everyone understands they are cooperating with enemy spirits. They make choices and do not necessarily know their decisions are highly influenced by demonic lies. Kraft further states,

> *There is an eternal competition for our allegiance, both kingdoms trying to draw us to their side, and at the same time trying to keep us from the other side. Satan's workings are frequently frustrated when people cooperate with God, and vice-versa. The difference in the competition is that God attempts to woo us with truth while Satan tries to draw us into his camp with deception. God tells us the truth about ourselves and about Satan; Satan tells us lies about ourselves and God.*

Those choosing to follow the leading of a demonic spirit may simply start out by believing demonic lies. In the case of a Jezebel-led person, it may be the lie that no one else can do a job as well as they can. Or, this organization cannot survive without them controlling everything to the finest detail. Another possible lie may be that everyone on the current team is incompetent and only the Jezebel-led person can fix it. Jezebel-led people look for gaps in ministry, places where things aren't as efficient as they could be and seeks to fill them. This is often the open door that Jezebel uses to gain access and control. The Jezebel-led person truly believes the organization needs them to control and fix the problem areas. Jezebel fights hard to establish and gain power within an organization and will strive to subvert anyone who stands in the way. After a Jezebel-led individual gets a taste of power, it's like an addiction. The more power they achieve, the harder it is for them to relinquish control. Highly influenced Jezebel-led people are seldom able to ever relinquish power on their own. It usually must be taken from them. Confronting Jezebel is no picnic. Demonically driven fear and intimidation can make it very difficult to accomplish. This is why it is imperative to uncover and deal with a Jezebel-led person as soon as possible.

If an organization can learn to protect itself by educating the leadership team, Jezebel-led individuals can be spotted in advance. In some cases where the level of influence a Jezebel spirit has over an individual is minimal, an organization may choose to keep that person under the watch of a strong leader. Even those people who are minimally influenced by Jezebel are capable of making life miserable for the people around them. So, the leader overseeing a Jezebel-led person must be strong and not be fooled by a controlling and manipulating individual. Jezebel-led individuals are capable of high drama, refusing to accept blame for anything—temper tantrums, emotional breakdowns, or anything else they can use to sway you into giving them whatever they want. Do not underestimate the intimidating nature of a Jezebel-led person. Very strong leaders crumble every day to the wiles and deceit of this spirit. Jezebel-influenced people can be very charming and deceptive and seek to remain hidden. You may try to extend grace to a person influenced by Jezebel, but don't be surprised if you are sorry for doing so.

If things start to get out of hand with a Jezebel-led person, a confrontation may be necessary. After speaking truth to the individual, provide the opportunity for this person to acknowledge their controlling ways, then look for a truly repentant heart. Here is the key: repentance means to be sorry enough to turn away from your sinful ways. Jezebel-led people are seldom able to accept correction, apologize, and rarely are willing to change long-term. Even when you do get an apology, it contains no personal responsibility on their part. An apology from a Jezebel might sound like this: "I'm sorry you were offended," instead of, "I'm sorry I offended you." Jezebel-led people can never admit anything is their fault.

A baseball slogan may be perfect here to make a point. Do not take your eyes off of the ball. What I am trying to say is this: Jezebel-influenced people will often change for a short time, but once they feel the heat is off of them, they will slowly step back into their controlling ways. In the meantime, don't be surprised if they try to win you over through flattery and hard work. By causing you to feel beholden to them, they know it is harder for you to discipline them. If a person with Jezebel-like tendencies cannot submit to any kind of discipline or authority, your department or organization is in jeopardy. Typically, if you give Jezebel an inch, it will twist it, and use it to do more harm. As soon as you know the Jezebel-led person will not submit to authority, make sure you protect the people working around them. I know it seems cruel, but it may be necessary to terminate the Jezebel-led person from the organization. But truly, which is worse—allowing an entire department to be bullied by one person, or removing one person from the team.

By understanding that a Jezebel-led person will be able to do greater amounts of damage the further they travel up the chain of command, those highly influenced by Jezebel should probably be removed as soon as possible. That may seem harsh, but in reality, it may be the only way to save the organization and the people within the organization from devastation.

A Jezebel-led individual doesn't have to be the leader to run an organization. In fact, it is in a better position of strength when it isn't the leader. When things begin to fall apart within a church, nonprofit, or an individual department, the leader is the one who receives the greatest amount of scrutiny. Jezebel spirits do not necessarily want the spotlight. If they can control things from a position of stealth, they can continue to cause havoc and not be blamed for any of the problems. If a Jezebel-led person can control a leader, they get to run the organization from a distance and let the leader take the heat when things fall apart or go wrong.

That's not to say that a Jezebel spirit will never try to convince a person to step into the leadership role, because they can and do. Jezebel-led leaders are very hard to work for. It is not uncommon for the organizational environment to be devoid of encouragement, idea sharing, joy, and other gifted leaders. Jezebel-led leaders are often seen as dictators who must have full control of nearly every aspect of the organizational structure. Their desire for full control chases away other strong and gifted leaders whose ideas and skills are ignored.

As the Jezebel virus spreads, it eventually touches everything in its environment. It starts with the person seeking control, it touches the leader of the department or organization. It travels to the co-workers, it affects the atmosphere of the organization. It eventually touches policy, it touches important decisions, it affects clients, volunteers, staff, hiring, promotions, and everyday operations. It can even negatively impact church attendance. The Jezebel spirit is like a vine that spreads out in all directions and tries to capture as much control as it can.

Those who work in a Jezebel-controlled church or nonprofit describe the atmosphere as being oppressively heavy. They feel as if they have heavy weights crushing and smothering them. Their hope is gone. There is a feeling that it will always be like this, and nothing will ever change. And for those unfortunate souls who try to confront the person with a Jezebel spirit, the backlash and punishment for trying is so great that you'll never want to try again. The backlash comes from several directions—the leader, the person with the Jezebel spirit, allies to Jezebel, and the spiritual forces of evil in the heavenly realms. It is easy to forget that the main force behind a person with a Jezebel spirit is a demon. The heavy atmosphere that is enveloping your environment is caused more by the demonic forces than the person who is the controlling dictator. Typically, the longer a Jezebel-led person is in your organization, the greater the level of oppression. As oppression increases, the more hopelessness and despair will impact the effectiveness of the team. Soon, gifted and highly skilled employees will begin to leave the organization to work for churches or companies where their skills and ideas will be used.

Another way to look at a Jezebel spirit is to imagine an octopus that can add tentacles at will. Each tentacle seeks to find areas it can control directly or indirectly through others. The mission of Jezebel is multifaceted. It seeks control in order to destroy, while the Jezebel-led person believes it needs control because they are the only ones who can fix the organization. If you can visualize the control-seeking tentacles of an octopus slithering throughout an organization looking for places it can slowly begin to dominate, you can start to picture how this spirit works. When all eight of its tentacles are actively engaged in controlling a specific area, it simply adds another tentacle. The longer Jezebel is allowed to function inside of an organization, the more tentacles of control it is able to amass. Never underestimate the depth and width of this spirit's ability to encroach itself within an organization. And with each area it touches, the virus-like symptoms begin to arise.

One more thing about viruses. We typically don't see them until the symptoms start showing up. Most Jezebel-led individuals are extraordinarily talented, skilled, and hard workers. They slip into organizations under the cover of their skill set and are capable of doing some very fine work. This is the protective covering that keeps them invisible in the early stages and untouchable when things start to fall apart. In John Paul Jackson's book, *Unmasking the Jezebel Spirit*, he shares this: *"If such a pastor is not checked by a strong board of elders, he or she will leave their church open to dominion and control by this demonic spirit. The church will quickly sink beneath an increasing weight of spiritual oppression, crushing healthy spiritual vitality and vision."*

Jezebel stays protected by its perceived value to the leader of the church or nonprofit while the destructive forces go unchecked throughout the organization. In her book, *The Jezebel Yoke*, Sandie Freed shares about how Jezebel advances its way into very secure positions within an organization:

Too many times I have witnessed leaders who are mesmerized (this is witchcraft) by a Jezebel who uses false flattery and manipulation to work her way into a prominent position. A Jezebel spirit threatens a church atmosphere by causing the pastor or leaders to believe that they cannot operate effectively without her. This has always amazed me—but this is what Jesus referred to as "tolerating" Jezebel. Jezebel performs well, prophesies well (though it is many times a false word), dresses really well, and is many times a large financial giver in the church. She will threaten to leave your church (ministry or business) if she does not have her way—and take others with her.

Important note: Even though the Jezebel spirit takes on many of the traits of Queen Jezebel found in 1 and 2 Kings of the Bible, this spirit can manifest itself in both men and women.

Just like Sandie Freed, I too, have witnessed several strong leaders fall prey to this spirit. On one particular occasion I watched a very gifted and experienced supervisor almost go into full panic mode when I confronted her about how a person in her department was demoralizing the rest of her team. This person literally shook in fear and announced to me the organization couldn't survive without so-and-so (the person demoralizing the team). At the time, it made no sense to me as to why this strong woman was suddenly overcome with fear and felt incapable of leading. I don't think I had ever seen this individual doubt her ability to lead. It wasn't until I became aware of how the Jezebel spirit works that I began to understand how the spirit of Jezebel (not an individual) supernaturally deceived her into believing the lie that she was incapable of leading. It was a twofold lie. It not only made her feel inadequate to lead, it also caused her to put extraordinary trust in the Jezebel-led person undermining her and her team—thus, allowing a Jezebel-led person to gain more and more control and continue to go unchecked within the organization. Many gifted leaders left, simply refusing to be controlled in unhealthy ways.

Our ministry has received countless testimonies from people who have been wounded by the spirit of Jezebel. As I have studied the carnage and damage wrought by the Jezebel spirit over and over again, I felt a calling from God to shed more light on how this spirit works. In the midst of doing research for this book, my eyes have been opened to a much broader attack against the church. In normal conversations with friends about the subject matter of this book, I have been surprised by the number of stories from people who have been negatively impacted by this spirit. The Jezebel spirit is on the prowl, looking to devour any unsuspecting organization or church. In Revelation 2:20 we read these words, *"Nevertheless, I have this against you: You tolerate that woman Jezebel, who calls herself a prophetess."* We are not to tolerate the Jezebel spirit. Many of us don't know what Jezebel looks like, or how to recognize the signs that a Jezebel-like virus has entered into our organization.

It is my prayer that this book will open up our eyes and give us the understanding we need to counter and remove this spirit from our midst. I know that exposing the Jezebel spirit is unpleasant business, and explaining how it works isn't exactly lighthearted stuff. That's why the first several chapters may seem darker and a little more unsettling to read. It's a little bit like explaining how cancer attacks the human body before you can begin to talk about how to treat the disease. As you continue to read, the book does turn a corner and offer strategies and solutions for dealing with this spirit. But first, we must deal with the less encouraging issue of describing the Jezebel virus. What you will read in the following chapters is the result of hundreds of clients sharing their stories with us, as they have sought healing for their wounds.

Chapter 2

What Are the Symptoms of the Jezebel Virus?

Because Jezebel works through people and every person is different, each Jezebel-infected environment will look different. It can be your secular job, your marriage, a friendship, your church, or other institutions. Trying to capture every possible environment in this book is impossible. So, I will try to focus most of my attention on how this spirit affects Christian organizations, but know full well its sphere of control can be found anywhere. There are several basic patterns (symptoms) that emerge in most Jezebel-influenced settings. It is important to know that not every symptom has to be present in each scenario in order for a Jezebel spirit to be present. There will be different scenarios and combinations of symptoms, and when you begin to observe multiple symptoms showing up in an individual or department, it is time to take a closer look. Jezebel-led people are compelled to control other people and the scenario they choose to operate in will vary.

There are a couple of ways to look for symptoms. You can monitor individuals by looking for specific behavior patterns, or you can observe entire departments, groups, ministry teams, and staff. It is quite possible that you will see the beginning signs of trouble in a group setting first, then by understanding how Jezebel works, you can begin to track the Jezebel-like behaviors back to the source. Do not be deceived. It is possible that the Jezebel-led individual may not be anything like what you might expect. The Jezebel spirit is amazingly adept at staying hidden.

Individuals with the Jezebel spirit are often highly productive and skilled. In a work setting they are exceedingly capable at managing upward in order to please the department head, leadership team, lead pastor, or organizational leader. Through flattery and going way above and beyond the norm to meet the needs of their supervisor, they are able to win over the supervisor's trust and, therefore, gain their loyalty and protection. If that doesn't work, they will try to manipulate the supervisor through guilt. Because of the extra work and favors, they strive to place a completely dysfunctional obligation upon the person they want to control. When the Jezebel-led person wants something, they have no problem reminding you of all the things they have done for you.

Jezebel is a demon, and yes, it is somehow attached to a person. Alarmingly, Jezebel is capable of extreme deception. It is able to mesmerize and blind leaders in seductive ways that can defy all logic. It may or may not be sexually seductive, but it most certainly is able to capture a supervisor's loyalty. A person with a Jezebel spirit will take on extra projects, compliment, charm, comfort, do favors, show compassion, and feed the ego of the supervisor or ministry leader with very subtle words meant to gain favor. All of these spellbinding tricks are for the purpose of self-preservation and advancement within an organization. They are also able to use other negative means such as blackmail, guilt, threats, anger, lies, and false accusations.

The Jezebel spirit must stay hidden in order to accomplish its destructive mission to divide and conquer until it gains power and takes control. Even when leaders being deceived by a Jezebel spirit are alerted to what is going on, they cannot see it. The supernatural spell of Jezebel blinds them to the truth, and then goes a step beyond. It then stirs up anger in the supervisor toward those who are trying to point out the truth of what a Jezebel-led person is doing. It also influences the supervisor to defend the person with Jezebel to extreme levels. The truth is, Jezebel-led people are masterful at playing the victim, and are able to play off of other people's sympathy to get their way. By using a victim mentality and self-pity, Jezebel is able to get people to feel sorry for them. This is emotional manipulation, and Jezebel will use it as a means to control you.

For everyone else in the organization who is being bullied, they are in a state of confusion at how the leader cannot see Jezebel's abusive control over the team. This may be the #1 reason why Jezebel is continually allowed to destroy churches and nonprofit organizations with little to no opposition.

Warning to Ministry Leaders

If you have a couple of individuals come to you complaining of a controlling and manipulative person in your organization, and you are acting or reacting in one of the following ways, you may be under the spell of a Jezebel spirit.

- Extraordinarily high levels of fear over losing the individual accused of being controlling. In your mind you may be overwhelmed by this thought: "We can't survive without this person."
- A flirtatious person of the opposite sex, or a highly productive person, regularly convinces you to overrule your established lead team to get their way and give them more power.

- Unexplainable anger and frustration at those who bring you complaints about the controlling person, before you know any facts.
- Driven by an intense desire to defend the person being complained about.
- Complete inability to see what several others are telling you about your loyalty to a difficult and controlling person on your team.
- Constantly looking for ways to excuse inexcusable behavior for the person accused of bullying your team.
- Extreme fear over confronting the individual being accused of bullying or controlling others.
- Compelled to protect the person being accused of being a dictator, bully, or manipulator.
- There is an unusually high level of loyalty between you and another person on your staff that supersedes common sense and conventional wisdom.

The truth is, most people with a Jezebel spirit are very gifted at pleasing the leader or leaders on the ministry team and are very adept at hiding how poorly they treat those who are considered equals or lower level staff. Remember, Jezebel believes it has no equal. Even though it goes out of its way to please the leader, it is only for the purpose of gaining their loyalty so they can eventually control the leader and, in time, the whole organization.

Symptoms of the Jezebel Virus

Heaviness

This is rather hard to describe, unless you are in an environment where Jezebel resides. The heaviness comes from two sources—the spiritual realm and the earthly realm. In other words, there is an invisible supernatural pressure that exists, and there is a human component. Because it is invisible, people feel like heavy weights are crushing in on them but they do not know why or where the pressure is coming from. It can sometimes take on the feeling of fear or anxiety. Some people describe the heaviness as a dark cloud that envelops everything. It drains you and causes you to feel tired and weary. It sucks the life out of you and steals your joy. Some have described the heaviness as an oppressive darkness that is invisible and yet is palpable. When you work in this kind of environment, you feel depressed and hopeless. It makes getting ready for work seem like it's an overwhelming act of futility.

On the human side of things, there is usually an individual who is responsible for most of the frustration felt by many in the organization. Feelings of hopelessness abound as one individual or group of individuals are able to dominate and dictate over the rest of the group. They are able to manipulate the emotional heartstrings of the rest of the group by their unchecked dominance and control. The deep frustration comes as the bullied and abused are usually left completely unprotected, while those doing the bullying are somehow embraced by the leader. As the Jezebel-led bully or bullies are embraced and given more authority, they become more emboldened to exert more and more control. These Jezebel-led individuals do not seem to have any consideration for how poorly they treat others. It appears that they think it is their God-given right to do so.

Imagine if you will, an eight-year-old boy on a school bus day after day being bullied by a fourteen-year-old boy. The absolute hopelessness and dread of the younger eight-year-old as he climbs onto the bus each day must feel like a thousand-pound anchor around his neck, crushing him under the weight of despair. Now, imagine the eight-year-old tells his parents and teachers about the bullying and no one listens! In fact, they tell the eight-year-old boy how wonderful the bully is, and how it is impossible for the fourteen-year-old to be a bully. When a leader or a leadership team allows an individual free rein to dominate and control others in their organization, it places the entire team under a heavy blanket of despair.

When you combine the heaviness of the spiritual realm with the frustration and despair that come from a human component, it is easy to see how this can destroy a department or an organization. In churches, people who are not even being affected by the bullying will sometimes discern or sense a heaviness over the church. They will often leave the church feeling a sense of foreboding and not even know why. If your church is losing people and there doesn't seem to be any reason for it, you might want to take a deeper look internally to see if there is any controlling or bullying taking place on your team.

I am the founder of a spiritual warfare and inner-healing ministry called Wellsprings of Freedom International. We travel to many churches for the purpose of training them and equipping them to do spiritual warfare ministry. One of the first things we like to do when we arrive at the church is to do a freedom session over the church. As we spend time corporately praying over the church with the senior pastor, our discerning team members will discern specific spirits that are attacking the church. Several years ago, we were praying over a church and several of our team members discerned spirits of heaviness and oppression. We worked as a team to command those spirits to let go of the church in the name of Jesus and they left. Our discerning team members saw them being forced to leave by the authority of Christ. Only our team and the senior pastor knew what had been done on that Thursday evening during our prayer time. Yet, the following Sunday, the pastor told us he had two people come to him and ask if the sanctuary had been painted the previous week. When he told them no, he then asked them why they thought so. Their answers were remarkable. They each said, "Well, it just seems so much lighter in here." They knew something was different, but because it was all in the spirit realm (something they were not familiar with), they didn't know how to put into words what they were sensing. So, they attached physical world observations to something that happened in the spiritual realm.

Heaviness is a co-conspirator that can work with the Jezebel spirit to cover organizations under a blanket of hopelessness and despair not seen by our human eyes. Team members will feel it; they just won't know what it is or where it is coming from. It is typically not until they leave the organization that they are surprised by how much the weight of heaviness had been crushing down upon them. After they step out of the organization, and the heaviness is lifted off of their shoulders, they begin to feel joy and hope once again.

Inability to keep good employees

When a Jezebel-led person is allowed to operate with high levels of authority, the symptoms of the Jezebel virus will begin to emerge. It may take a little time to see a pattern take shape, but losing good people is a common indicator that something is wrong. I'm not saying that every time you lose a good employee it is because of a Jezebel spirit. However, if you see a trend of good people leaving over the course of a year, it could be there is a Jezebel-led person in your midst. I recently had lunch with a friend who shared with me that last year in his former church, nine of ten staff pastors either quit or were fired and replaced. A pattern that keeps repeating itself every couple of years. The only person who remains on staff year in and year out is the controlling and abusive senior pastor. He continues to get by with it because he has surrounded himself with a board of directors who are completely loyal to him. Because of their blind loyalty, spiritual abuse is allowed to continue, and an angry dysfunctional leader is never confronted and held accountable to change.

Team members who have outstanding leadership skills are especially vulnerable. Jezebel-led individuals need to be in control and cannot tolerate other gifted leaders being on the team. Because the Jezebel-led person has typically earned the trust of a department head or the organization leader, they are allowed to dominate others on the team. Jezebel doesn't want other leaders on the team; it wants only loyal followers who will do its bidding. Jezebel-led leaders will drive you crazy by telling you that you are in charge of a project or division and never let you make a single decision. They will make important decisions for your department without ever consulting you or asking for your input.

Gifted leaders are a threat to Jezebel because Jezebel-led individuals don't ever want their strategies and plans scrutinized. They cannot handle tough questions or any kind of accountability for their actions. Anyone who questions a Jezebel-led person's decisions will eventually be pushed to the sidelines. Good leaders typically have good ideas for how things can be done better, but a Jezebel-led person always thinks they know better than anyone else. Only Jezebel's ideas can be used as Jezebel-led people usually refuse to listen to anyone else's ideas.

Good employees and good leaders will only put up with a restrictive and limiting environment for a little while. Eventually they will move on to where their ideas and abilities will be appreciated and used to make a difference. It is not uncommon for Jezebel-led individuals to be perfectionists, always finding fault with everyone else on the team, except with themselves. Jezebel-led environments cause very talented and hard-working individuals to feel incompetent and doubt their abilities.

Poor attitudes from normally good people

When many of the effects of a Jezebel spirit begin to show up in a department or organization, attitudes will naturally begin to slide downward. It will even affect those long-term employees who have been the most loyal and faithful. Most organizations have a couple of employees who are prone to being frustrated and unhappy. However, when a group of normally happy and satisfied employees begin to exhibit frustration and discontent, it would be wise to look into the matter. I believe there is a normal ebb and flow in the emotional atmosphere of most organizations. By that I mean, there are ups and downs as people interact with one another, but the basic emotional rhythm of an organization is subconsciously felt and known by the whole team. We may not be actively aware of every problem or frustration, but as a whole we have a sense of the overall emotional health of the organization. When an organization's emotional barometer begins to fall, almost everyone in the organization will begin to sense something is wrong. They may not be able to identify the source of the problem at first, but as the problem persists, it will affect the basic emotional rhythm of a department or organization.

It would be wise for departmental or organizational leaders to pay attention to this subconscious emotional rhythm, or at least pay attention to the employees who are trying to express a perceived downward trend. Especially when it is being spoken by those who have been the most loyal and most concerned about the overall health of the organization.

Jezebel-led individuals (who are usually causing the problems) are almost always able to feign innocence, while blaming the rest of the team for having poor attitudes. When leaders who are deceived by Jezebel ignore the most loyal in the organization, Jezebel is allowed to continue to wreak havoc and the overall attitude of the organization suffers.

Important note –

Do not be deceived by whom I am referring to as the most loyal and concerned about the organization. The Jezebel-led person will have already established its loyalty to the leader, not so much to the organization. This is where leaders get confused. They confuse loyalty to themselves as if it were loyalty to the organization, thus they listen to the Jezebel-led person above those who have been faithful long-tenured staff members. Jezebel-led individuals are notorious for blaming everyone else for problems and bad attitudes, trying to keep the spotlight off of themselves. When leadership ignores faithful employees who are only trying to make things better, while taking the side of the controlling individual, bad attitudes will be a natural consequence. It is a frustrating place to be when those who are dominated and controlled by a Jezebel-led person are regularly blamed for bad attitudes. While at the same time, the controlling Jezebel-led person who is causing the plunging attitudes is never confronted for their dominating behavior. As this crazy cycle continues to play out, the bad attitudes sink only lower while the frustrated and bullied team members continue to be lectured and reprimanded for their bad attitudes. It never seems to occur to anyone to look for the source of the bad attitudes and remove it from the organization.

Sudden loss of trust from the leader toward his or her leadership team

This one may be extraordinarily deceptive, but it is one of the ploys that Jezebel sometimes uses in the midst of a Jezebel-influenced environment. We must never forget that a Jezebel spirit has an all-encompassing desire to destroy Christian organizations. It is easy for this fact to get lost in the confusion that occurs as we try to separate the person being used by Jezebel from the actual Jezebel spirit. I'm not convinced that all Jezebel-led individuals are completely aware that they are being used to destroy an organization. It would appear that Jezebel is able to lie to the Jezebel-led person and deceive them into believing that their actions are to advance their careers and help the organization.

When a Jezebel-led person truly believes they know more about leadership and ministry building than anyone else, it sets them up as a puppet for Jezebel to use.

As the talented and hardworking Jezebel-led person becomes more trusted by the leader, the leader increasingly relies on them for advice. Slowly, Jezebel starts to point out all the flaws of the anointed team surrounding the leader masqueraded as wise business counsel. Meanwhile, what is really going on is a slow separation of the leader from the leadership team in an attempt to isolate and cause division on the team. Jezebel hates anointed leaders and wants to remove them from effective service. If in the process of removing them from a specific job they can drive them out of ministry all together, then that is an ultimate win.

The secret mission to isolate the leader from their trusted leadership team is to eventually replace each one of them with an ally to Jezebel. It is very subtle at first, but as time goes by, the delicately placed attacks increase. Little by little, the Jezebel-led person chips away at the character, talents, and competency of the targeted team member. Jezebel will seek to exploit every mistake a team member makes in order to drive home their point. This includes mischaracterizations and completely manufactured lies.

Even though a Jezebel-led individual strives to project the persona of a mature believer who is above reproach, they are very capable of lying. It is not uncommon for a Jezebel-led individual to exaggerate stories to make things appear much worse than they actually are, or totally invent fabricated tales to further destroy the confidence of the leader toward a team member. They are also very adept at hiding information, making sure that anything good the targeted staff member does is kept from the leader. Jezebel-influenced people will do whatever is necessary to destroy the trust a leader has in one of his or her team members, and that includes creating absolute lies. This is very hard for a leader to see because of the trust they have placed in the Jezebel-led person, and the almost supernatural persona of righteousness projected by the Jezebel-led person. Because Jezebel-led people often recruit allies, it is not uncommon for the leader to hear disparaging remarks being made from more than one person. If a leader took some time to evaluate all who are speaking negatively about a long-time employee, they might very well discover all speaking badly about a person are part of the Jezebel-led person's team of allies. These are complete followers of the Jezebel-led person who do exactly what they are told or influenced to believe.

Jezebel seeks to cause division. I recently received this story from one of our network team members:

> *A few years ago, a gentleman entered into our ministry. He seemed to be highly religious and was able to say all the right things. He was very complimentary to me and offered to do special projects for me that were very labor intensive. He would often tell me how anointed I was and that there wasn't anyone else he knew that had the kind of favor that God had given to me. This person went through our training and spoke very highly of the ministry. Eventually he began to serve on one of our ministry teams. He was a very confident person and was able to project his self-assuredness in his use of spiritual gifts. After a period of time, he was able to convince many of our team members that he was more gifted than most. Whether he was or not didn't matter as he had convinced people he was. As team members began to place higher levels of trust in his spiritual gifts, he used that to sway people's opinions. This man was a Jezebel-led person who was striving to control and persuade people in our ministry team to follow him.*
>
> *It took time, but little by little he won the trust and confidence of many of our team members. After a while, we began to notice that people who served on teams alongside*

of him began to quit. As we began to meet with them and ask them why they were quitting, we got the same answer: "Oh, I'm just not gifted enough to serve on a team." Upon further investigation, we discovered another pattern developing. Team members from one team were getting frustrated with team members on a totally different team. These were people who didn't even work together except for one person who happened to serve on both teams. Yep, the confidently gifted man. We eventually found out the man was telling the team members on one team that the team members he served with on the other team didn't think they were gifted enough to be in our ministry. This led to people quitting because they believed his lies, and it led to division between ministry teams who also believed his lies.

The spirit of Jezebel is a spirit that pursues the destruction of Christian organizations. It will seek ways to enter into an organization and win over the trust of the leader, then, slowly begin its mission to cause division and mistrust between the leader and his/her leadership team, board, and followers. In John Paul Jackson's book, *Unmasking the Jezebel Spirit*, he writes,

> *Flattery can also become a catalyst for causing division. Usually this ploy is accomplished through creating destructive "relational triangles." In a triangle, Jezebel will befriend person A and person B. However, Jezebel will slowly convince person A that person B does not like him or her. She will also convince person B that person A does not like him or her. Then, Jezebel will appear as a peacemaker who has a deep desire to see each one succeed. By pitting each one's gifting or wisdom against another's, this individual produces jealousy, strife, and contention—even in the strongest relationships.*

Jezebel strives to cause division by pitting one person against another, or causing strife between two departments.

Once the leadership team is dismantled from around the leader, Jezebel will attempt to replace the leadership team with people who are under the control of the Jezebel-led individual. When Jezebel has established a team of its loyal allies around the leader, they may then choose to control the leader, or attempt to remove the leader. Sometimes it is so Jezebel can take control of an organization, and sometimes it is to destroy the organization so it can move on to another one. If you are a leader, and someone fairly new to your organization has suddenly found their way into your inner circle, keep a close watch. They may be a legitimate blessing brought into your life from God. But they could also be someone the enemy is planting in your midst to bring destruction.

Of course, not every Jezebel-influenced plan will follow this pattern. This is just one of the ways it might happen. There are many strategies a Jezebel spirit might choose to use against you. In an attempt to win over the leader, Jezebel will flatter the leader and work hard to diminish the confidence and friendship the team leader has toward his/her team. Jezebel must do whatever it can to destroy the base of trust previously established with the leader before Jezebel arrived on the scene. Once the leader's trust in his or her team has been destroyed, Jezebel can more easily maneuver into a position of power.

An atmosphere of intimidation and fear

When a leader allows and even defends an abusive individual within an organization, fear will naturally dominate the organizational culture.

I am reminded of Jeremiah 23:1-4:

> *Woe to the shepherds who are destroying and scattering the sheep of my pasture!" declares the* LORD. *Therefore,*

this is what the LORD, the God of Israel, says to the shepherds who tend my people: "Because you have scattered my flock and driven them away and have not bestowed care on them, I will bestow punishment on you for the evil you have done," declares the LORD. "I myself will gather the remnant of my flock out of all the countries where I have driven them and will bring them back to my pasture, where they will be fruitful and increase in number. I will place shepherds over them who will tend them, and they will no longer be afraid or terrified, nor will any be missing," declares the LORD.

It is the leader's job to protect the team. When they fail to do so, the team will be overcome with mistrust and fear. The leader or leadership team are the only ones who can provide a culture of safety. If they fail to do so, who is left to protect the team? How can a lower-level employee stop an abusive supervisor or co-worker if the leader refuses to do anything about it? Imagine that the abusive and controlling supervisor or co-worker is protected by the leader or lead team. Then what? Intimidation and fear will prevail over the department or organization. It is also important to mention that if you confront a person with Jezebel or call them out for their controlling behavior, you will be targeted for retaliation. Jezebel will get even. It's all part of its intimidation strategy meant to control you with fear. It is also a tactic of self-protection. If you mess with Jezebel, you will pay such a high price you will never try again. This is where a leader should protect the anonymity of those who come to them with their concerns. If the Jezebel-led person ever discovers who complained about their behavior, Jezebel will try to make that person's life miserable or try to get them terminated from the organization.

Good team members will stay in an environment of fear for only a short time. They will usually give the leadership team a chance to fix the problems before they choose to leave. If good team members begin to leave your organization expressing an unwillingness to work in an environment of fear and intimidation, you may have a Jezebel-led person on your staff, or you have a controlling leader who likes to abuse people. Either way, the leader must step in and do whatever is necessary to protect the team. Leaders, don't dismiss the cries for help, and don't ignore multiple complaints about an abusive controlling person just because they are part of your inner circle of trust. Jezebel-led people hide out in inner circles and use their closeness to the leader to deflect blame.

Interestingly, paranoia and fear can seep into the Jezebel-led leadership team as well. This is a little harder to see, but it is often there. Because the Jezebel-led person works behind the scenes in very deceptive ways, there is a high level of fear that it will be uncovered. The Jezebel-led person is afraid that the truth of how things are failing and falling apart will be exposed. Seldom does a Jezebel-led environment stay healthy enough to grow as an organization. In time, Jezebel's influence over the organization will begin to be noticeable. As finances and attendance numbers begin to decrease, high levels of paranoia will set in. In Steve Sampson's book, *Discerning and Defeating the Ahab Spirit*, he talks about tendencies found in wounded Jezebel-like people. He writes, *"Additionally, they are suspicious of everyone. Whenever there is a disagreement with someone, they not only try to attack the person, but they try to collect as many people as they can to get on board with them and agree that the other person is bad"* (p. 71). Anyone trying to ask questions about why things are declining will cause deep fear in the leader and the Jezebel-led individual. The fear of looking bad will drive them to deception and denial.

Sampson goes on to explain, *"When you deal with a Jezebel personality, it does not seem to matter what course of action you take, because they do not take responsibility or blame for anything. If you take action concerning something, they will blame you; if you do not take action, they will blame you. You never win. Jezebels are slick, always excusing themselves from any responsibility"* (p. 69). Manufactured and deceitful stories of how wonderful things supposedly are, and attempts to hide real problems or deflect blame onto others, are all part of the denial strategy. The fear of people discovering the organization is broken will often create an environment of trying to hide, alter, or sugarcoat uncomfortable information and sinking statistics.

The overarching concern that what's really going on will be exposed, leads them to isolation. Only those truly loyal to Jezebel are allowed into its circle of trust. This isolated group invents their own truth and becomes suspicious of anyone not in their group. Jezebel fabricates its own version of reality, and keeps the loyal followers believing its propaganda. The paranoid Jezebel-led person and the leader they control must cover up the real problems affecting the organization. They do this by stepping into victim mentality and currying sympathy with false excuses for the bad numbers. Jezebel invents false stories blaming everyone but themselves for all that is going wrong. The worse things get, the more the stories and blame depart from the truth. The leadership culture within the organization becomes one of fear and mistrust. People asking tough questions, or those pointing out how the organization is failing, are seen as threats and cannot be trusted. Fear dominates the culture from top to bottom.

Regular complaints of an individual who is controlling, abusive, and manipulating

Jezebel-led people are typically spiritually abusive. And when they are the leader, or feel hidden and protected by the leader, they often become domineering dictators who can make life miserable for nearly everyone. The effects that one abusive person can have over an entire department or organization is mystifying, as you contemplate why it is allowed to happen.

As we talk about abusive behavior, I think it might be helpful to look at a definition of abuse that can help us clarify what we are talking about. In a recent post from a Church Leadership blog article, I found the following definition:

Abuse is a pattern of coercive control based in an abuser's feeling of entitlement to power over another person. An abuser gains and maintains control through various tactics that can be physical, emotional, verbal, financial, sexual or spiritual.

Controlling and abusive behavior destroys the morale of the team, it chases good people out of the organization, and negatively affects production. Creativity is squelched, people are needlessly tormented, and energy and life are sucked out of the department. There is no joy in coming to work, people take time off just to get away from the excessively domineering person. I have observed departments that were running at full capacity, filled with people excited about their jobs, who loved coming to work, be completely shut down by the addition of one controlling bully. I'm convinced that most organizations would be far more productive simply by removing a pushy and domineering person from their midst.

Looking back at each of those situations where bullies were allowed to have free rein, I have identified two reasons why they were allowed to continue to abuse people.

1. They intimidated their supervisor to such an extent that the supervisor was afraid to confront them.

A friend of mine once told me a story about approaching his supervisor and asking him why a certain person in his department was never required to do any work. He was pretty sure he knew the answer as this person had a fiery temper and had learned to use it to bully other people. The supervisor's answer to my friend was quite revealing: "She's my pet, she can do whatever she wants, and never talk to me about this again!" My friend had watched her on multiple occasions flatter the boss and on different days dress him down with her anger and rage. Or, she would go into such an emotional tirade of "woe is me, everyone is against me," that she manipulated him into believing all her problems were somehow his fault and it was his job to make her feel better—which he typically did by giving her whatever she wanted. She taught him to seek her approval and never cross her path or there was a steep penalty for doing so. Jezebel-led individuals have a supernatural ability to manipulate people, and project a frightening level of fear and intimidation upon others.

2. They were friends with the organizational leader who would protect them and punish anyone who complained about their abuse.

Jezebel-led individuals seemingly have a supernatural ability to mesmerize the leader, charm them, and use them as a defense shield. It's almost like Obi Wan Kenobi in "Star Wars," who could wave his hand over a storm trooper's face and convince him of something completely the opposite of what was occurring right before the trooper's eyes. Of course, it doesn't really work that way, but Jezebel-led people are often abusive and are almost always protected by a leader. It doesn't make sense, yet, it is a pattern that occurs time and time again. Here is a story I received from a friend that perfectly describes how this works:

> *At one of the former companies I used to work for, I was made aware of a highly controlling supervisor who stole one of her employee's cars over lunch break. She had to run some errands and noticed that one of her employees had left their keys in their car. This bullying supervisor had a reputation of stealing things and taking advantage of her employees who were often teenagers. Many complaints had been lodged against her for this behavior, but the vice*

president of her department always protected her. On this occasion she got caught red-handed taking her employee's car without permission. As she was pulling back into the parking lot, the teenage employee was outside frantically trying to find his car so he could go to lunch.

Almost everyone in her department had been negatively impacted by her and all thought this was finally the day that she would be fired. She was not fired. She was not reprimanded, and this only led to her being even more blatant in her bullying behavior. If you can steal a car, get caught and be protected, you now know you have free rein to do whatever you want. As you can imagine, that is exactly what she did. She strutted and flaunted her power over everyone. For years, she went out of her way to make life miserable for the people in her department.

A couple of years later, I had a conversation with an employee who worked in the HR department at the time this event occurred. I asked him how this particular employee had gotten away with stealing a car. He told me that the HR department was ready to fire her, but the vice president stepped in and completely blocked it from happening.

This is why this symptom has been included in this chapter. If you are the leader of an organization, and you are presented with complaints about bullying and abuse, you need to take them seriously and not make excuses for people close to you who might be perpetuating the abuse. Also, don't be fooled into thinking that abusive bullies are always explosive and angry jerks. Some manipulate through emotional coercion. Flattery, favors, playing a victim, emotional meltdowns, eliciting sympathy, and using guilt to get people to obey are other forms of control. I had a friend tell me a story about a person who at one time used sheer anger and domination to control people. However, when that was frowned upon by the management team, the individual changed to become a smiling and domineering person. They still fit the description of an abusive person as they felt entitled to control others, but somehow doing it with a smile made it acceptable. Don't think you are above being deceived; this is happening in organizations all over the world. Jezebel can be found in any denomination and any size church or nonprofit ministry.

Diminished anointing

As God's anointed servants are chased out, and as an environment of control increases, God may choose to withdraw His anointing. In one of his messages, Reverend Jimmy Evans gave a wonderful description of God's anointing. He said, "The anointing is a completely revocable, divine advertising and enablement to do what God wants you to do." He goes on to say, "God will never, ever, anoint unrighteous control." I have seen this amazing anointing multiple times in my life. I attended a church that went from 50 people to nearly 3,000. It was a joy to watch and participate in. People came from all over. Yes, we worked hard, but people just showed up. It truly was like God was advertising for us and sending people our way. God came alongside of us and did the heavy lifting. I feel like God is doing the same thing for the ministry I serve in today called Wellsprings of Freedom. God is going before us to do the heavy lifting. As we follow Him using our God-given gifts, He blesses our efforts and allows us to do far more than we could ever do on our own.

In Romans 11:29, the Bible is clear that our spiritual gifts are irrevocable, God does not take them away. I have seen this firsthand. I once attended a conference and heard a pastor teach one of the finest messages I've ever heard. But sadly, we later discovered he was having an affair at the same time. In light of this, it is important to understand that just because your spiritual gifts are working as they always have, doesn't mean that everything in your life is honoring God. On several occasions I have observed spiritually gifted believers fall into patterns of sin. They rationalized that because their spiritual gifts were still working, God wasn't upset with their sin. The spirit of Jezebel will absolutely use this lie to its advantage. It will convince a Jezebel-led person that their abusive and controlling ways are completely acceptable to God, all because their spiritual gifts are still functioning. Jezebel will rationalize into their mind: "The organization is falling apart, but since your spiritual gifts are as sharp as ever, it can't be your fault." In other words, if your spiritual gifts still work, you must still have the approval of God.

What is interesting is when the irrevocable gifts of God are combined with the anointing of God. Amazing things happen as God does the heavy lifting and unexplainable blessings are poured out over an organization. What a wonderful place to be and we should always strive to live under God's anointing. Conversely, when God removes His anointing and we are left to do things on our own, things become hard. You may still use your spiritual gifts, but you will do it without God's heavy lifting. Ministry becomes difficult. Where things used to just naturally and smoothly unfold before you, it will now feel like you are walking in quicksand. You will work as hard or maybe even harder than before with little to no results.

I'm not saying that good things won't happen, God will still use your gifts to bless others. It's the overall dimension of things that begins to diminish. God does not bless unrighteous control. If your organizational environment is a controlling environment where people are being oppressively controlled, God can't bless that. He is not going to stand over your organization and supernaturally advertise and woo people to come to a place where people are being manipulated and mistreated. Nor is He going to persuade His anointed young leaders to come to a place where their gifts and talents will be ignored, where their God-given leadership gifts are squashed, and where they will be criticized and driven from the ministry. When God withdraws His supernatural advertising because our organization is wounding both the shepherds and the sheep, we are in trouble. Worship will become harder, outreach will become harder, everything becomes harder.

It is possible, even likely, that the Jezebel-led person will be clueless or pretend to be clueless to the reality that things are falling apart in the organization. If things are brought to their attention, their first instincts will be to deny things are broken, rationalize and make excuses, or blame others for the problems. If you are the controlling and manipulating leader, or the one being controlled by a Jezebel-led leader, chances are you live in a bubble of false reality. It may be an isolated bubble of one or two, or because Jezebel typically recruits allies, there may be several in your bubble. This makes total sense. Your allies know better than to cross you, they aren't going to tell you the truth. Jezebel-led leaders seek those who will be loyal supporters and shun those who are dissenters. They just expect their loyal followers to accept their decisions without question. Whatever size the bubble is, their reality of things will most likely be distorted. Things may be falling apart, but the Jezebel-influenced leader will deflect the blame and refuse to take responsibility for it. This is because the Jezebel-led person and the allies live in a fantasy world of their own making. They may know there are problems, but the problems are never their fault. Blame is cast everywhere else, sometimes toward those who try to expose the truth. If you are the Jezebel-led leader, the one dominated by a Jezebel-led person, or those in the ally bubble, you most likely won't see the controlling environment that is causing frustration and hardship for others. Life is good for the ones in control. A good friend of mine used to say, *"It's good to be the king."* They're not the ones being dominated, so those in leadership, or in the ally bubble, live outside of the oppressive environment, but certainly contribute to the abusive culture.

Recently, one of our Wellsprings team members sent me an article on "25 Signs of Spiritual Abuse." It is found on the website of Jill Monaco Ministries. As I read through the list, I was astounded at how parts of it so perfectly confirmed what often takes place in the ally bubble. I won't include all twenty-five signs, but five of them fit perfectly with this chapter:

- *Spiritually abusive leaders have their minions do their dirty work and isolate, intimidate, or manipulate those who don't comply.*
- *Spiritually abusive leaders surround themselves with the elite and don't interact with the sheep.*
- *Spiritually abusive leaders use their charisma to create a cult-like following that will defend them when they are questioned.*
- *Spiritually abusive leaders create the culture of a popular inner circle. If someone raises a concern, they are put out of the clique and other inner circle people are afraid to speak up.*
- *Spiritually abusive leaders surround themselves with people who only praise them, fear them, or submit to them.*

For those in control, being in control means they get to establish the blame for why things are broken. They are blind to the oppressive atmosphere because it isn't happening to them. The overall attendance of your organization may be down, your financial numbers may be down, you're working harder than ever with lower overall results, but no one inside the ally bubble is responsible. Because those in the ally bubble get to affix blame, they can assign responsibility for the organizational problems to anyone or anything they want.

Because the team of allies have endeared themselves to the leader, they are part of the leadership team. When people outside of their loyal inner circle attempt to point out the controlling abuse of the Jezebel-led leader, the whole core of allies rise up to defend the leader, just like the article above suggests. This makes it more difficult to bring corrective action against the Jezebel-led leader. Those on the outside of the inner circle trying to highlight and expose the spiritually abusive environment are condemned by the whole group. It's not just the Jezebel-led leader denying obsessive control issues; it is the whole leadership team. If a board of directors gets wind of abusive tendencies, all of the loyal followers who have been promoted to the upper echelon of leadership stand together in denial that anything is wrong. As a group they deny allegations of abuse and as a group they secretly banish and isolate those who brought the charges. It is not uncommon for the ally group to be the board of directors who are more devoted to the leader than the organization in trouble. Sometimes, sins committed by the leader will be buried by a group of long-time board members who have become loyal friends.

Unfortunately, individuals in an organization who try to express that the controlling environment is the problem will no longer be considered loyal, and will become outsiders. People who leave—not wanting to be part of the oppressive environment—will be considered untrustworthy and a traitor. As staff, volunteers, and attenders leave the organization, those who are in the ally bubble further isolate themselves from the rest of the organization. They view each person leaving the organization as a personal offense, and that often leads to resentment. Their collective isolation, and loyalty to one another, allows for a dysfunctional and false narrative of group think, group propaganda, and group lies. As they commiserate together over the perceived offenses of those leaving the organization, they are so wrapped up in their own version of reality that they are blinded to the truth. They circle the wagons of denial around themselves as a protective shield, and continue in their destructive ways—oblivious to the fact that their patterns of control and oppression are what are causing people to leave.

When the controlling leader and faithful allies refuse to change their controlling ways, or hide secret sins, the wonderful supernatural blessing of God may be withdrawn. If the overall results of your organization have been going the wrong way, you might want to take a closer look. If you are the leader, are you a lone ranger? Have you dismissed complaints of excessive control directed at you or someone on your team? Do you function from day to day in an isolated bubble with others who follow only your orders? Do you place loyalty above competency? Is your organization in a downward spiral, and you are blaming everyone but yourself for what's broken? Do you get angry and defensive at those who try to point out the truth? Do these questions stir up feelings of anger and frustration? Do the symptoms listed in this chapter define your organization? You can't be afraid to discover the truth. If you are the leader, get away from your close-knit group, and ask yourself the tough questions. Don't make excuses for you or your team. Are you the controlling leader? Is there someone on your team who is controlling you and the team? Follow the truth no matter where it leads you. You can't fix what you don't know is broken and you can't fix what you deny is broken.

Chapter 3

Jezebel—Under the Spiritual Microscope

"Jezebel?" "Is there really a spirit named Jezebel, and where did that name come from?" For those who do not spend much time studying spiritual warfare, it is easy to get confused about the names given to specific demons. I remember in the early days when I was just starting out in freedom ministry, people were upset with me when I would call a spirit by name. "Demons are demons, they don't have names," people would say to me. I understand their frustration and confusion as most churches don't teach on spiritual warfare and a lot of Christians are in the dark on the subject. Because of this confusion, it might be best if we address this issue first, before we go into detail on the Jezebel spirit.

Do demons have names? This is a great question, and the answer is found in Scripture, and is based on common sense, and years of practical hands-on experience confronting demons in the name of Jesus.

First, let's go to the Word of God. In Luke 1:26, we read, *"In the sixth month, God sent the angel Gabriel to Nazareth."* In Jude 9, we find this writing, *"But even the archangel Michael, when he was disputing with the devil about the body of Moses, did not dare to bring a slanderous accusation against him."* And in Hebrews 1:2-4,

> *But in these last days he has spoken to us by his son, whom he appointed heir of all things, and through whom he made the universe. The Son is the radiance of God's glory and the exact representation of his being, sustaining all things by his powerful word. After he had provided purification for sins, he sat down at the right hand of the Majesty in heaven. So he became as much superior to the angels as the name he has inherited is superior to theirs.*

I think it is clear that angels have names. But, what does this have to do with demonic names? In Revelation 12:7-9, we find the answer:

> *And there was war in heaven. Michael and his angels fought against the dragon, and the dragon and his angels fought back. But he was not strong enough, and they lost their place in heaven. The great dragon was hurled down— that ancient serpent called the devil, or Satan, who leads the whole world astray. He was hurled to the earth and his angels with him.*

Most modern-day theologians believe that demons are fallen angels, and because a case can be made that good angels have names, it would stand to reason that the fallen angels or demons have names too. In fact, in the last Scripture above, we see a perfect example of this as the fallen angel who led the revolt against God is called out by name—Satan.

But that isn't the only place we see demons called out by name. In Mark 5:9, we see another example: *"Then Jesus asked him, 'What is your name?' 'My name is Legion,'* he replied, *'for we are many.'"* In 1 John 4:3, it refers to the spirit of antichrist, and in

Luke 11:15, "Beelzebub" is called the prince of demons. Also, in Mark 9:25, Jesus commanded a spirit of deaf and mute to come out of a little boy.

Demons do have names and experience has taught us that usually their name coincides with what it is they are doing to the person they are tormenting. A demon called itself "Legion" because there were many demons all attacking one man in a graveyard, and a spirit of deaf and mute kept a boy from being able to speak. Today, we see a very similar pattern. Spirits that call themselves "Night Terrors" are responsible for placing horrible nightmares in little children and adults. Spirits that call themselves "Anger" are able to influence people to fits of anger. Spirits of "Pride" lead people into patterns of pride. In many cases, if you can identify the behavior a person is struggling with, you may have uncovered the name of the demon negatively harassing them. However, that is not always the case.

Some demons take on the names of Bible characters who acted in specific ways. For example, in Acts 13:6, there was a Jewish sorcerer and false prophet named "Bar-Jesus." Today, we come against many spirits who call themselves "Bar-Jesus" and their mission is to give believers false visions and false prophecy in hopes of casting doubt on the gifts of the Spirit. There are some spirits that take on the names of mythological gods. Molech (Leviticus 18:21), Asherah, and Baal (Judges 3:7), just to name a few. Often a demon will take a specific characteristic from a Bible character or a false god and try to influence or project those dreadful attributes onto a human being.

Who is Queen Jezebel?

As we begin to take a deeper look at the spirit of Jezebel, we can see how this spirit takes on the characteristics of Queen Jezebel found in the books of 1 Kings and 2 Kings. The spirit of

Jezebel is capable of high levels of control, much like is found in Scripture as Queen Jezebel controlled her husband, King Ahab. She not only controlled her husband, but she controlled the whole country through him. So much so that she was more like the king than the queen. 1 Kings 21:25 reveals Jezebel's influence: *"There was never a man like Ahab, who sold himself to do evil in the eyes of the LORD, urged on by Jezebel his wife."*

In 1 Kings 16:29-33, we begin to see how Jezebel's influence began:

> *In the thirty-eighth year of Asa king of Judah, Ahab son of Omri became king of Israel, and he reigned in Samaria over Israel twenty-two years. Ahab son of Omri did more evil in the eyes of the LORD than any of those before him. He not only considered it trivial to commit the sins of Jeroboam son of Nebat, but he also married Jezebel daughter of Ethbaal king of the Sidonians, and began to serve Baal and worship him." [It is interesting that Ethbaal means "like unto Baal"] He set up an altar for Baal in the temple of Baal that he built in Samaria. Ahab also made an Asherah pole and did more to provoke the LORD, the God of Israel, to anger than all the kings of Israel before him.*

We get a further look into the control Jezebel had over Ahab and Israel from 2 Kings 9:22: *"When Joram saw Jehu he asked, 'Have you come in peace, Jehu?' 'How can there be peace,' Jehu replied, 'as long as all the idolatry and witchcraft of your mother Jezebel abound?'"*

Ahab married Jezebel, who was an idol worshiper, and took on her religious practices by serving and worshiping Baal himself. From the very beginning Jezebel influenced and manipulated Ahab to do her bidding, even to the point of worshiping idols.

The name Jezebel in the *Jones' Dictionary of Old Testament Proper Names* means "without cohabitation." In his booklet called *The Jezebel Spirit*, Francis Frangipane comments on this definition or translation: *"This simply means she refuses to live together or cohabitate with anyone. Jezebel will not dwell with anyone unless she can control and dominate the relationship. When she seems submissive or servant like, it is only for the sake of gaining some strategic advantage. From her heart, she yields to no one."*

The Overall Mission of Jezebel

In the Old Testament, Queen Jezebel set out to kill and destroy all the prophets of God and lead the Israelites into idolatry. Today, this spirit is still obsessed with destroying the church. The spirit of Jezebel is a powerful and deceitful spirit that is capable of destroying churches of all sizes. Its number one goal is to destroy. The spirit of Jezebel knows that the best way to take out an entire church is to conquer the lead pastor and the team around him or her. John Maxwell says that *"everything rises and falls on leadership."* Demons are well aware of that fact and will do everything they can to undermine the leadership team, knowing that by so doing, they can possibly destroy the whole church or organization.

Because Jezebel is an evil spirit, it has the capacity to attack and influence human beings to the point of controlling them. But it is not limited to just attacking an individual. It can also have high levels of influence over a church, ministry, or territory. This spirit is simply following the footsteps and orders of its master, Satan. In John 10:10, Jesus reveals to us the mission of Satan: *"The thief comes only to steal and kill and destroy."*

All evil spirits, no matter their title or level of power, are focused on destruction. However, they all seem to be armed for battle in different ways. Jezebel is no different. This spirit has its own unique set of weapons or methods it uses to cause devastation. By looking at Jezebel under the microscope and learning more about its specific characteristics, we might be able to push this destructive virus back from our organization before it completes its mission.

There are hundreds of strategies the Jezebel spirit uses to destroy small groups, departments, and organizations. Trying to uncover and highlight all of those strategies is impossible. Nor have I seen or experienced all the ways a Jezebel spirit works. As I unpack some of the strategies and characteristics of Jezebel, and try to unveil some of the tactics I have seen or heard from others about how Jezebel works, I understand some will be familiar to you, while others will not. There are some definite patterns to how Jezebel operates, but each and every organization will have its own specific version dependent upon unique situations and personalities. There are no identical acting Jezebel-led individuals, but there are common threads. Each Jezebel-led individual is a blend of characteristic threads commonly associated with Jezebel. The varying degrees of each characteristic found within a Jezebel-led person causes each one to look a little different. But by knowing the basic threads or characteristics most often found in a Jezebel-led person, we can hopefully uncover where there is suspected Jezebel activity at work within our organizations.

A Closer Look at Jezebel

Jezebel's playing field is not limited to the office. It will attempt to show up wherever there is an anointed work of God being accomplished. This means it can show up in a Bible study group that's impacting lives. It can show up on a worship team, or a prayer group that is too powerful for Satan's liking. Healing prayer teams, deliverance teams, addiction recovery groups are all susceptible to an attack from Jezebel with the hope of destroying the group from the inside out. Anywhere people are finding Christ, or supernatural life transformation is happening, you can expect Jezebel will attempt to target them for destruction. Slowly but surely Jezebel will try to creep into the inner circle of the leader or leadership team with a mission to destroy. Hopefully by knowing some of Jezebel's most common characteristics, unsuspecting ministries can protect themselves from harm.

Control – Strategically, this just makes sense. The enemy wants to take control of our churches, so it stands to reason that Satan would send in Jezebel-controlled agents who are highly capable of dominating and controlling people. Hundreds of real-life stories confirm how the spirit of Jezebel seeks to gain as much control as it can. The more control it can wield over an organization, the greater the leverage it has to implement destruction. Over the course of time, a Jezebel-led individual will strive to take control from whomever and wherever it can. It might be the highest levels of leadership or it might be to subvert control from a small group leader. Wherever there is a potential opening for Satan to plant an agent of destruction, he will do it. Size doesn't matter. A Jezebel-led person is often described as being super controlling or dictator-like. Jezebel-led people typically set their sights on the highest-level leader within the department or group they want to control and begin to win over their trust.

Once the Jezebel-led person wins the trust of the leader, they begin to set their sights on more and more areas where they can quietly gain access and control. Information is a source of power and Jezebel-led people will try to monopolize all the information to flow through their position. This is so they can maintain control over people and situations with their incredible knowledge of what is going on in an organization. This information will often be used to impress the leader and can be leveraged for positional advantage. Jezebel-led people always seem to know everything about everybody, and they know how to use that knowledge to their benefit.

Jezebel-led people are very adept at creating a loyal spy network of people who keep them informed of all the latest scoop going on in the lives of people inside the organization and information about what is happening within the organization. The information-gathering agents may not even know they are being used for underhanded purposes. People who are influenced by a Jezebel spirit can be very bold and are not afraid to ask very direct questions to try and draw information out of people that can be used later. The more information gathered by a Jezebel-led individual, the more they can use it to their advantage. They may even use it to gain the respect of their supervisor by sharing things with them to help the supervisor make important decisions and cause the supervisor to rely on them for future reports.

One strategy of a Jezebel-led person is to highly serve the leader, striving to build trust, while secretly maneuvering to gain more and more control over the staff. As they become more entrenched and trusted by the leader, the more of a bullying dictator they become in the area or department they work in. Eventually, they will start decimating and destroying other team members in their department, or if they are allowed by the leader, will target the anointed staff around the leader.

A Jezebel-led person may not just settle for taking out team members from around the leader; they may choose to take out the leader. A strong-willed controlling board member may target a pastor by manipulating and controlling other board members into a coup against the pastor. It may be to remove the pastor, or it may be to steer a vote on something the controlling board member wants or doesn't want to happen. All too often, the controlling board member actually runs the church through the board. This Jezebel-led person may have controlled the board for decades and has repeatedly stopped any positive momentum or forward progress of the church. The spirit of Jezebel does not want any church to succeed and will strive to place willing representatives wherever it can to manipulate, block, or destroy the anointed work of God. If the controlling board member can't control the pastor, or if the pastor makes an attempt to remove the controlling board member, all-out war will be declared upon the pastor. The board member will target the pastor and lead a charge for his or her removal.

It is not uncommon for a Jezebel-led person to set their sights on a particular staff position, and regularly undermine the person currently serving in that position to the leader. The ultimate goal of the Jezebel-led person is to get the leader to remove that person and replace them with the Jezebel-led person or a person recommended by the Jezebel-led individual. (Those individuals recommended by the Jezebel-led person who are promoted become indebted followers of Jezebel.) It is frightful to watch this happen. But Jezebel uses this tactic to move itself or an ally up the leadership ladder. In so doing, Jezebel gains a new level of control, and subtly strikes fear into the remaining team who watch it happen. They become trained to obey the controlling person for fear the same thing will happen to them. As the leadership team watches the leader acquiesce to the Jezebel-led person's proposals, they begin to see who is really in control. Even though a Jezebel-led person may not hold a supervisory position, they have no problem exerting authority over others as if they do. There is certainly a supernatural component to all of this, as there is a boldness to control others on the part of the Jezebel-led person that is staggering and certainly not normal. In addition, Jezebel is able to place an extremely high level of fear upon those being controlled. Paralyzing fear that invokes obedience.

As the leadership team is slowly replaced with Jezebel allies, department meetings begin to subtly change. Ideas presented by the leader are challenged by the Jezebel-led person, and Jezebel's team of allies overrule the leader. But this is only the tip of the iceberg! One by one, the anointed leadership team is replaced by manager types who lead on the basis of title and not so much on relationships and influence. As they lead their departments and areas of responsibility, faith-driven ideas and programs are scrapped, spiritual vitality diminishes, and because of their controlling ways, joy is replaced by heaviness and hopelessness. Little by little, Jezebel gains more and more control by controlling the leaders placed over the organization. Soon, the organization begins to die a slow death. Remember, Jezebel's goal is to destroy.

There is an alternative way the spirit of Jezebel can attack an organization or a small group through control. Jezebel may not need to replace the lead team around the leader, if the lead team is willing to side with the Jezebel-led person to neutralize the leader. This tactic is often more effective in destroying smaller sized groups. For example, picture if you will, a Bible study group that has been meeting for over a year. The leader of the group is truly gifted at discerning and teaching the Word, and lives are being changed as a result of the precious teaching. Satan influences a Jezebel-led individual to join the group. This person is really gifted at flattery and winning people over with their relational charm. In a few months, the Jezebel-led person begins to quietly undermine the Bible study leader to one or two within the study group. Seeds of doubt and deception against the Bible study leader begin to emerge, and division and disunity destroy the group.

Jezebel-led people want to control everything, and they will seek to have control over every detail and decision. They will especially strive to have control over budgets and specifically have control over where money is spent. By controlling the money, their control and power over the organization soars. It is not uncommon for them to offer extra funds to a specific department, in order to gain the department leaders' support over an important issue. On the flip side, they can pull finances from a department leader who doesn't agree with their plans. They will seek to flatter and win over the largest givers in the organization so if they need extra funds for a special project, they have a source no one else may be able to tap into. It is also not uncommon for a Jezebel-led person to have large financial means of their own that they can use to control leaders and organizations. If you don't do what they want, they threaten to pull their money from the organization and leave.

Pride – Jezebel is never wrong, it must always be right. You will seldom win an argument with a Jezebel-led person because they truly believe they are right. They believe their ideas and plans are always the best. They have an inflated view of themselves, a selfish and delusional view that props themselves up in their own minds. They truly believe they have all the answers, and unfortunately, are often gifted communicators who can manipulate others to side with them. When a Jezebel-led individual has control, there is no collaboration with a team, and no one else's ideas matter. Though Jezebel-led people will falsely insist that they are open to new ideas, the truth is they manipulate and coerce people to accept their concepts and plans. This will eventually shut down the creativity of the team and cause team members to feel unheard and unimportant. In meetings, ideas presented by other people will sometimes be ridiculed and mocked as being silly by the person with Jezebel. This slowly teaches them to remain silent in future meetings or only share things they know will be acceptable. I have watched Jezebel-led individuals lead meetings where they communicate up-front that they want to hear the team's ideas. However, when none of the ideas match the direction they want to go, they completely dominate the meeting with their own concepts. They get very frustrated with anyone who dares to question their ideas, and it becomes clear that there was only going to be one set of ideas that would be acceptable—the ones presented by the Jezebel-led person. Everything in the early part of the meeting was simply a show put on to make people think the Jezebel-led person was open to other people's ideas.

Jezebel-led people refuse to submit to anyone. You almost have to see this to believe it. Jezebel-led individuals have a seething disdain for authority. They will not bow to anyone, unless it is an act in order to gain an advantage over someone. A number of years ago, a good friend of mine who was vice president of a fairly large organization shared this story with me. He told me how he was walking down a hallway one morning and saw a woman walking toward him who worked in one of the departments under his leadership. She was not a supervisor or a direct report to him and he seldom had had any direct communication with her. He did know about her reputation for being a rather loud-mouthed bully, so he put on a smile and told her good morning. His intention was to be kind and friendly. Unfortunately, her intention was to show him that she didn't bow down to anyone. He was dumbfounded by her response. She told him in very crude language that I won't use here, "Shove off and mind your own blankety-blank business." She was a part-time employee who held no position of leadership but hated anyone who represented authority.

This pride and disdain for authority is why it is so hard to help a Jezebel-led person find freedom. When they are confronted, they refuse to believe they could be wrong. Whether this is stubbornness on the part of the individual or a blindness placed over them by a demonic spirit, I do not know. However, what I do know is that when you are given the unfortunate task of confronting a person with the spirit of Jezebel, you can't give enough evidence for them to accept that they are wrong. I once had to confront a Jezebel-led woman who was spreading damaging lies throughout an organization. I shared with her evidence

I had gathered from other people who each heard her in separate moments and on separate days tell a very distinct lie about an individual. Their stories of what they heard the Jezebel-led person say all matched perfectly. As I shared what each person had told me, the Jezebel-led person denied ever having said anything even close to what her accusers were saying. And she did so with an indignant attitude that seemed to communicate: How dare you even question someone of my righteous standing in the Lord?

There is another place where pride has a tendency to show up with a Jezebel-led person. It can show up in a twisted prophetic gifting. Through years of leading spiritual warfare ministry, occasionally we have had discerning team members get caught up in the false notion that they are discerning things at a higher level than anyone else. This is dangerous and is the reason why we teach our team members how to test the spirits and why we use more than one discerner on each of our freedom teams. Sadly, we have discovered that Jezebel-led discerning people see their discernment as being much more advanced than anyone else's. They have a tendency to believe that only they are truly hearing the voice of God, and anyone who questions or disagrees with them have flawed or limited discernment. Remember, Jezebel is always right, and wants to dominate and control others. Even when several other discerning people see a twisting of the Jezebel-led person's gift, they will not accept that they could be wrong. These controlling and prideful discerners will often position themselves around lead pastors, small group leaders, and other ministry leaders, and use their distorted discerning gifts in an attempt to control them in the name of God. For example, "Pastor, last night I received a vision, and God told me to tell you that you are supposed to _____." All too often, their vision is an emotionally distorted version of what they want done. What makes this difficult is that they sometimes can and do discern some important things. In our ministry we teach that discerning people are messengers only. They may pass on to a ministry leader what they see, but then it is up to the ministry leader to interpret what God might be saying. It is not a discerning person's job to interpret or control a pastor or leader through visions, dreams, or words from the Lord.

Seduction and flattery – The Jezebel spirit has a way of seducing the leader, not necessarily in a sexual way although that is possible. Jezebel-led people have a way of winning over the leader in an almost supernatural way. It can be through flattery, or the appearance of high levels of loyalty. It can be through acts of kindness, an over-the-top work ethic that lightens the leader's workload, or verbal compliments that regularly build the leader's self-esteem. Over the course of time, the leader feels beholden to the Jezebel-led individual and all that person does for the leader. The Jezebel-led person causes the leader to think that he or she cannot survive without the person who has Jezebel. This unnerving form of seduction causes the leader to protect the person with Jezebel, while at the same time is blinded to the way the Jezebel-led individual abuses the rest of the department or leadership team. This causes a hopelessness on the team as the leader is incapable or unwilling to protect the team.

Imagine if you are the president of a fast-paced growing company. You are working seventy to eighty hours a week and barely have time to think about time off or family commitments. It's lonely at the top and there are few people who understand the price you are paying to keep the company moving forward. Your employees are dedicated and hardworking and you appreciate all they do. As the company expands, you are able to hire your first vice president. Within a month, the new vice president is working as many hours as you are and is taking giant projects off of your desk. Your workload is diminishing and you discover the new vice president is working more hours than you. After a few more months, the new vice president has become your greatest encourager and is the one person with whom you can share your deepest concerns and fears. Multiple conversations over lunch and staff meetings where the vice president demonstrates high loyalty to you in front of the team become normal. Your life slowly changes and your workload is nothing like it used to be. The new vice president continues to take on all the new projects in order to keep your workload very light.

As time progresses, you realize the vice president is running much of the company and is very happy to do so. During a lunch break, one of your longest and most reliable employees asks to speak with you. You are happy to talk with them and invite them to sit down. They are clearly nervous as they sit down with you. Their eyes constantly scan the room as they whisper, "May I have permission to speak honestly, sir?" "Why absolutely yes," you reply. "Sir, the staff is frightened and confused. Many want to quit because the environment has become so toxic and unbearable." You respond by saying, "What are you talking about? I've always prided myself in making this a great place for our employees to work." The employee replies by saying, "We know that, sir, but things have changed since you hired the new vice president. Sir, he is a demanding bully who threatens to fire anyone who doesn't measure up to his standards, and no one is ever good enough." The employee continues, "He is mean and abrasive, he belittles people and makes fun of them in front of the whole team. We used to be able to share new concepts and ideas freely in meetings, but our ideas are no longer welcome. Plus, he has told us that if anyone ever attempts to speak with you without his knowledge, they will be severely punished!"

As you walk back to your office, you are fuming with anger. You think in your mind, "How dare he, how dare he violate this company in such a way." You then march into the vice president's office and demand that he reprimand the employee for telling such horrendous lies about your loyal VP.

Sadly, that's often how it works. Then, when other trusted employees come and share similar stories with the president, the president begins to blame the employees for having bad attitudes. Deep resentment builds up in the president toward his employees for their lousy attitudes, while the person causing the poor work environment is untouched and allowed to continue to wreak havoc on the employees. The employees are regularly rebuked for their perceived rotten attitudes instead of the person responsible for it all. Eventually, hopelessness sets in and good people begin to look for jobs elsewhere. No matter how many people come to the president, the blind loyalty to the vice president persists. This can become even more confusing to the president if the Jezebel-led person has a team of allies who are all standing in defense of the Jezebel-led person. Imagine the confusion when all the allies cast blame for bad attitudes upon the very ones who are being abused.

When people under the dictatorship and oppression of a Jezebel-led individual try to explain to a leader or supervisor what is going on, the ones trying to point out the abuse and dysfunction will usually become targets. Jezebel-influenced people will convince the leader that those complaining are the troublemakers trying to stir up dissention and division in the ranks of the organization. The oppressed individuals are disciplined and reprimanded for speaking out, while the Jezebel-led person gains more influence with the leader for their perceived loyalty. The oppressed are silenced as the Jezebel-led person is able to shift the blame for the toxic attitudes onto the backs of the innocent. This ensures that no one will ever try to speak against the Jezebel-influenced person again. Meanwhile, those who are only trying to speak truth about an abusive situation are marginalized and trapped under the oppression until they choose to leave. And when they do leave, the leader celebrates. The leader thinks that the source of the bad attitudes has left the organization, not realizing the real source of the trouble is the abusive Jezebel-led person they have embraced.

Dominance – Once the Jezebel-led person has the loyalty of the leader, they will become a bully and will use the authority given to them by the leader to dominate and control the leadership team or employees within the department. The leader is deceived by the serving nature demonstrated toward them by the person with the Jezebel spirit, not seeing how the Jezebel-led person bullies and demands obedience from other employees. The servant heart goes only one way…up to the leader. The Jezebel-led individual expects the leadership team and other employees to serve them. Special favors will be granted to those loyal to the person with Jezebel, in order to keep them loyal. Jezebel-led people will identify team members they can win over and manipulate, and they are masterful at creating loyal allies to their cause. They often find people who are failing or who are insecure, and begin to win them over by propping them up or moving them into leadership roles they could never achieve on their own. This develops unwavering loyalty to the person with Jezebel. Anyone who dares to undermine the person with Jezebel will become a target for the Jezebel-led person and its allies to take out. If the Jezebel-led person is the boss, those who the boss discovers are in disagreement will be targeted for removal or harassment until they quit.

False prophet – The person with a Jezebel spirit often sees themselves as a prophet seeing things that no one else sees. This is self-diagnosed but is also supported by the leader and those who bow to Jezebel. Satan is cunning and will mix enough good into the mind of the person with Jezebel to make them appear to be wise. But under closer examination, the prophetic thoughts are often critical and driving in nature, creating a guilt-produced vision of the future that can drive the leadership team toward chaotic busyness that keeps the team on the verge of burnout. It can also create an unattainable perfectionistic environment that weighs heavy on the whole team as they feel compelled to be perfect in all they do. No one ever feels good enough but keeps chasing after this elusive goal.

Jezebel-led individuals are able to use their reputation of being prophetic and being able to hear the voice of God to their advantage. They can conjure up multitudes of supposedly God-driven ideas that on the surface all look good. Because the ideas usually make sense, and seem to be godly, no one dares to stand against them. Much of the time the ideas are of monumental heart-tugging proportion, and have to be, in order to draw the leader and team off mission. Often, this is the beginning of chaos, confusion, and weariness for the team. Jezebel-led individuals spin off so many new big ideas that must be done now, everyone is caught up in a tornado of activity that never ends. New projects are launched on a regular basis, but nothing is taken off of the team's plate to compensate for all the new activity. The atmosphere of the organization begins to shift as people are driven to accomplish all the new while still expected to maintain the old. The team begins to feel used, tired, overwhelmed, and like incompetent failures. All the busyness and chaos of doing what appears to be good, takes away from the overall plan and mission. Because the new ideas have good in them, the leader can point to and highlight those successes while the rest of the overall mission is falling apart. Satan is no fool; he will allow small portions of an organization to succeed in order to cover up for the overall destruction of the whole.

Division – The Jezebel spirit strives to create conflict between individuals, between team members and the leader, between departments, between campuses, between church members and leadership, between board members, and between lay ministry leaders and the leadership team. It uses strategically-placed individuals who are highly influenced by the Jezebel spirit to accomplish its mission. Jezebel will attempt to create division between small group leaders and the small group. People within Bible study groups will begin to fall away as a person in the group tries to take control away from the leader. Jezebel-influenced people will create overlapping leadership structures within an organization to give multiple people authority over the same area. This causes confusion and frustration between leaders and departments that will eventually lead to anger, mistrust, and disunity. Jezebel-led leaders will favor those who are loyal to them by allocating money to them for special projects, while taking funding from those who are not part of their inner circle. This contributes to high levels of resentment from one department to another.

Jezebel-led leaders will sometimes surround themselves with an insular team of loyal favorites, and it is abundantly clear to all who the favorites are. This is much different than a highly gifted and talented leadership team who work together to build the organization. One of the common strategies used by Jezebel when someone disagrees with them or confronts them for a mistake or bad behavior is to attack them. Nevertheless, they seldom try to do this alone. Jezebel will enlist her loyal followers to join in the attack.

When Jezebel is at work building a leadership team, it is more often than not filled with less competent loyal followers. Loyalty to the Jezebel-led person is more important than competency, which causes two things:

• It promotes resentment across the team as they watch less competent people being given more and more control. Many of the competent team members will be placed under the supervision and control of less competent leaders who are completely controlled by the Jezebel-led individual.

I recently read in one of John Maxwell's ministry blogs the following story about failed leaders:

> President Harding surrounded himself with loyal people, not competent people and his administration failed. The cabinet was filled with followers who could not lead, but only follow, they were only there to tell Harding how good he was and agree with his ideas. No critical thinking or alternative ideas seemed to originate from the team surrounding him.

• It may eventually cause good leaders to leave the organization and subtly influence the rest of the team who remain to chase after loyalty rather than competency.

When people see there are rewards for following the Jezebel-led person, others on the team not in Jezebel's inner circle may decide to strive harder to make it into the inner circle. This is a subtle way for Jezebel-led people to increase their sphere of control over the organization as people clamor to please the Jezebel-led person in order to get ahead. When they please the Jezebel-led person and get recognized for it, they become even more loyal followers. Those who follow a Jezebel-led person are expected to dominate and control their departments much the same way as the Jezebel-led person controls them. This leads to a culture of conflict and divisiveness within the organization.

Perfectionism – Jezebel-led people often demand perfection that is almost impossible to achieve. You can seldom do enough to please a person with Jezebel. When a person with Jezebel is in a high level of leadership, it can cause great frustration within a department or an organization. People strive to please the Jezebel-led person; however, no matter what they do it never seems to be good enough. The team can never win, but the

Jezebel-led person keeps them tied up in knots of anguish striving for Jezebel's approval. The person with Jezebel can bring a critical oppression over an entire organization. Seldom is anything good enough for the Jezebel-led individual, which is all part of the long-term strategy as it is a way of driving people into a trap. People become obsessed with trying to please the Jezebel-led person, which in a sick and twisted way is how the demonic spirit is generating obedience to itself. Driving them into a willing compulsion to obey leads them further into its control. Perfectionism becomes a heavy weight placed on the whole organization, which leads to a joyless existence and brings about a weariness from trying and never succeeding in being good enough. Criticism is the dominant theme within the department or organization and heaviness and fear are close behind. No one is allowed to be good enough and every task or project is marked with disapproval of some sort. An overarching fear begins to dominate the work environment. Anxiety sets in as the team knows that no matter how hard they try, their work will somehow miss the mark. They know they will be told by the Jezebel-led person all the ways they could have done it better. Eventually, much of the team will lose their self-confidence and will struggle with issues of self-worth. They will doubt their ability to make good decisions and will gradually look to the Jezebel-led person for deciding future projects and programs.

In David Johnson and Jeff VanVonderen's book, *The Subtle Power of Spiritual Abuse,* they write this observation: *"Spiritual abuse has the effect of making people extremely self-focused, preoccupied with doing things right and keeping happy those who are in places of authority. Recovery begins and continues with keeping our focus on God, what He has done, and who we are because of that."*

Brashness – I don't know if brashness is the right word, but I have watched Jezebel-led individuals say very harsh and mean things to people and feel absolutely no remorse for doing so. It is as if they have no conscience. Jezebel-led people can at times feel as if the world revolves around them. Their words cut people down, hurt people's feelings, and cause people to walk on eggshells around them. This is partially why people do not like to confront Jezebel-led people. They have sharp tongues, and little to no understanding of other people's feelings. And yet, if anyone does dare to speak back to them in the same manner, Jezebel-led individuals become highly offended. They let the offense simmer, and then turn themselves into a victim. "How dare they speak to me in such a way?" becomes their battle cry. Revenge and getting even becomes their main obsession. It is a one-sided street. They can criticize others verbally, but they cannot take it when it comes back at them. They simply cannot submit to anyone! When you couple that with the understanding that a Jezebel-led person is never wrong, they take on a godlike complex. They are always right, they are never flawed, and anyone who tries to tell them any different must be punished. The punishment may come in the form of a verbal tongue-lashing, or it may be much more hidden. Some Jezebel-led people can be passive-aggressive and work behind the scenes to get you fired. The bottom line is this: They are highly sensitive to criticism coming at them but have no awareness of how they hurt others. It may be that they see themselves on a throne, and it is their right to hurt others. Plus, their false prophetic pride leads them to believe they are too far above everyone else to be criticized.

Chapter 4

The Tenacity of Jezebel

I did not originally intend to include this chapter in the book. However, as I looked back at my personal experiences with Jezebel, and the stories of others, I realized this must be addressed. There is a hidden trait of Jezebel that is often overlooked. *Jezebel is tenacious. It never gives up!* It is like a super-virus that never goes away, and just when we think it is on its way out, it comes roaring back. If we can't find a way to stop it, it can be fatal to an organization or to a relationship.

Of all the qualities and characteristics of Jezebel, this may be the one that most explains the difficulty in removing the spirit from the organization. It is rigorously stubborn in its pursuit to destroy the kingdom of God. Never underestimate or dismiss Jezebel's ability to survive. It is like a cat that has nine lives. I'm reminded of the movie *"Butch Cassidy and the Sundance Kid"* in which Paul Newman and Robert Redford were being hunted down by a group of professional trackers. No matter where they went or tried to hide, the trackers relentlessly pursued them. Jezebel never gives up on its mission to destroy.

If I had to describe this ability it would be something like this: It has an ability to stay invisible. It wears a suit of Teflon that deflects all blame. It can masquerade as a source of good.

When you think everyone sees its destructive capabilities, it gets promoted. This spirit is like a crafty lawyer who finds all the loopholes. It has persuasive powers that charm others into protecting it from harm. Strategically, it is like a master chess player thinking four moves ahead of you. It has a supernatural ability to intimidate you, even when you know there is no reason to be afraid. The ability of Jezebel to spin truth and cast doubt upon those who speak truth against it is simply remarkable. It seems to be indestructible. When it appears to be captured, it is an escape artist that always manages to find a way out.

A good friend of mine spent years supervising a very controlling pastor in his district. This controlling pastor had chased away over two-thirds of his congregation. He resisted any and every attempt of my friend to help him. In fact, he would become furious if my friend even offered him any kind of advice. Because of Jezebel's influence, he was always right and my friend was always wrong. The congregation had even reached out to my friend begging for help. The church was dying a slow death as people were wounded by the pastor. Little by little, many drifted away from the church. My friend began working with his immediate supervisor, and they worked out a one-year plan to bring health back into the church. The plan included removing the abusive pastor and working hard to reach out to those who had been wounded by the pastor. My friend had talked to enough people to know that many of those who had left would be willing to return, knowing the source of the emotional hurt and pain was gone. My friend and his supervisor worked together on the plan for many months.

When it came time to implement the plan, my friend's supervisor came into town to implement step one—removing the controlling pastor. My friend was filled with hope again as he believed the church was about to enter into a new phase of healing and hope. The supervisor met with the Jezebel-led pastor for well over an hour. When he came out of the meeting, my friend was ready to begin to implement step two of the plan. However, what happened next demonstrates the frightening ability of a Jezebel spirit to survive. My friend's supervisor told him the plan had changed. The abusive pastor was not going to be removed, and instead, my friend was being removed as the pastor's supervisor. The abusive pastor was being placed directly underneath the authority of my friend's boss. The abusive pastor remained in charge, continued to abuse, continued to rebuke the wisdom of his new boss, and continued to drive the few remaining people away. The Jezebel-led leader, through the power and deceit of Jezebel, was given the authority to finish its mission…destroy the church. The church dwindled down to around fifteen people and the abusive pastor finally left.

This Jezebel-led leader was within minutes of being removed from power and was still able to overturn months of planning in one short meeting. With all the evidence stacked against the controlling pastor, Jezebel not only survived, but was also able to take out the person who was a threat to its existence. Story after tragic story told to me by others follows this same pattern. Jezebel not only finds ways to survive, it finds ways to win. It not only stays in power but is able to neutralize those who stand against it.

At this point, I can almost feel your sense of hopelessness in dealing with a Jezebel-led person. I am sorry for projecting that kind of image. You may even think I have exaggerated the ability of this spirit to survive. I assure you I have not. We dare not ignore this threat. I think the part of its ability to survive is our inability to see how strong this spirit really is. If we continue to underestimate the ability of this spirit, it will continue to ravage our organizations.

The stories of how this spirit is decimating churches around the world weigh heavy on my heart. I know that by painting such a dark picture of what this spirit is capable of could lead to fear and hopelessness. But that is not my intention. It is only by seeing the truth that we have any chance of removing this spirit from our midst. A long time ago, when I was just getting started in spiritual warfare ministry, I received a word from the Lord while leading a freedom session. We were dealing with an arrogant and stubborn spirit that was refusing to leave. One of the discerners on my team handed me a message we believe came from the Holy Spirit. It said, "Remember, you are not dealing with puppy dogs and butterflies. Be strong and courageous, take the authority I have given you and remove this spirit, for I Am with you."

Wow, within just a few minutes the spirit was removed. Jesus is all-powerful and there isn't a demonic spirit that has been created that doesn't have to submit to the authority of Christ. In Ephesians 1:18-21, we find these encouraging words:

> *I pray also that the eyes of your heart may be enlightened in order that you may know the hope to which he has called you, the riches of his glorious inheritance in the saints, and in his incomparably great power for us who believe. That power is like the working of his mighty strength, which he exerted in Christ when he raised him from the dead and seated him at his right hand in the heavenly realms, far above all rule and authority, power and dominion, and every title that can be given, not only in the present age but also in the one to come.*

A significant problem with Jezebel (or any spirit of evil) occurs when the person who Jezebel is controlling doesn't want to repent and be free of the Jezebel spirit. Their freewill decision blocks this spirit from being removed from the person. Jesus chooses not to interrupt a person's freewill right to make their own decision. He doesn't want any of us to sin, but He doesn't stop us from doing so. It's not that He doesn't care about our decision, because He does care. In fact, He is actively working on us right up to the point of us making the decision. Think of your conscience. How many times have you had the Holy Spirit nudging you and saying, "Please don't commit that sin"? And how many of us have completely ignored the Spirit's prompting and have gone forward with the sin? All of us!

So, what do we do with this conundrum? How do we help the person and the organization when the Jezebel-led person doesn't want to be free? This is why this chapter is hard to write. But this is also why I think this chapter is necessary. It is hard to hear how tenacious this spirit is, and how hard it is to remove. In my opinion, it is only by facing this truth that we will have the courage to do the hard stuff. What is the hard stuff? Understanding that we can't play nice with a Jezebel-led person who doesn't want to be free. We have to be strong and courageous. We have to do whatever it takes to remove the person from the organization. And as we are doing this, know that the Jezebel spirit has an ability to place high levels of blame upon you. You may feel overwhelmed with guilt and confusion. The Jezebel spirit will project thoughts that promote fear and tie you up in knots of shame at the idea of firing them after all they have done for you. Combine that with how easy it is for Jezebel to influence people to be its allies, and all of a sudden other people are telling you what a mistake it is to let go of the Jezebel-led person.

Before I was called into ministry, I had the privilege of supervising large groups of people. Most of those people were wonderful and I enjoyed working with them. On rare occasions, I had to fire people. This was never something I looked forward to doing and I pretty much hated having to do. When the day came for the final confrontation, it was never fun. Your emotions are all over the place, especially as a Christian. However, what I have learned firsthand is that if the person you have to let go is a Jezebel-led individual, the emotional torment prior to the meeting is ten times worse. The spirit of Jezebel begins an all-out war with your mind and emotions in an attempt to stop you. It does not want its agent removed. Here are a few examples of how Jezebel might attempt to influence your decision.

Supernatural fear and anxiety – It's unimaginable the level of oppression that can be placed against a person or group of people who are trying to remove a Jezebel. Waves of confusion, fear, and anxiety can be brought to bear against those attempting to correct or remove Jezebel. These are invisible waves of fear that come out of nowhere. They can be paralyzing if you are not ready to fight them off with prayer. Even then, they can rock your world. The secret words directed into the minds of the people trying to remove Jezebel are all fear-based: "Back away from this, it's not worth the anxiety and fear you are feeling." "Keep it up and this anxiety and oppression will only increase. Stop and it all goes away." Everything is sent by the Jezebel spirit to paralyze you with fear and make you stop. Anyone who is ever put in the position to remove a Jezebel from power must understand they will be attacked at a level they cannot comprehend. If they don't understand it is not flesh and blood, but spiritual forces of evil in this dark world, they will most likely lose.

The spirit of Jezebel has a way of digging into your feelings. It can supernaturally intensify your emotions and twist them to work against you. It's like an orchestra conductor who with the wave of a wand can cause a whole section of the ensemble to increase in volume. Every insecurity you have ever dealt with will rise up to discourage you—all in an attempt to paralyze you. Then, by pointing the wand to another section, fear and anxiety will rise up, or anger and frustration. Jezebel is also capable of pulling up debilitating lies from your past. Thoughts that you are a failure or that you will never measure up will come crashing into your mind. You will be reminded of mistakes you have made and critical words falsely spoken over you by others. Jezebel is constantly stirring the pot of your emotions to discourage you and get you to doubt yourself. Each wave of intensified thoughts and emotions are part of Jezebel's strategic plan to disqualify you mentally. Through all of this, the Jezebel spirit will try to get you to give up your attempt to remove the Jezebel-led person from the team. By filling you with doubt, it can cause you to believe you are the broken one, and that you can't survive without the Jezebel-led person. It will try to convince you that you are not morally strong enough, or mentally tough enough to take on a person with the Jezebel spirit. All of this is partially why so many people back down from a Jezebel-led person and allow them to remain in power. The supernatural ability of the Jezebel spirit to cause anxiety and confusion can be debilitating.

For those who are tasked with the assignment to remove a Jezebel-led person from your team, I highly recommend you enlist two or three people who are not tied to the Jezebel-led person and who fully understand how Jezebel operates. You will need their mental support as a check and balance against the lies Jezebel will be throwing at you to try to stop you. You will need to surround yourself with people who will keep you grounded in truth about you, and focused on the destructive actions of Jezebel in your organization. Otherwise, Jezebel stands a good chance of getting you to disqualify yourself, and convincing you to take yourself out of the game.

False repentance - The Jezebel spirit can sometimes have a flare for the dramatic. It is not uncommon for a Jezebel-led person to manipulate your emotions to gain back control. It is the "rhetoric of repentance" without actual repentance. For example: An abusive, controlling husband, who has repeatedly abused his wife and is confronted with separation from his wife, will go into an emotional charade that could win an Oscar. The emotional grandstanding will include weeping, apologies for past behavior, promises of change, and gut-wrenching appeals for mercy and forgiveness. The abused person is pacified by Jezebel's false repentance. The act is so convincing that they are filled with compassion for the abuser. Sadly, over time, the routine gets repeated over and over again because of the same abusive behaviors, and little-to-no change. This might shed light on why some who are in long-term abusive relationships are never able to walk away from them. Jezebel sees compassion as a form of weakness and uses false repentance to manipulate the compassion of an individual to its advantage. Jezebel will attempt to use the same strategy of false repentance to persuade a boss not to fire them.

Distorted truth - Jezebel can at times twist things to such an extent that an abused person can sometimes be made to feel like they are the one who is really the problem. Jezebel is masterful at turning the table on those who are confronting the Jezebel-led person for their unacceptable behavior. Somehow, those confronting Jezebel for significant violations of controlling or bullying are made to believe it was all their fault. It is a lie, but it throws confusion into the situation and can sometimes keep the abused person, or the confronting person from continuing the battle to remove Jezebel.

I recently read a quote by Shannon L. Alder that was posted on Facebook. Though it is referring to a narcissist, it fits perfectly with the actions of a Jezebel-led person:

> You will never get the truth out of a narcissist. The closest you will ever come is a story that either makes them the victim or the hero, but never the villain.

Oh, how this describes a Jezebel-led person. They live in a world of false reality. They can be selfish, mean, and hurtful to others and it is never their fault. It's like an ultra-controlling husband who is defending himself for losing his temper with his wife over a dirty spot on a dish. "If you would have done a better job cleaning the dishes, I wouldn't have to treat you this way. It was your mistake that made me lose my temper. Somebody has to teach you how to do things right!" Because they have a highly distorted view of themselves, nothing can ever be their fault. They can always justify their bad behavior, and it is usually by putting the blame for their actions on you. They don't need to address their anger issues; after all, if the wife would simply live up to the Jezebel-led husband's impossible expectations, he wouldn't need to get angry. So, the poor wife is always on the wrong side of things. She can't win. It's her fault the dish was dirty and it's her fault her husband lost his temper. This is just another form of abusive control based on distorted truth. She is always in a position of defending herself, while her abusive husband never accepts any responsibility for his abusive ways. This is one of the ways Jezebel is able to deflect any blame being placed on themselves and keeping people in bondage to them. If it wasn't a dirty dish, it would be a misplaced remote control or running out of a favorite snack food. There will always be something not right enough, so the Jezebel-led spouse can always keep their partner in a cycle of feeling like they never measure up. This leads to the abused spouse falsely believing they deserve the verbal or physical abuse. As long as the abused spouse accepts the blame, they lock themselves into a lifetime of abusive control.

Another strategy of the spirit of Jezebel is to twist things in the mind of the Jezebel-led person. When someone tries to speak truth into their life, they become deceived into believing that the truth presented to them is a demonic spiritual attack. In Jack Deere's book, *"Surprised By the Power of the Spirit,"* he explains how this happens:

> *Some people seem to assume that every negative experience, every obstacle in our path, is a result of personal opposition to our endeavors. This assumption can keep us from hearing God. If God has permitted a trial to lead us to repentance or to refine us, and we assume it is only Satan hindering us, we will never seek the repentance nor the change God wants to bring us.*

Jezebel is frequently able to take spiritual advice from well-meaning friends, and turn it into a spiritual attack. Things that are actually true about the Jezebel-led person get distorted, and turned into an offense. Words spoken out of love and meant to be a blessing are twisted into something they were never intended to be. As the offense festers over the course of time, it causes the Jezebel-led person to see themselves as a victim.

The victimization trap – Once they see themselves as a victim, the truth spoken to them by others, in an attempt to help them grow in Christ, morphs into what they see as an all-out spiritual attack. When they see it as an attack instead of wisdom from a friend or a boss, they miss out on an opportunity for repentance and real-life change. This is magnified when Jezebel convinces the Jezebel-led person that they are incapable of being wrong.

Well-meaning advice intended to encourage them to become more Christlike is turned into something it was never meant to be. As the Jezebel-led person takes on a victimlike attitude, the advice giver becomes the bad person, and the Jezebel-led person doesn't feel the need to change.

In John Paul Jackson's book, *"Unmasking the Jezebel Spirit,"* Jackson shares this thought: *"Someone with a Jezebel spirit will seek to gain sympathy from many people, especially when confronted. Such individuals will claim they have been spiritually abused."* By becoming a victim, the broken Jezebel-led person can cause people to feel sorry for them. Through emotional manipulation, the Jezebel-led person is able to attract sympathy from others, while demonizing the person trying to help them to change. It is like a prophet in the Old Testament going into a city and pronouncing a need to repent. But the announcement from God to repent is met with stubborn resistance and the prophet becomes the hated and despised one. Some Jezebel-led people will take those who have presented truth and attempt to turn their warnings into a spiritual attack upon themselves and their ministry. They just can't handle anyone telling them they are wrong. In their mind, the Jezebel spirit convinces them that they are the truly called ones, they are the only ones who truly hear the voice of God. When what they are doing is challenged, it can't be coming from God, because only they hear from God, so it has to be an attack from the enemy.

Many Jezebel-led people believe they are highly gifted with prophecy, and typically their prophetic gift is distorted by pride. Pride leads them to believe a lie. They believe they are the only one gifted enough to truly hear God's directives. When real truth is presented to them by another person, their pride and distorted prophetic gift will not only reject the truth but will also twist it, and influence them to be highly offended. Anything that is shared from another person that doesn't match their own distorted perception of themselves must be wrong. Therefore, they see it as a spiritual attack sent against their perceived calling and spiritual gifts.

These are some of the reasons why it is so difficult to help a Jezebel-led person to find freedom. They are seldom open to receive any form of correction or advice, as it goes against the deceptive thoughts being fed into their mind by Jezebel. It is frustrating to see the level of deceit Jezebel can spin to deflect blame off of itself, and turn well-meaning advice from friends into a spiritual attack.

Empty apologies - Apologies can be diversionary tactics used by Jezebel to disarm their opposition. Once the apology is given, the one confronting Jezebel is led to believe that the Jezebel-led person understands and will begin to change. The apologies are usually a dramatic act without repentance. They are used to confuse or sidetrack the opposition on the surface, but underneath, Jezebel's secret mission or plan will keep moving forward. Jezebel might slow down toward achieving its goal, but only for appearances and only for a short time. Apologies will usually be void of any remorse or personal responsibility to change.

These empty apologies have the secondary effect of coming across as being godly and religious. Jezebel-led people will try to appear to be godlier than the person confronting them for poor conduct. This causes the confronter to doubt themselves in their disapproval of Jezebel's behavior. Putting on the appearance of godly sorrow can divert or cause those opposing Jezebel's plan to pause or relent. It can be confusing, because as Christians we want to forgive and are commanded to forgive. I think we can forgive...but keep our eyes open looking for real change. Abusive controlling men use this ploy over and over again to divert attention and win back the loyalty of their abused spouse. They use it because it works over and over again. It even works to win over outside influencers—those friends and family of abused people who take the side of the abuser over the abused. This may happen because of the abuser's persuasive apologies that can be over-the-top dramatic presentations meant to elicit sympathy. And, oh how Jezebel knows how to elicit sympathy. It is like a supernatural seduction into its web that ensnares people and turns them into allies. It partially explains why abused people defend the abuser.

Imagine a leader confronting a Jezebel-led person for their proven bullying and controlling behavior, and leaving the meeting filled with guilt and shame for trying. As Jezebel used all of its defensive maneuvers, the leader not only didn't fire them, they were filled with compassion toward the Jezebel-led person and gave them more responsibility. As Jezebel begged for another chance and promised with tears to do better, the leader let down his guard. When Jezebel saw the leader beginning to soften, the siren-like demonic power to ensnare kicked in. Through tears the Jezebel-led person said, "Haven't I worked hard for you? All the hours I have put in trying to make this place a success. I know I may come across as bossy, I'm sorry that people felt bullied, it won't happen again. I'm only trying to help people be better. I'm such a perfectionist that I just think people should be giving their best. What's wrong with that?"

Once the empty apologies are spoken, then, the case for being a victim can begin:

"Nobody understands me, I work so hard, and all I get is a slap in the face. Nobody works harder than I do."

"They are all just out to get me because I work so hard and they are jealous of how much I get done. I make them all look bad, and they don't like it."

"If you only knew what goes on when you are not around, they all talk bad about you; they goof-off and make mistakes. I'm not allowed to be in their little cliques, because I stand up for you. I'm the only one in the whole department who defends you, and here you are firing me."

"I'm the only one with my nose to the grindstone and you are going to let me go. That's not fair."

After they have enticed you into feeling sorry for them, the stage is set for drawing you into an alliance with them:

"If you let me go, the whole department will crumble, there's no one left to defend you and get the work done right. I am the only one loyal to you. They are certainly not. They make jokes about you behind your back. They

think you are an embarrassment to the organization. But I don't. This place can't survive without you. Please let me stay, I'll be your right-hand person. I'm sorry you feel let down. Please give me another chance. Please! I'll let you know everything going on behind your back. You can trust me; in fact, if you put me in charge of the department, I'll make sure the production goes way up. I know where all the mistakes are being made and I know all the ones who are goofing off. Please give me a chance to prove myself and I promise, you will not be sorry. You know I love Jesus, you know I am loyal to you, this is all an attack by Satan to destroy me and keep my spiritual gifts from being used for the kingdom. Besides, you are a Christian, I thought Christians forgave one another."

It is a perfect storm of Jezebel tendencies and strategies that all lead to confusion.

Lies, false repentance, drama, loyalty, guilt, empty apologies, sympathy, twisting of truth, and being under a supposed spiritual attack; it's all there. Plus, the hidden seduction emanating from the spirit of Jezebel that no one can see, drawing the leader into its web, turning the leader into an ally.

Over the years, I have been dumbfounded by the resiliency of this spirit to remain in control. Its ability to take advantage of our kindness and compassion is what often propels it forward and allows it to continue to dominate and control. Here is the good news!! This spirit can be removed from your organization. We have removed several Jezebel-led individuals from our ministry over the last eight years. It was never fun, and it was never easy, but it can be done. It takes courage and determination to expel it from your organization. When confronting a Jezebel-led individual, stay on mission and don't negotiate. Don't face it alone. Bring in a trusted staff person or board member to help you remain strong. In most cases, removing the Jezebel-led person is your best option. Create a list of truth statements to counter Jezebel's attempts to persuade you from your mission. Build your case of bullying and control. Re-examine the characteristics found in Chapter 1 and make a list of the ones that match the actions of the person you are confronting. Watch for the defensive tactics highlighted in this chapter, and avoid falling for them. Stay strong and quickly cut off the Jezebel-led person's ties to the organization. Expect high levels of anxiety before you meet. However, once the confrontation is over and you have cut ties with Jezebel, the anxiety will subside and the heaviness over the organization will dissipate very quickly. You will feel like the organization is able to breathe again. You will be a hero to your staff and team for being willing to protect them. Remember, if you don't protect them, no one else will.

Chapter 5

How Jezebel Affects the Team

Shelly was a hard-working employee. She had built a great relationship of trust with her long-time customer base. They loved Shelly and valued her ideas for improving their business. They appreciated her willingness to listen to their feedback on new products, and how she worked hard to iron out any problems they encountered. Shelly spent years nurturing relationships with her customer base and seldom if ever had any complaints from any of them. Shelly got along great with her upper management team and was highly respected by them for her years of excellent service to the company and to her clients. Shelly loved her job and loved helping her client base find solutions to their problems. Things in general were good for Shelly and her future with the company looked bright.

Over the course of time, the company announced there would be changes in the management structure. Shelly was informed that she was going to be working for a new boss. At first, everything seemed to be going very well. Her new boss would often flatter her with compliments. She called Shelly "sweetie" and "honey" at the weekly meetings and really made

Shelly feel appreciated. She would emphasize weekly to Shelly how she was on Shelly's side and how Shelly could absolutely trust her to always have Shelly's best interest in mind.

Unfortunately, her boss's actions did not match up to the words she regularly uttered in Shelly's presence. It wasn't long before Shelly began to discover she was being set up by her new boss. The supposedly kind and supportive boss was sending out false emails depicting Shelly as incompetent and incapable of doing her job. In addition, her boss sent out emails where she falsely accused Shelly of mistakes, and then would position herself as the hero who had to come to the rescue and fix all of Shelly's errors. None of this was true. In each case, Shelly had already worked through the problems presented to her by her customers and had provided wonderful solutions to each one. The customers, as always, were very pleased with how Shelly quickly responded to their needs. However, this is not what was being conveyed to the vice presidents by Shelly's boss. Upper-level management was receiving reports that were chocked full of lies depicting Shelly as failing the customers, and stories of how the boss had to continuously save the day. It wasn't long and Shelly's boss was able to create an ally with a vice president in another area of the company. It was clear that Shelly's boss was trying to gain more power and control by manipulating stories to impress the vice president. Her new boss's ability to flatter people just like she did to Shelly served her well to win over the trust of the unsuspecting VP.

Shelly was beside herself. She hadn't done anything wrong; her customer base assured her they were very happy with the service she was providing them. Yet, she was in a fight for her job. Her boss tried to control her and micromanage her at every opportunity, always looking for ways to make Shelly look bad and make herself look like a hero to her vice president. It got to the point where Shelly was spending more and more time retrieving email conversations with her client base just to prove her innocence. It wasn't long and Shelly went from totally loving her job to fear and frustration. One nightmare situation after another created by Shelly's boss in an attempt to undermine her and gain more power left Shelly feeling helpless and hopeless.

Shelly still loved the work she was doing for her clients and continued to have great relationships with them. Only now, she was doing so under a heavy weight of oppression. The only thing that changed was the addition of one flattering, selfish, controlling and manipulating boss who had no problem lying to gain power at the expense of others. A perfect description of what Jezebel does.

When you work alongside a Jezebel-led person, it can be a very frustrating experience. The Jezebel spirit will eventually affect everyone over the course of time, and seldom in a good way. Many friends have shared with me painful stories from their past work experiences that include the secular, church, and nonprofit worlds. They have witnessed firsthand how the Jezebel spirit is able to oppress individuals, small groups, departments, lead teams, churches, nonprofits and other organizations. Jezebel seldom works alone. The truth is that almost all demonic spirits work in conjunction with other evil spirits. They combine forces to bring about division and destruction. After Jezebel gets established in an organization, Jezebel invites a whole host of other demons to help carry out the overall destructive assignment against the team.

Demonic Tag Teams

When I was growing up, I remember our family watching "All-Star Wrestling" on TV. It was filled with outrageous drama and staged confrontations between the most popular wrestlers to allure people into coming to the next title match. Some of those events were called "Tag Team Matches" as two wrestlers would combine forces to take on another team of two. Each team could only have one wrestler participating at one time. But if one of the wrestlers got tired and could tag the hand of his partner outside the ring, his teammate would jump into the ring and take his place.

After years of doing this ministry, I have come to realize there are what we might call demonic tag teams. Sometimes there are more than one demon tag teaming against us at one time. I want to share some of the more common demons that combine forces with Jezebel to destroy or severely hinder organizations. The following list highlights some of the more frequent demonic alliances we find working with Jezebel.

Apathy – This is very sad to see, especially when you have a team of great leaders who love to be inventive and think outside the box. Once a Jezebel-led leader reaches a high enough position to control a team, creativity is pretty much stifled. Ideas presented in meetings where Jezebel resides are usually dismissed and sometimes even mocked or laughed at by the person with Jezebel.

A friend of mine shared a story with me about a meeting he sat in where a person with Jezebel was invited to lead the meeting. It was supposed to be a brainstorming meeting, and the team was looking for new ways to market a new product. The Jezebel-led person was in the inner circle of the vice president and was given permission to take the lead. Everyone in the room knew about the close relationship the meeting leader had with the vice president. At first, there seemed to be a lot of energy and excitement as they started sharing new ideas and concepts, but that ended very quickly. As each idea was presented, the Jezebel-led person openly laughed and criticized each person who tried to share an idea. My friend said it was frustrating to watch this leader bully and put down nearly every idea presented. Little by little the room got quieter and quieter as those in the room simply shut down and stopped sharing. As the ideas from the group began to cease, the Jezebel-led leader began to write down all of his ideas on the white board. If anyone in the room dared to criticize or explain why his ideas might not work, they were made to feel like they were simpletons who had no clue how to run a business. It became obvious that there was only one person in the room who was smart enough to know a good idea from a bad one.

This is just one meeting and one example of how Jezebel works. One bad meeting isn't going to have a significant impact on your organization. The danger unfolds when the Jezebel-led person begins to run entire departments in this manner and gets away with it. As Jezebel controls every idea and shuts down the creative ideas of other talented leaders, apathy will begin to set in. The talented and gifted support team will become indifferent. They will think, "Why bother to brainstorm or suggest new ideas? My ideas and plans for improvement don't matter." They will eventually become bored and uninterested in their job and seek employment somewhere else where their ideas will matter. Over time, your organization will exchange gifted employees, who could significantly impact your future, for people who are simply trained to follow the ideas of Jezebel. Before you think that might not be so bad, remember Jezebel's overarching mission is to destroy your organization. If Jezebel-like leaders are the only ones who are allowed to strategize for your organization, difficult and challenging days are ahead. When you really need your most creative team members to help you pull the organization out of the nosedive, they will be stifled by fear, they won't care, or they will have already left your organization.

Anger and resentment - When the bully in our ranks is protected by the leader, hopelessness invades the culture. Before long, anger and resentment will build up toward the bully and toward the leader who allows it to happen. There may also be resentment toward any of the allies Jezebel has managed to win over. These are the ones who follow the Jezebel-led person's every command and use their close position to Jezebel to power over other people or receive favors. When the most loyal to the organization are habitually bullied, put down, and forced to deal with completely insane and unacceptable circumstances, anger and resentment will rise up within the ranks. When a few long-term employees attempt to approach the leader of the organization for help and are squashed for doing so, the anger intensifies. In many cases, those who go to the leader are punished. As the anger and resentment builds up and spreads across the team, the destructive Jezebel virus works its way throughout the organization. Good people become disillusioned, and since they have no one in leadership they can talk to, they huddle together and share their disappointments and fear.

As the anger and resentment spread, the overall corporate atmosphere is deeply affected. The longer leadership tolerates Jezebel's antics, the greater the chances for a slow but steady exodus of good employees. In addition, during the process of hurt and angry people leaving, the organization inherits a bad reputation. Once an organization gets a reputation for being a difficult place to work, it dissuades other talented people from applying for a job. Over the course of time, this will undercut the overall level of leadership within the organization.

We must not think demons are stupid. Instead, we must understand they are tactical and patient. Once they initiate a plan, they will coax it along for whatever length of time necessary to achieve their overall goal of destruction. If it takes five years to deplete an organization of good leadership, then so be it. The enemy knows that by depleting an organization of strong leadership, it will eventually crumble.

Fear – One of the dominating undercurrents of a Jezebel-influenced environment is fear. The sense of fear may or may not be realistic, but it is certainly prevalent within the group being controlled by a Jezebel-led person. Evil spirits can attack us in many ways, but one of the more prominent ways is by attacking our minds and emotions. As I mentioned before, Jezebel has an ability to intensify our emotions. In other words, if we struggle with fear, demons can ramp it up to a higher level. For some this can include panic attacks. When they attack our minds, it is usually with a lie, a false perception of what is real, or a hyperintensified version of reality. They can increase the number of times they project lies into our minds. Think about how the enemy projects temptations into your mind and you get a glimpse of how they are able to do this. This partially explains how a Jezebel spirit so easily intimidates individuals. They can attack our minds with false, exaggerated, worse-case scenarios that paralyze us. When the environment we work in is already unhealthy, it is not difficult to see how demons will use that to torture us with inflated ideas of what could possibly happen.

Of course, there is another factor that produces high levels of fear. Jezebel-led people can be ruthless in their need to control people. The fear that can be unleashed within a department is hard to imagine. When the Jezebel-led person is the leader, or is protected by the leader, despair can quickly overtake an individual or a department. Often the fear is very real as the Jezebel-led person bullies people and there is no one to protect those being bullied. When abusive control is allowed to go unchecked, the spirit of fear will intensify the emotions of those being intimidated by a dictatorial environment. Some will refuse to be dominated and will leave, while others will be overwhelmed with insecurity. The fear of not being able to find another job will cause them to stay. Their fear keeps them trapped under the rule of Jezebel.

Because the team outside of the Jezebel-led person's inner circle of allies has watched employees be demoted, isolated, or fired, they become filled with fear. They are afraid that if they don't fully agree with the dysfunction of the organization, they too will be let go. There begins to be an overshadowing atmosphere of fear within the ranks of the organization. Even people who have held very secure positions for many years within the organization will begin to doubt their value and importance to the overall team. This is magnified only by Jezebel's unchecked dominance and bullying of the team. It soon becomes very clear that any attempt by a team member to try and expose Jezebel's deeds to the leader will result in negative consequences for the person trying to speak out. Fear of making a mistake, fear of being reprimanded, fear of confrontation, fear of being belittled or put down in front of others, fear of losing their job—coupled with the reality of how demons induce and magnify fear through our thoughts—all contribute to an environment of dread.

Fear of rejection – Jezebel-led people have a very sick and twisted way of fostering a need in those they abuse to apologize to them. It stems from a fear of rejection. In Steve Sampson's book, *Discerning and Defeating the Ahab Spirit*, he shares his own personal story with this issue:

> *In my own experience, I struggled most in situations where I was offended and verbally abused. I would actually go to the person who offended or hurt me and apologize! I rationalized that I was taking the high road, but really, I was denying my true convictions. Worse, the aggressive person would not accept my apology. I was naïve enough to expect at least an "I'm sorry, too." Instead, I would get a response such as, "You should be sorry," or "Okay, just don't let it happen again."*

I also learned that Jezebels (control freaks) never truly forgive you; they save your "offense" as ammunition for future conflicts. The next time a problem arises, every past issue or offense will be brought up in your face. And you were naïve enough to believe it was forgiven and forgotten.

He goes on to write about controlling people:

They are usually defensive, cutting and unforgiving. They act as if your opinion or input is worthless, and they believe theirs is right and even in alignment with God's truth. An inflated ego masks their own low self-esteem (p. 50).

As we have previously stated, Jezebel is never wrong, totally believing it is the only one who truly hears from God. It is our fear of rejection and need to please other people that drives us to apologize and hope we can somehow appease the person who is upset with us. Unfortunately, Jezebel uses our fear of rejection to its advantage. It is this tactic that keeps us subtly under its control. We seldom can see how going overboard trying to please them keeps us in bondage to them. Our desire for their approval keeps us subservient to them.

Doubt – When Jezebel-led people are permitted to bully and dominate over people and control the leader, people on staff begin to doubt the leader's ability to lead and protect the team. They also begin to doubt the goodness of the organization that allows it to happen. If the organization is Christian-based, they may also doubt the goodness of God. If the Jezebel-led person is the leader, they may even doubt the leader's call into ministry.

The longer the dominating person is allowed to go unchecked, the more doubt builds up that anything will ever change. Hopelessness sets in as the team has nowhere to go for help inside the organization. Most Jezebel-led people have been given free rein and are seldom accountable to anyone. Even if there is some form of accountability, Jezebel's refusal to submit to any kind of authority usually means they walk all over the person they are accountable to, or they schmooze them with false flattery. In many cases, the Jezebel-led individual slowly sets things up so everything, including complaints, must go through them first before being presented to the overall leader. It is not uncommon for the Jezebel-led person to use their given authority to block employees from any meetings with the senior leader until they know the purpose for the meeting. If they don't like your topic of discussion, you are not allowed a meeting. If by chance they find out you veered away from the topic in the meeting, you can probably expect an interrogation on what you did say and a reprimand for doing so. Jezebel must maintain absolute control.

There is another form of doubt that begins to occur after being under the thumb of a Jezebel-led person. *Self-doubt*. I have observed this over and over as people are stripped of their confidence by a Jezebel-led person who is always right. Jezebel-led people have a way of promoting their superiority over everyone and have an ability to make everyone around them who disagrees with them feel stupid. They carry a persona of arrogance about them that projects outward to the people they work with that says you are incompetent. Partly because they believe it to be true, and partly because of the overarching demonic spirit's influence that we tend to forget. Demons project lies into our mind. So, when a Jezebel-led person criticizes you and humiliates you, there is a demon that starts projecting those same thoughts into your mind in an attempt to persuade you into accepting the lie. Just like in the Old Testament, Jezebel hated the anointed servants of God and did everything she could to destroy them. In the Old Testament, Jezebel tried to physically kill them, but today, the demonic attacks are more geared toward the mind. On one of our past mission trips to Mexico, we performed freedom sessions for twenty-one pastors. Every one of them was on the threshold of quitting the ministry. They were listening and believing the lies that were being projected into their minds. Lies that told them they were incompetent failures and that they didn't measure up to being a pastor. Satan was on the verge of convincing them to take themselves out of ministry by filling their mind with self-doubt.

Today, the Jezebel spirit, and the Jezebel-led individual, both directly assault the self-esteem and confidence of gifted and called men and women of God. The longer they are subjected to Jezebel's dominating and disparaging ways, the more apt they are to fall prey to its lies. This certainly happens in work environments, but perhaps a good way to describe this is by looking at an abused spouse. Think of how the abuser works to convince them they are worthless and no one else would ever want them. Beautiful, kind, and loyal souls that are subjected to horrific lies by abusive partners are deceived into believing that they are ugly and unlovable failures. The abused person is so filled with self-doubt that they spend years trying to make changes in order to please the abusive spouse. Sadly, the controlling partner will never approve of their spouse's changes. This is another tool they use to keep people in bondage. If the abused spouse never feels good enough, they are caught in an unending cycle of striving to *be* good enough. And of course, this is exactly the strategy Jezebel uses to keep people under their control.

Over the years I have watched strong and confident leaders get drawn into the web of Jezebel's deceitful ways. Usually the leader doesn't even see it coming. As the Jezebel-led person appears to be loyal to them, the leader is won over by their charm and hard work. Little by little the leader gives more and more responsibility to the Jezebel-led person. As time goes by, the team around the leader is dismantled and replaced by

Jezebel followers. Eventually the leader begins to doubt his/her ability to make decisions. The Jezebel-led person and their allies slowly undermine the leader and question nearly all of the leader's decisions. The self-doubt of the leader is multiplied by the spirit of Jezebel projecting thoughts in the leader's mind. As this self-doubt increases, the leader will often back away and allow the Jezebel-led person and their team to make decisions for the organization. This will seem like a good idea to the leader in the midst of their self-doubt; however, Jezebel's ultimate mission is to destroy the organization. Putting them in charge only speeds up that process.

Because of my years of traveling to other churches, I have heard stories about how wonderfully talented, young leaders just starting out in ministry were browbeaten and made to feel like they are incapable of making good decisions. Sometimes because of an older leader who was insecure, but often because of a controlling individual who always had to be right. After years of being told they were not good enough to lead, or incapable of preaching, or running a department, many just quit and stepped away filled with self-doubt. In their mind they believed the lie that they weren't good enough to be used by God. The self-doubt was so strong they couldn't see how truly anointed and gifted they really were to lead others. Some went on to new churches and have soared to new heights under encouraging administrations, while others still struggle with self-doubt and are unable to get their confidence back. Here is an actual testimony from a young pastor who was battling this spirit in his church. It is amazing to see how he describes the doubt and fear that he experienced:

> *I was the lead pastor of a church which was deeply influenced by the spirit of Jezebel. It seemed to work only through a handful of people... but I encountered it through one specific individual more often than others. As a leader*

in that dynamic, here are three of the things I personally experienced:

1. **Feeling of removed anointing and giftedness** - *One of the first things I experienced in that dynamic was the feeling that God had somehow removed his anointing from my life. I felt ineffective and not up to the task. It is not a bad thing to feel this in a "my weakness is HIS strength" type of way. But this was different. I was made to feel that my weakness equaled the removal of God's hand on my personal ministry. The spirit of Jezebel made me feel like I was cut off from the presence of God... and that all of my gifts would be ineffective moving forward.*
2. **Diminishment of "power" and joy** - *This second thing confused me for a long time. There would be certain moments of great ministry momentum in the church. These would be short seasons of small victories that should have led to great joy in my heart. Often, these moments would be short-circuited through manipulative actions of several in the church who were influenced by the Jezebel spirit. These were always done behind the scenes, through email or hidden personal interactions. I would always feel like something was under the surface ready to strike... and I wasn't wrong most of the time. The ability for me to experience joy was slowly taken away. Eventually, I became aware that I wasn't myself anymore. I felt small, isolated, and powerless to change the situation.*
3. **Panic and anxiety before confrontation** - *I was surprised to learn (and experience) the difficulty in confronting the Jezebel spirit. I remember one particular situation where I knew I would be meeting with someone who was heavily influenced by the Jezebel spirit for a much-needed confrontation. The whole week prior was awful. The heaviness that*

surrounded that impending meeting was overwhelming. It caused stress fractures in other relationships that week... relationships that were normally solid. There were times when I felt like I couldn't breathe and I just had this urge all week to run and hide... to cancel the meeting. Reflecting back, I believe it was the Jezebel spirit intensifying my anxiety because it knew that direct confrontation was the only tool I had left that would work. I eventually had the meeting and things almost instantly got brighter following that meeting.

This young pastor was crushed under the weight of fear and doubt, both tag teaming with the spirit of Jezebel to try and take him out of ministry. Thankfully, he stood up to the Jezebel-led person, but even that was extraordinarily difficult to do. The spirit tried to convince him to run instead of confront. This is the very reason many Jezebel spirits are allowed to run rampant in our organizations. The fear to confront is so high that many leaders simply collapse under the extreme pressure. They feel like it would be easier to just avoid the confrontation. Unfortunately, avoiding the confrontation only gives the Jezebel spirit greater confidence to control the organization. If the spirit knows it will not be confronted, it knows it can do whatever it wants without fear of reprisal.

In Jezebel's attempt to maintain absolute control, any strong leaders on the team must become faithful followers or be taken out of commission. Jezebel fears other strong leaders, knowing they are a threat to its domain. Jezebel is also threatened by strong leaders who are well liked by staff, volunteers, and congregation members. Often, some of the most loved on staff are targeted by Jezebel precisely for this reason. Jezebel wants absolute loyalty from the staff and volunteers, and anyone else who develops a devoted following is intensely despised by Jezebel.

Those who are deeply loved—simply because they passionately care for people—don't have a clue as to why they are targeted by Jezebel. Usually they are made to believe they are incompetent failures, when all they really did wrong was love people so well that people wanted to follow them. That is a threat Jezebel cannot tolerate.

As these demonic tag teams manifest within a department or an organization due to Jezebel's control, it's just a matter of time before morale, trust, confidence, attitudes, and production will all be impacted. The old adage that one spoiled apple can spoil the whole bunch is still true. Unfortunately, many leaders do not see how one individual can have such a far-reaching impact on the team. Left unchecked, Jezebel will continue to unleash its destructive viral infection throughout the organization. Because dealing with Jezebel can be very difficult and intimidating, most leaders tend to look the other way. They take the easy way out and purposely evade confronting Jezebel-led people. Their refusal to tackle the tough issues leaves the organization vulnerable to Jezebel's advancing forces of evil.

Chapter 6

Understanding and Interacting with Jezebel's Host

Demonic spirits operate at varying levels of power. Higher-level spirits may be able to rule over a country, state, region, or church, whereas, lower-level spirits need a person it can use to accomplish its hellish mission. Lower-level Jezebel spirits seek individuals they can influence to do their bidding. For the sake of this chapter, we will call those demonically influenced individuals Jezebel's "host." In biology, a host is an organism that harbors a parasitic guest, and lower-level Jezebel spirits need a "host" in order to function. The challenge of writing this chapter is trying to be merciful to the Jezebel host, while at the same time being mindful of its destructive capabilities. With the possible exception of those who practice occultic rituals on purpose, most people don't willingly shake hands and invite spirits into their lives. If the devil came to your front door and said, "Hey, I'm the devil. Can I come in?" Most of us would slam the door shut and run for cover. Evil spirits are always looking for hosts they can use, but must do so in very sneaky and subtle ways. There are multiple ways for them to achieve this goal and perhaps the most efficient way is through our mind.

A couple of years ago I was at a missionary conference in Germany sponsored by the missionary arm of The Wesleyan Church. At this conference they brought in Dr. Johannes Reimer, who came to teach on a variety of subjects. During one of his seminars, he taught on how we can listen for the voice of God to guide us through tough issues. He shared an amazing story of how a group of church planters in Europe listened for the voice of God to determine where to plant a new church in their city. They had been wrestling for months on which part of the city they should plant a church and where they could possibly find a building. He taught them the many ways God might use to speak to them and invited them to meet together on a weekly basis for a time of listening prayer.

During a meeting, one of the church planters got a very specific vision of an unusual looking building. It all seemed rather odd, but Dr. Reimer had them write down the details of the vision. In another meeting a different person in the group got an image of a particular part of the city. In another meeting the Lord revealed that they were supposed to go prayer walk the part of the city revealed in the vision. As they were walking through the neighborhood praying, they came upon an unusual looking building. As they compared it to the details of the vision, they realized that it matched the vision. In absolute amazement they went into the building. They quickly realized it was perfect for their needs. Within a short amount of time they were able to meet with the owner of the building. He was delighted to be able to rent out part of his building on the weekends for Sunday services. By listening for God's voice, they were able to find the perfect location to plant a new church in their community.

In the midst of this seminar, Dr. Reimer shared with our group something that Wellsprings has experienced almost from the very beginning of our freedom ministry. He explained to those attending the conference that three voices speak into our mind each and every day—our own thought voice, the voice of God, and the voice of enemy spirits. The story above is a beautiful illustration of listening for the voice of God. For many of us this is easy to grasp, although not so much for others. But the harder part for many of us to accept is the idea of a demon speaking into our minds. It might be easy to dismiss this idea until we contemplate the reality that Satan is not omnipresent. If we are honest, we are tempted in our minds with evil thoughts nearly every day. We all have them. If Satan is not omnipresent, then where do the tempting thoughts come from? In addition, many of us hear our own thought voice condemning us on a regular basis. Thoughts telling us we are no good, that we are failures, or that God could never love someone like us.

Most of the time, these negative thought voices are simply demons projecting thoughts into our minds. Their hope is that we will pick up the negative thoughts and begin to believe them. The negative thoughts are lies, but when we hear them almost every day, they begin to sound true. When an evil spirit perceives you are listening and accepting the lies they are projecting into your mind, the level of their attack increases. There are times when the lies projected into our minds are nothing more than simple, one sentence condemning statements. In some cases, the lies resemble strategies for how we should live our lives. On the surface they seem to make sense and appear to be protective in nature, perhaps for the purpose of keeping us from being hurt by others. And this is a key factor for how the Jezebel spirit entwines itself into the mind of an individual and creates a host.

Almost every person who is controlled by a Jezebel spirit has been deeply wounded by another person, group of individuals, or a severely traumatic event. Sometime after the wounding event occurs, the Jezebel spirit begins to offer deceptively enticing advice: "You need to be in control." The advice to control everything is fairly common, but the purpose for doing so can vary depending upon each person's wounding experience. For example, a parent who suffers the loss of a child may be told they need to control their remaining children to keep them safe. The parent or parents become obsessively controlling believing it is a good thing, only to discover later that they will eventually lose their children to anger and resentment. As parents keep an excessively controlling grip on their children, the children become filled with deep resentment. The controlling nature of the parents drives the children away. That was not the parents' intention, but the lie of the enemy deceived them into believing what they were doing was good, while hiding from them the truth that they were pushing their children away. Most demonic advice is a form of bait and switch, offering something that seems to be good, only to later pull the rug out from under you with a consequence you could not see.

There is another strategic way that demons lie to people about needing to be in control. They will often tell a person that by staying in control of everyone and everything they protect themselves from ever being hurt again. By dominating and controlling people you hurt them before they can hurt you. This is another form of bait and switch. Yes, they are often able to keep others from hurting them, but the hurtful way they do it drives people away from them. Sadly, this causes the Jezebel-led person to feel even more rejected.

Those who are wounded and become controlling for protection will often build up walls of defensiveness and live inside those walls. In the end, they still end up feeling rejected and alone, which drives them into a cycle of wounding. The more they try to control people to keep from being wounded, the more people avoid them, which leads them to feeling rejected. These people feel like they are walking on eggshells when they are in the presence of a Jezebel-led person. They do whatever they can to avoid conflict and keep things calm and peaceful. Most people will appear to be the Jezebel host's friend on the outside, while on the inside they are boiling over with anger and resentment. They secretly hope the Jezebel-led person will quit or be fired, but dare not speak of it out of fear of retaliation.

The defensive wall the Jezebel host builds around themselves hardens their emotions so that they can't feel any remorse for the way they treat others. They can bully, belittle, and criticize others and feel absolutely no guilt or shame for having done so. However, no one had better go near anything approaching the appearance of correction toward them, or else they are highly offended. They will not submit to authority or correction of any kind without a highly charged emotional response. It is totally a one-way street. They have no sorrow or regret for verbally abusing others but are extremely sensitive and reactionary toward any criticism directed at them. It's like a deep cut that gets infected and never heals as even the slightest touch sends tremors of pain. That's how a Jezebel-led person experiences correction. It is deeply painful to them and their defensive walls go up. Their inability to accept correction of any kind will cause them to avoid accountability and seek to only recruit people who will submit to them.

Imagine a person who is very broken and dysfunctional, someone who desperately needs people to come alongside of them and speak truth into their life. They are a mess; their life is in complete disarray. When they listen only to their own thoughts, they sink deeper into isolation and despair. Nothing they try seems to work for them; however, when a person does come into their life speaking truth, they can't hear it. Because of their defensive walls, almost any and all corrective truth spoken to them is rejected. They rebuff and ignore the very thing they need to get well, which almost guarantees a lifetime of brokenness and sadness. It appears like the spirit of Jezebel is establishing its domain within a person and the defensive posturing locks it in place for years to come. This is partially why many who work in the field of spiritual warfare have portrayed the difficulty in removing a high-level spirit of Jezebel. Most attempts to help a person with the Jezebel spirit is met with tremendously elevated levels of resistance to any kind of truth spoken to them. The Jezebel spirit attached to them perverts the truth being spoken and twists it into an attack on their character. It is a perpetual demonic trap. It can be very frustrating when we consider the intentional plot of how this demonic cycle cements ongoing control over an individual. Truth spoken to them is twisted into a personal attack which leads to feelings of rejection. The rejection leads to defensiveness, which leads to the need to control. Excessive control leads people to tell them they are being controlling, which leads them to feeling attacked.

Even when a spirit of Jezebel is removed from a person, they must be very careful. For if they feel like things in their life are sliding out of control again, the temptation to control everything may quickly come charging back. And the cycle begins again.

It can be very difficult to have compassion for the Jezebel host. Usually when we go out of our way to show love and care for a person, it is appreciated. But with a Jezebel-led person it is not appreciated, it is expected. They see the world through a very selfish lens. It's all about them. The only modification to this statement is when the Jezebel-led person is going above and beyond with flattery, favors, and manipulation to win over a leader's loyalty. Even then, it is for selfish gain. *A word of caution here: We must be very careful who we receive flattery and favors from as we don't want to become beholden to a controlling Jezebel.* The person with the Jezebel spirit will repeatedly hurt and wound other people without even the slightest remorse. Their inability to experience any regret over how they treat others is part of the numbing defensive shield they put around themselves for protection. As they hurt others with absolutely no visible signs of sorrow, the people they wound become ensnared in deep anger and resentment. It makes it very difficult for those wounded at the hand of Jezebel to offer forgiveness and grace. But it can be done.

Once as we were helping one of our Wellsprings clients deal with unforgiveness toward a Jezebel-led person in their life, the Lord gave one of our discerning team members a sobering vision. The vision was a depiction of the inmost core of the person with Jezebel. In the vision they saw a little girl in a large park sitting on a swing. Although she was sitting on a swing and could have been having fun pumping her swing higher and higher into the air, the swing wasn't moving. As the little girl sat in the swing, a look of deep sorrow reflected the sadness and loneliness of her heart. The playground was large and had room for many children to come and play, but instead, the playground was empty. There was not another person in the park; it was completely void of other people. The controlling little girl had chased them all away. It was a sad little vision, portraying the deep loneliness that exists in the depth of the Jezebel host's soul.

When our client was able to see the Jezebel-led person being deceived by demonic lies, it helped them to find the strength to forgive. Forgiveness has nothing to do with the abuser, it is something between us and God. It's simply choosing to release our anger and resentment toward the Jezebel-led abuser and giving it to God. Choosing to forgive is a very good thing for us to do. The deep bitterness we hold within ourselves really only hurts us and steals our joy. Unforgiveness is like a poison pill that we take expecting it will harm the abusive person, only it doesn't. The poison of resentment and unforgiveness only destroys us from the inside out. Forgiveness restores our relationship with Christ and allows us to release the anger and the need for revenge. This is something we choose to do on our own. It is not dependent upon an abuser's apology. Otherwise, the forgiveness so necessary for our healing may never occur. In many cases the abuser is never able or willing to say they are sorry. If we wait upon them for an apology, the precious healing that comes to us through forgiveness may never happen. Forgiveness is for our well-being, not the abuser's. It is a gift from God that leads to the healing of our emotions.

Forgiveness is not going to the abusive Jezebel host and offering an apology. They have abused and manipulated you; thus, you have nothing to apologize for. Forgiveness is not an apology and you are not asking them to forgive you. Until they receive healing, going to them and offering forgiveness would lead only to further abuse. In their demonically infused state of mind, they truly believe they have done nothing wrong. Your offer of forgiveness would most likely be met with an arrogant sneer of denial. But that should not deter us from releasing our grudge toward them. The beautiful thing about forgiveness is that it is not dependent upon the abuser's cooperation, apology, or blessing. It is a personal decision and is given without any expectation of change or restoration from the abuser. For example, sometimes we need to forgive someone from our past who has died. Forgiveness is releasing our resentment toward an offender and is completely one-sided. It doesn't mean you have to suddenly have a relationship with the abuser. If they are abusive to you, stay away from them. Their refusal to change is on them, not you. It is also something you may have to do on a daily basis if the abusive Jezebel continues to hurt you. There are times we cannot immediately get out from under the controlling abuse. If the abuser is our boss, co-worker, or a family member, it may take some time to create a plan to get out of the abusive situation.

Typically, when we release our resentment and forgive the person with Jezebel, it is restorative only for us. It does not fix the person with the Jezebel spirit. In most cases, their controlling and offensive behavior is from a demonically induced numbness.

They falsely believe it will shield them from ever being hurt again. It is supposed to protect them from further wounds, but in reality, it sucks them into a pit of self-victimization that justifies their abuse of others. Yes, we need to forgive them for *our* spiritual health, but we must also understand it will not fix our day-to-day interaction with the Jezebel-led person. We must never beat ourselves up or blame ourselves for their poor behavior. No matter how hard you try, you will most likely not be able to please them on a regular basis. You may even find yourself in a pattern of regularly apologizing because you aren't meeting their expressed wants and needs. Stop the madness. Don't let their dissatisfaction of you be used as a way to manipulate you into being their slave. It is important to understand that nothing you do will be good enough. Their brokenness is not your fault. The brokenness is inside of them, and until they are able to see their need for help, they will not change.

I'm convinced the spirit of Jezebel loves conflict and strives to draw as many people as possible into battle. The spirit's job is to destroy and it will use any means necessary to accomplish that goal. This spirit will use the emotional angst that is stirred up in conflict to distract the team from building the kingdom. The host containing the Jezebel spirit is a demonically equipped fighter who will submit to no one. Skirmishing with people does not affect a Jezebel-led person. They feel no remorse for words they speak or actions they take to destroy you. If you try to fight them using their emotionally charged techniques, you will be consumed by your own guilt. The Jezebel spirit does not fight fair and will lead the Jezebel host to fight unfairly. Those who go into battle against a Jezebel host will feel like they are up against a buzz saw. Jezebel will lie, cheat, argue, control, go into fits of rage, manipulate, spin the truth, and use tears and emotionally charged outbursts to win people to its side. They will intimidate or flatter others to stand against you. They will use self-victimization to elicit sympathy for themselves and try to convince others that you are the problem. In some cases, sexual favors are given to ensure they get their way. If that isn't enough, they have an ability to seemingly switch personalities. They can turn on their spiritual charm and appear to all as if they are innocent servants of God being persecuted for using their gifts to advance the kingdom. Jezebel is a cunning foe and will use anything at its disposal to defeat you or your organization. We dare not fight Jezebel using the demonic techniques it uses, or we might stifle God's blessing. What I mean by that is, Jezebel wants to draw us into battle. It wants us to lie, to lose our temper and go into fits of rage. It wants us to say things that we will feel sorry for and that it can later use to manipulate us through guilt and shame. Plus, if we are loving and compassionate people, we must be careful not to open a door for a Jezebel spirit to seize us in the midst of our rage as we strive against Jezebel.

The following true story was written by one of our team members. Though it did not take place in the church, it perfectly illustrates some of the weapons Jezebel uses and how God led a Christian manager not only to survive, but to win:

> *There are no boundaries capable of containing the Jezebel spirit; nothing is off limits or safe from its potential invasion, including corporate America.*
>
> *For the last twenty years, I have proudly worked for a large Midwestern Fortune 500 company. Our core values are all-American; business ethics are taken seriously and employees are typically good, hardworking people. Over half of my career I have spent formally supervising others and successfully navigating the ups and downs that come with leadership responsibilities. It wasn't until my current role that I experienced a challenge like never before, something dark that rattled me to my core.*

It was late 2011 when my spiritual walk with God began transforming. The Holy Spirit began moving in me like never before. I was reading scripture and when I came to Isaiah 6:8, I recognized God was calling me. Those words to this day still cause my eyes to well up; I know God was speaking to me, calling to me, and I consciously submitted completely to his will for me and my life. It wasn't long after that significant changes began to take place in my life. My family and I relocated for my job, all of which brought incredible growth, challenge, and joy. The time had come for us to return home and I had prayerfully requested my next position knowing full well that whatever position was offered to me would lead me to where God intended. He had placed me right where I was for his will and purpose, and now, he was calling me once more to which I again responded, "Here I am, Lord, send me."

Within the first few months of my new role, I quickly discovered that the position I had accepted was riddled with problems. The team I was now responsible for managing consisted of eleven people around the world, four of which were not performing to expectations. Countless peers, customers, and managers lined up to share their frustrations with my team's performance and their abhorrence for my entire staff. What was God thinking? I had no doubts that he had placed me here in this position. I trusted him, but I couldn't imagine how I was going to overcome all the problems I was facing. I knew he would see me through it but frankly I was unsure as to how it would all unfold.

During one of the first meetings I had with my new manager I was warned about one of my employees. He was an entry level manager that had consistently done just enough to stay out of trouble, but not enough to *accomplish anything. On a personal level, he was a nice guy. The kind of guy that enjoyed arranging employee luncheons and afterhours social events. People liked him as a person despite his pessimistic, "woe is me" mentality, much like that of Eeyore from Winnie-the-Pooh. My manager shared with me the challenges my predecessors had experienced with him and their inability to motivate him. He recommended I keep my eye on him as his patience had grown thin and expected I would need to take action to address his performance deficiencies.*

It didn't take long for me to determine that this employee's performance was below average and formal action would be required to address his gaps. In order to ensure he understood expectations, I conducted regular meetings with him to review his defined goals and to discuss progress. With each meeting he became more resentful and defiant, silently refusing to execute his job responsibilities. Given his inaction and insubordination, my leadership supported my decision to rate his performance at below average, a rating seldom given and certainly the first time he had received such a rating. Much time and energy were put into articulating the basis for his rating as well as expectations for successful performance. Despite my efforts, he refused to accept my feedback or acknowledge any of his shortcomings and instead was convinced my manager would see things his way and that I was mistaken. (Jezebel can never be wrong.) He proceeded to meet with Human Resources and my manager, all of which supported the assessment and final rating I had given him.

The year that followed initially started off well and he appeared to be genuinely working harder to accomplish his goals. By midyear, I was optimistic that if he continued to make progress, he would earn a successful performance rating. However, not long after conducting his midyear review, he became complacent and refused to make hard decisions, execute his responsibilities, or hold others accountable. His inaction put the credibility of our entire team at risk as well as my reputation as a leader. Given the severe consequences resulting from two consecutive below average performance ratings, I met with my leadership to ensure alignment and support prior to taking the required next steps. Human Resources confirmed that a second below average rating would result in a mandatory performance improvement plan. Such plans consist of clearly defined goals, success measures, and milestone dates. Failure to achieve the plan within the defined timeline results in disciplinary action up to termination.

In addition to challenges I faced with this domestic employee, I was struggling with my team in Europe. My team's performance incited the same response from my European colleagues and leadership, who also repeatedly shared their frustrations for my employees. Given the workload in the region, I spent much of my time in Europe coaching, working, and meeting with local leaders to complete the tasks my staff failed to complete. Through the grace of God, two European employees left the company and I was able to bring on an incredible employee to take their place. He quickly understood his responsibilities and began fulfilling each, which removed the burden from me. I was then able to again place my focus on my domestic team and my underperforming employee.

The sudden departure of two of their colleagues generated a significant amount of fear in my remaining staff. Given confidentiality requirements, I was unable to assure my remaining staff that performance issues drove their resulting separation from the company. My underperforming domestic employee understood that and used the fear of his colleagues to his advantage. He knew he was on the same path as his departed colleagues and began his counterattack to avoid experiencing the same fate. He used passive-aggressive tactics to "innocently" plant seeds of dissention within the team towards me as their manager. I knew something was wrong but was unable to convince my employees they had nothing to fear. They no longer trusted me and I realized I had become the outsider. They were a team and together, they had begun working to expel me. (Jezebel recruits allies.)

During this time, I had requested the support of an internal professional coach. I recognized I was dealing with numerous, highly confidential challenges and needed to have someone I could consult with. My assigned coach was a seasoned manager located in another part of the company, and someone that I had never met. I was grateful to have him and connected easily with him. In a short amount of time, I discovered that he too was a Christian. He and I met regularly and he helped me separate fact from fear, to put away my feelings so I could think clearly as a manager, and to not lose sight of where I was going during this difficult journey. (Jezebel incites fear.) The internal coach was an incredible blessing, and I know he was truly a gift from God.

As the year came to an end, it was clear my problem employee did not meet expectations and had rightfully earned his second below average performance rating. Given the resulting consequences, I met with Human Resources to begin developing the next steps. My leadership was totally supportive of my rating, knowing full well the seriousness of such. Despite all the feedback the problem employee had received prior to this point, when he heard he was again rated below average he became combative. (Jezebel will submit to no one.) He once more was convinced that I was mistaken and that a conversation with my manager would result in a different result. I encouraged him to speak with my manager which he eagerly did. My manager confirmed his support in my rating and informed my employee that his boss did as well. My manager shared with him that such ratings require leadership visibility and approval, all of which I had received prior to delivering his review. Despite all he had heard, he refused to accept the feedback and take responsibility for his shortcomings. Instead, he elected to use the discord he had created within our team to take me out once and for all. (Jezebel must win.)

I was invited to a meeting with Human Resources to discuss my poor performer's progress toward his defined improvement plan. He had a set period of time to achieve the plan which, as I pointed out earlier, consisted of clearly stated goals, success measures, and milestone dates. Failure to successfully complete his plan within the defined timeline would result in disciplinary action up to termination. When I arrived, my Human Resources manager looked concerned, and for good reason. She shared with me that an anonymous complaint had been submitted claiming I was creating an environment of hostility at work. Such claims are taken very seriously and required further investigation. The investigation team was there to speak with me about what they had found and she then excused herself from the room. I couldn't believe it. I knew who submitted the claim and was so angry! He vengefully attacked me in order to destroy my reputation. (Jezebel will lie and does not fight fair.) I didn't realize at that moment what I was up against but recognized this was the work of Satan.

The investigation team somberly entered the room and sat directly across from me. They shared the claim with me and the follow-up work they had done to determine whether the claim had merit. They informed me that my team didn't trust me and that while they were not pleased with me, the complaint was not substantiated. No further disciplinary action would be required. They asked me for a response as they stared at me unsympathetically. I paused, listening for God's still small voice. My eyes teared up as I replied, "I'm sure there are things I could have done better, things I could have said nicer, but my intent was always good. If this is truly my team's perception of me, then I need to change." I didn't fight back, I didn't deny anything, and instead I humbly accepted the feedback of my hurting team recognizing that my poor performer was likely leading this attack.

In the weeks that followed, I was paired up with a mentor, a woman whom I have immense respect and admiration for. She genuinely cared for me, encouraged me, and challenged me as I continued to walk through the remainder of my employee's performance improvement plan. Those months were the hardest of my entire career. I described it to my coach, Paula, as if I were walking in a dark forest, so dark I could not see the path forward. I had never felt so alone. What I later realized is that circumstances created intense isolation. My leadership backed away from me after the compliance issue was raised due to their own fear of potential damage to their reputation. I was on my own. My decisions, the results of this performance plan were all on me and I was afraid. I had never faced something of this magnitude and I began questioning myself. Was I doing the right thing? How do I adjust my management style to regain my leadership's support?

I started second-guessing myself and losing confidence in my ability to make the right decisions. My mentor recognized what was happening and helped me see it for myself. She told me not to lose myself in all this. What she said reminded me that I was a great manager and that I needed to be true to myself. She asked me if I wanted my employee to be successful or not and why? She helped me to see that I knew what I needed to do; I wasn't lost, just a little disoriented. She was so right.

God had given me everything I needed and he reminded me of that fact through the wisdom of my mentor. I stopped trying to prove my employee was the problem and instead began praying for him. I asked God to help me love him, to see him as Jesus does. That prayer changed me. The darkness began to make way for the light and I could again see the path forward. I embraced humility and the knowledge that God was in control. Being right wasn't important, but doing right was.

Ultimately, my employee failed to successfully complete his performance improvement plan. When asked for my recommendation for disciplinary action I advocated that he not be terminated, but instead placed in a position in which he was capable of successful performance. When the time came to notify the team, my message was positive. I shared the exciting opportunity he had in this new position and had a farewell celebration for him during which I thanked him for his contributions to our team.

After this experience, with the help of Wellsprings of Freedom International, I came to realize what I was truly up against. I had encountered a spirit of Jezebel and successfully survived its vicious attacks. Looking back, I can see clearly how it operated, how it manipulated and how it responded when confronted. There was no way I could have overcome this spirit head-on. Every attempt to do so backfired and instead brought me one step closer to my own demise. What I now understand to be the secret to my success was humility and love. The truth of 1 Peter 3:8-9 was the antidote to the poison of Jezebel for me. It states, "Finally, all of you, live in harmony with one another; be sympathetic, love as brothers, be compassionate and humble. Do not repay evil with evil or insult with insult, but with blessing, because to this you were called so that you may inherit a blessing." I have been blessed beyond measure! God has transformed my leadership and my team! We have become a high-functioning, highly aligned team producing incredible results! While we still encounter challenges and difficulties, we are able to address them together with the knowledge that we will overcome!

Every encounter with a Jezebel spirit is different. Each situation is different based on what position the Jezebel host holds in the organization. Is the host a staff member, board member, upper management, employee, volunteer, large contributor, friend of the leader, or a family member of the board or leadership team? Is the Jezebel host the senior leader? Has the host won over the senior leader or the department leader? Does the host contribute large amounts of money? Has the host formed an alliance with other key leaders? How much control has the host been able to secure over the organization? If the answer to that last question is that they have a lot of control, how will you replace them? Can you put a plan in place to do so before confronting the Jezebel host? How can you minimize the damage they could inflict upon leaving? Is the host able to submit to authority to any degree? Do the confronting members have the courage and strength to remove the highly manipulative Jezebel host?

Organizations forced to confront a person hosting a Jezebel spirit will have to seek their own solutions. There is no cookie-cutter perfect solution that works for everyone. Some organizations will figure it out and some will not. Jezebel is tenacious, and it will take prayer, discernment, wisdom, and self-control to defeat this spirit. Because we can only help people to the level they will allow, successful options for defeating this spirit are limited. The Jezebel host either truly repents and is willing to fully submit to leadership, or it is removed from the organization. And due to Jezebel's treachery, the first option which we would all prefer to see cannot include leaving the Jezebel host in a position of power. Jezebel will influence the Jezebel-led person to weep, beg, and plead with emotionally charged petitions to keep their job, along with passionate promises to change and repent. It all appears to be real, but very often it is simply a ploy to remain in power. Unfortunately, the first option usually leads to another more difficult confrontation down the road.

I believe most of the organizations that are struggling with a controlling Jezebel host just don't have enough information to make wise decisions. There must be a balanced approach when confronting a Jezebel host. You cannot fight them using their ungodly tactics; it just doesn't work. Humility, self-control, truth spoken in love, coupled with strength and courage are some powerful weapons. But even then, it comes with no guarantees. The success of almost all organizations rises and falls on leadership. If the senior leadership team or board of directors is under the deceitful spell of this spirit, and cannot wake up to its destructive ways, there is little hope for removing the spirit. The spirit will be able to continue its destructive course and the organization will die a slow death.

If the leadership team is awakened to what this spirit is doing, there is definitely hope. Confronting Jezebel as a unified leadership team and avoiding the emotionally charged atmosphere that usually surrounds the Jezebel host are solid steps to begin. Compiling all the facts and presenting them to the Jezebel host with a humble and gentle spirit will keep the leadership team from getting sucked into a three-ring circus. A chaotic shouting match usually ends up working to Jezebel's advantage. Staying calm but remaining unified and firm are significant keys to success. Jezebel will look for any disunity on the leadership team and use it to its benefit when it can. So, stand together. Be prepared for anything. Going over a list of possible reactions to expect from Jezebel before the confrontation meeting will be very valuable. If you suspect that Jezebel may fly into an emotional tantrum in the meeting and you have laid out your counter strategy in advance, you will be way ahead of the game. Jezebel is often like a spoiled child who is used to getting its way. Giving in to their demands only appeases them for the moment and demonstrates a weakness they will continue to exploit in the future.

Confronting Jezebel can be very draining, but taking back control of your organization is liberating. When Jezebel is removed or stripped of its power, the overarching oppression will lift off of your organization and new life will begin to flow. Freedom will reign again. You will be amazed as you move forward at how many things Jezebel controlled, touched, and negatively influenced. A time of peaceful joy will flood over the organization along with a sense of being safe and secure. However, we dare not bask in the feelings of security for very long. For just around the bend, or in the days that follow, the spirit of Jezebel will be looking for a new host to insert into your midst—sometimes even more powerful than the last one. Hopefully, your newly-trained eyes will spot them on the horizon like a shepherd spotting a predator. And being good shepherds, you will keep them away from your flock.

Sometimes Jezebel-led individuals are believers in Christ who are broken and deceived. Their deep emotional wounds keep them in heavy bondage. I don't believe they are going to hell, nor are we called to get revenge. However, their dysfunction and abuse cannot be permitted to harm the people in our organizations. As leaders, it is our responsibility to protect our people. That puts us in a precarious position: How do we protect the team and help the Jezebel host? The answer to that question will vary from person to person, and on how they respond to corrective action. The truth is many Jezebel-led individuals don't want help because in their minds they aren't broken. To even suggest they need help is an insult to them that will lead them to feeling rejected and angry. Don't experiment with trying to fix them by keeping them in a position of power on your team and coaching them in that position. Remove them from their position of power and place them in a job where they cannot bully people. Also, cut them off from anything that they control, especially finances, budgets, and people. You can offer outside counseling if you feel led to do so. If this is your choice, monitor them closely, continually asking the people around them if they see any signs of the host trying to control others. If this option is your choice, make sure it is not based on guilt and shame placed upon you by the host. Keeping a Jezebel host in a position without power may cause them to resign anyway, as not being in control is too difficult for them to handle. Or they will stick it out, hoping they will someday be restored to a position of power again.

Be careful. I once counseled a controlling, abusive Jezebel-led husband who had been separated from his wife for several months. He agreed to counseling. For a full year, he completely changed and became the husband that he needed to be. It was remarkable to see him interact with his wife. He was loving, kind, and caring—the model of what a husband should be. After a year of change, his wife wholeheartedly agreed to allow him to come back home and within two weeks he reverted back to his controlling, abusive ways. Giving the Jezebel host a second chance is risky and should be done only with extreme monitoring.

Earlier in this chapter I shared the importance of not being lured into confronting the Jezebel host using Jezebel tactics. Perhaps this moment is the perfect time to shed light on why. Staying calm, speaking truth, and remaining firm but kind, has a far greater chance of influencing the Jezebel host to seek outside help. I also suggest staying away from name calling. Don't say, "You are a Jezebel," or "You are a bully." Instead of using names, strive to gently, but accurately, describe their behavior. For example: "The reason we are meeting with you today is to discuss some deeply disturbing issues in your behavior. We have observed, and received complaints, about your controlling, demanding, and manipulating behavior. It is important that you understand that it is not acceptable in our organization."

It is pretty tough to convince someone you care about them and believe counseling could help them after you have been shouting at them and calling them names. Satan knows this and will try to entice you into a battle royal. Jezebel is crafty and will attempt to provoke you with something that may totally catch you off guard. In an instant, you may find yourself enraged by the words being thrown at you by the Jezebel-led person. This is what Jezebel does. Stay alert. It might be a fabricated story about you. It could be the most blatant lie you've ever heard, or it might even be a disgusting insult hurled at you. On many occasions it is an over-the-top temper tantrum. Sometimes it's a tearful emotional appeal for a second chance. And sometimes it's an accusation that you don't care about people when you don't give in to the Jezebel-led person's demands. Jezebel is not used to losing. It must win, and will use any tactic that it thinks will bring a victory, including guilt and shame.

Strive to resist losing your temper for the sake of the host, and for your own spiritual health. If you happen to fail at this, remember you are not fighting against flesh and blood, but against the powers of this dark world. Give yourself a break, ask God for forgiveness, and strive to do better next time. Many of Jezebel's tactics are to throw you off of your game and get you to give in to its all-out attempt to survive. Survival means it deceives you into letting it stay on your staff so that it can continue to destroy from within.

I don't know exactly how, but there is a supernatural mesmerizing aspect to Jezebel that is beyond comprehension. It uses it in the midst of confrontation, like a sleight-of-hand magician. As leaders, we walk into the meeting with the Jezebel-led person, fully expecting to remove them from our staff or board. A little while after we leave the meeting, we wake up to the realization that somehow, we allowed Jezebel to stay. They somehow managed to survive. Realizing this in advance may help you to remain strong. Always avoid meeting with a Jezebel host alone. Make sure you have a witness to back you up and lend you support. Never underestimate what a Jezebel can do. So be strong!

Chapter 7

Ahab

I'm convinced that wherever there is a Jezebel-led person, you will find an Ahab-led person close by. Yes, there is a spirit called Ahab that works very closely with the Jezebel spirit. Though a person with the Ahab spirit may sometimes be the leader, that leader will usually surrender their authority over to Jezebel. The Ahab leader will appear to be in charge, when in reality, Jezebel is behind the scenes controlling almost everything Ahab does. Ahab-led people don't see it that way, but just as a person with the Jezebel spirit will vehemently deny they are influenced by Jezebel, so will those with Ahab deny they are influenced by Ahab. Both deny they are being influenced but for different reasons. Jezebel-led people deny it because they can't be defective, and to have a demon would mean they are defective. And Ahab-led people deny it because of a deep selfish need to look good to others. There is such a high-level need for Ahab to appear to have it all together that they will avoid anything that even remotely could make them look bad. Other ministry leaders have shared stories with me of how a person with the Ahab spirit will attempt to manipulate numbers, omit important information, or spin stories to their advantage in order to appear as if they have it all together. Well-intended advice given to them from others is often viewed as an attack on their ability rather than a helpful suggestion. Sometimes truth spoken to them will be twisted into an imagined spiritual attack against them.

Jezebel and Ahab spirits are so totally opposite of one another that you might not expect them to work together. However, in a demonically dysfunctional way, they complement each other. Jezebel needs people to control and Ahab willingly allows for that. Ahab-led people typically hate confrontation and don't mind letting Jezebel handle that for them. The aggressive bullying nature of Jezebel will dominate a person with Ahab. This is because the person with Ahab will do whatever it takes to avoid conflict. Plus, many passive Ahabs take on a victim mentality. Some might even say it is their calling in life to suffer, expecting it to follow them throughout their life. They might even believe the lie that they deserve to suffer. Unfortunately, if they choose to believe this lie, there are plenty of demons waiting to help them make this a certainty. For many Ahab-led people, their suffering is directly connected to their relationship with a Jezebel-led person. They are blinded to this reality, as they spend the majority of their time obeying and protecting a Jezebel-led person who manipulates them through guilt and shame.

Even though these two spirits are very much opposite of one another, they both enter into our lives in a similar way—through deep wounds. It is precisely these deep wounds that contribute to both Jezebel and Ahab spirits being able to gain access. Individuals who are deeply wounded will often react to those wounds in one of two ways. They will become super aggressive or super passive. The aggressive Jezebel-led person will determine to never allow anyone to hurt them again. Usually this is done by attacking other people before others can attack them. The passive Ahab-led person takes a different approach. They do everything they can to be people pleasers, taking abuse rather than causing conflict. Both extremes are rooted in the fear of rejection.

In the book of 1 Kings, we see how Jezebel and Ahab operate together. It is interesting to note that Ahab, who was the passive one under Jezebel's control, is actually the king. He was the recognized leader of the country. However, the aggressive Queen Jezebel was actually the one making most of the decisions. This is a fairly common pattern for how these two spirits influence their hosts to interact with one another. It is not always the case, as some Jezebel-led individuals do step into top leadership positions, but Ahab-led individuals typically hold the leadership position while surrendering control to a Jezebel-led person working behind the scenes.

It might be quite easy to be fooled by an Ahab-led person because they are not the aggressive one. Their quiet, passive personality might cause you to think they are above reproach, but as we look at Ahab in the Bible, we can see that isn't always the case. I alluded to 1 Kings 16:33 earlier in Chapter 3: *"Ahab also made an Asherah pole and did more to provoke the Lord, the God of Israel, to anger than did all the kings of Israel before him."* Because Ahab-led people are often people pleasers, it is easy to be deceived by their less aggressive personality. In many situations, a person with the Ahab spirit can be more dangerous than a person with the Jezebel spirit. This is because Ahab protects Jezebel and gives it freedom to openly bully and control. They also strive to please Jezebel by doing pretty much whatever the person with Jezebel wants. For most Ahab-led individuals, it is easier to try and smooth over Jezebel's mistakes after the fact, rather than directly confront Jezebel and prevent the mistake from happening in the first place.

It is not uncommon to find an Ahab-led leader spending great amounts of time defending and making excuses for a Jezebel-controlled person on their team. A person who worked in an Ahab–Jezebel environment once told me that the Ahab leader spent the majority of his time going around and putting out fires created by the person with the Jezebel spirit. The truth is, Jezebel-led people ruffle many feathers and Ahab-led people work very hard to smooth them over. Amazingly, out of a completely broken sense of loyalty to Jezebel, Ahab will at times take the blame for the things Jezebel has done. There is a driving need to protect Jezebel, no matter what kind of destructive actions Jezebel has taken, or mean words it has spoken. The Ahab-led person is there to clean up the messes with a charming smile, people pleasing personality, and an ability to spin reality into a fabricated story chalked with misdirection, missing facts, and lies. Their goal is to quickly ask for forgiveness of the individual who was hurt by Jezebel in order to pacify and bring the matter to a close. Ahab-led people know Jezebel is incapable of truly asking for forgiveness and must somehow do it for them. Unfortunately, about all it does is take the heat off of Jezebel. It doesn't fix Jezebel or prevent Jezebel from continuing in its destructive ways.

It is important to see that the Jezebel–Ahab relationship is demonically twisted and empowered to accomplish one mission—to cause destruction. While Jezebel wreaks havoc within an organization, the blinded Ahab leader provides a covering of protection over the Jezebel-led person to complete the mission. The Ahab leader may or may not see that they are enabling Jezebel to do harm. A friend of mine recently told me a story of how a former Ahab leader didn't see how he had been protecting an abusive Jezebel-led person on his staff until he changed jobs and got out from under the demonic spell of Jezebel. Then, looking back on the situation the fog lifted and he saw clearly how he had been deceived and was used as a pawn. Part of the problem is that even if an Ahab-led person does see there is abuse occurring, they can't imagine confronting the Jezebel-led person. Supernatural fear overtakes them and they simply look the other way. For the passive Ahab, it's just easier that way.

In Steve Sampson's book, *Discerning and Defeating the Ahab Spirit*, he writes about how the Jezebel spirit tends to operate differently in men and women:

> *God has given women a gift in their emotions. They are intuitive and usually come across as far more sensitive than men. Therefore, the enemy of their souls tries to take advantage of this giftedness and tempts women to use their emotions illegitimately to get their way, often through manipulation. On the other hand, God has gifted men as leaders. They possess strength and can offer protection. But the enemy then comes along and deceptively lures men into controlling others through domination and intimidation (p. 65).*

I have heard stories about how this works. In one instance, I heard about an employee who was completely thrown out of his company's business meeting simply because he offered a new idea to the planning team that was slightly different than what the Jezebel-led leader was proposing. In another instance, a friend of mine who was sitting in a corporate meeting, witnessed a female Jezebel-led person completely dominate a leader and his staff by using highly animated emotional outbursts. These manipulative outbursts included rage, tears, tantrums, and overly dramatic body language. Like a crafty lawyer, she was able to draw sympathy from her audience and turn herself into a victim by casting guilt and shame on everyone in the room who dared to disagree with her. She manipulated them with her emotions and played them like a violin. As you can see, both intimidation and emotional manipulation work to control people.

Those influenced by an Ahab spirit are often seen as puppets that are completely controlled by Jezebel. It's almost like they are caught up in a spell, or like robots unknowingly programmed to protect and please the Jezebel spirit. Ahabs are loyal to Jezebel and have an inward compulsion to take care of them. They know Jezebel's tendency to hurt and walk over people, and are compelled to smooth out the waters after Jezebel creates waves of discontent. Ahab is a people pleaser and spends enormous amounts of time picking up the broken pieces left in Jezebel's path. It is their solemn duty! Ahab is the excuse maker and defender of Jezebel's frustratingly controlling ways. Though they may not know why, they simply must guard and protect Jezebel. It is a blind loyalty that makes no human sense to anyone but them. To them it is as natural as breathing. It is the abused woman who cannot step out from under her controlling and physically abusive partner. Only it's worse than that as she willingly defends and makes excuses for the abusive behavior.

You might even find a whole group of Ahab-influenced people who practically bow down and worship the Jezebel-led person. Jezebel likes to create obedient allies who willingly follow its instructions. Sometimes it's hard to know if these allies are being influenced by an Ahab spirit or if they are just survivalists. There are those who will do whatever is necessary to protect their job, and if they need to align themselves to a controlling person to survive, they'll do it. Most likely both exist on a Jezebel-controlled team. When Jezebel can surround itself with a group of willing loyalists, it becomes far more powerful. The more people Jezebel controls, the more control it has over the organization. Imagine a whole group of people who take up the responsibility to protect Jezebel and keep it in power. If a leader does wake up to what the Jezebel spirit is doing within an organization, they may have to confront an entire group who are loyal to Jezebel.

In an organization, it is not uncommon for the Ahab leader to place the Jezebel-led person's wishes above the needs of the entire organization. It is often felt that the need to protect Jezebel is more important than the health of the team or organization. Some have told me that they feel like the Ahab-led leader is more interested in pleasing Jezebel than building the kingdom of God. That is hard to imagine, and yet it sometimes does seem to be true. Jezebel's needs supersede the needs of the whole. It is mostly about Jezebel getting its way over everyone else. One Jezebel-led person will dominate a whole staff or department while the Ahab leader makes sure everyone submits.

The person with the Ahab spirit will move mountains in order to please the person with Jezebel, including the disregard of company policy and rules. Ahabs can't see it, but they must please the person with Jezebel above everything else. Friendships, long-standing work relationships, church memberships, volunteers, and even relatives who attempt to warn Ahab about Jezebel's domineering control over them will be isolated and removed from Ahab's inner circle of friends. It's far easier for an Ahab-led person to step away from well-meaning people than face the fear of confronting or disciplining a Jezebel-led individual.

If we can remember how critical and manipulative Jezebel is of others, we can begin to see how this spirit controls Ahab. When a child learns they can get anything they want by using temper tantrums to get their way, they basically control their parents. Jezebel uses all forms of manipulation to get its way. It can dominate and bully. It can throw very embarrassing temper tantrums. At times, it will lead the Jezebel host to use guilt and shame to elicit control or it may go into long seasons of pouting, isolating those who do not obey. When Jezebel is able to make an Ahab person subtly feel like they never measure up, the criticality of Jezebel drives an Ahab-led person to do whatever is necessary to receive approval from Jezebel. When Jezebel seldom hands out high praise and approval, it keeps the Ahab in a very disguised form of bondage. Typically, Ahabs find themselves in a wild and addictive life cycle of striving to please Jezebel and never quite achieving the goal. Jezebel-led parents can keep their children in a very destructive cycle of bondage as the grown-up kids spend much of their lives striving for their parents' approval, but never quite getting there. It seems the harder they try to please Mom or Dad and fail, the more determined they become to somehow accomplish that goal. Sadly, these children who spend their whole lives seeking a parent's approval may never receive it before their parents die.

Real Life Story

In the midst of writing this book, but after I had written this chapter on the Ahab spirit, I had something very amazing take place. A sixty-one-year-old man came in for a freedom session. We do twenty freedom sessions a week at our facility in Illinois, and out of all the freedom teams he could have been assigned to, he was assigned to mine. As the freedom session unfolded, we discovered that he had been dominated and controlled by a Jezebel mother his entire life. It started when he was two-years-old. His mother was a very broken and dysfunctional woman. It was through deep wounding in her life that she became demonized with Jezebel. When she was a little girl, her mother passed away and her father told her that it was all her fault, so she grew up hating men.

As a result of her wounding, Jezebel was able to attach to her through a very deceptive lie: *"If you follow me, no one will ever hurt you again."* The Jezebel spirit told her that by burying her emotions, becoming numb, and dominating other people, no one would be able to hurt her ever again. My client told me that his mother was the most selfish person he has ever known. Everything was for her needs, she had no ability to meet anyone else's needs. He told us that his mother had basically committed emotional incest with him. He was raised from two-years-old on to please her no matter what, or there would be deep emotional consequences. She would subject him to a form of emotional torture. If he didn't do exactly what mom wanted, she would manipulate him through very intense guilt and shame. He was trained by his mother to obey or else he would suffer unbelievable periods of condemnation and guilt until he followed her selfish instructions to the letter.

Because she hated men, she didn't want her son to be a man, so he was forced from as early as he could remember to be feminine. If he stepped out of that role, he was emotionally abused by her until he conformed. She demanded perfection from him and when she didn't get it, he was emotionally chastised. He strived his whole life to please her, and was never allowed to measure up to her standards. She emotionally tortured him by demanding perfection and always made him believe he wasn't good enough and that he had to try harder. He told us that he spent his whole life trying to be good enough for her approval and never achieved that goal. He also shared with us that if you didn't obey his mother's every desire, she emotionally cut you off from her. She was either able to control you or you were dead to her. Because she was so mean, dominating, and controlling, she had no friends. Our client told us that it was deeply imbedded within him that he was her only friend and that it was his responsibility to please her and make her happy, which he could never do. He was told in his mind that if he stopped trying to please and obey her, there would be no one else to serve her and she would die. In his mind he served her to keep her alive.

In the midst of his freedom session as we were walking him through our inner healing process, we discovered the spirit of Ahab was attached to him and had controlled him since he was nearly two-years-old. Toward the end of his session, he was able to hear the demonic spirit speaking into his mind. Demons regularly project thoughts into our minds (think of all the tempting thoughts you have endured throughout your life). When this happens, we can command the spirit to reveal to the client its mission and lies. This is very helpful for the client as it helps them to understand how demons speak into our minds to influence what we believe about ourselves, others, and God. Demons project thoughts into our minds every day. What our ministry team did was expose the demonic thoughts he had already been hearing for years. We do this so our clients will know the source of where the evil thoughts are coming from and be able to reject them going forward. As I commanded the spirit to reveal its lies to the client in the name of Jesus, the exact answer to my questions popped into my client's mind. We have used this technique to help our clients for many years. As he received the thought, he was able to tell us what he heard the spirit saying to him. And we were able to take those answers to reveal to the client how the enemy had been deceiving him for years.

Here is the transcript of the actual interrogation of the Ahab spirit from his healing session.

> **Team Leader:** "Spirit of Ahab, what is your mission in Jon's life?"
> **Jon:** "The thought that it wants to destroy me just came to the forefront of my mind."
>
> **Team leader:** "Spirit of Ahab, why do you want to destroy Jon?"
> **Jon:** "I just received the thought: Because we hate him, he has been created to do good works for God, and we have to stop him."
>
> **Team leader:** "How do you try to destroy him?"
> **Jon:** "We destroy him through guilt and emotional pain."

Team leader: "How do you do that?"

Jon: "We gave him a perfectionistic standard that we raised higher and higher and was impossible for him to achieve."

Team Leader: "Ahab, what were the lies that you told him?"

Jon: "We told him he was special, but not because of God. It was because of his special attachment to his mom. We kept his and her identities entwined."

Team Leader: "Why did you do that?"

Jon: "So he would never be able to become who God wanted him to be."

Team Leader: "What were the other lies you told Jon?"

Jon: "We told him he must obey his mom. If he didn't, she would die. We told him this from childhood. We trained him to obey his mother from a very early age by threatening to kill his mother if he didn't obey."

Team Leader: "What other lies did you tell him?"

Jon: "We told him his mother was a victim and he needed to feel sorry for her. She was really mean to him, but we told him he deserved to be treated that way."

Team Leader: "What made him believe he deserved to be treated so badly?"

Jon: "He was male, and we told him because he was male, he was bad. We made him feel guilty for having fun."

Team Leader: "Why?"

Jon: "Because it's his responsibility to care for his mother, and if he was having fun, he wouldn't be alert to her problems and crisis situations. We told him he must stay vigilant at all times to care for his mother."

Team Leader: "Ahab, how did you convince him to obey his mother at all cost?"
Jon: "Vows he spoke at a young age that set in motion his compulsion to protect his mother no matter what. Even when she hurt him."

Team Leader: "Ahab, how did you keep him in bondage to you?"
Jon: "Through his mother's manipulative guilt and shame."

Team Leader: "Ahab, what other lies did you tell Jon?"
Jon: "He is a bad son, he is not perfect, so he is not good enough. Of course, he could never be good enough because we continually raised the bar so he could never be good enough. We told him he must try harder to be perfect for his mother. We locked him into a cycle of obedience for all of his life starting at a young age. And we never let him out of the cycle."

As you can see, the Ahab spirit's job was to destroy him and use him to protect his Jezebel-led mother—which is what he did faithfully for sixty-one years. He was demonically brainwashed to obey through his mother's emotional punishment. It was because of the emotional torment that the demons were able to take him captive and reinforce a supernatural bondage to his mother that defies all logic. Those in bondage to Ahab must protect their Jezebel cohort no matter what, and they are completely blind as to why.

When we deal with a Jezebel-led individual, we are dealing with both a human being and a spirit of evil. Yes, there are controlling and manipulative people in the world, perhaps because they have learned how to use these kinds of techniques to get their way. But when you add in spiritual realm realities, the ability of a Jezebel-led person to control an Ahab-led leader approaches a whole new level. It can be very frustrating for employees and volunteers who watch their leader be dominated and controlled by another individual who manipulates them into making bad decisions and allowing toxic work environments. The need for Ahab to please Jezebel supersedes everything.

A number of years ago, a friend of mine shared a story with me about a business meeting that took place in his company. He told me how a Jezebel-led staff member lost her cool in a meeting with several members of the leadership team. It was an ugly scene of shouting and angry outbursts toward members of the leadership team with what the team thought was a very important twist. It was done for the first time in front of the Ahab leader. They had tried to tell their leader about the angry outbursts but were pretty much met with unbelief. Now, the team was sure something was going to happen to stop the crazy angry temper tantrums. The normally quiet and mild-mannered Ahab leader put up his hands and yelled, "Silence, stop!" Once the room became still, amazingly, the normally mild-mannered Ahab leader began to yell. The team thought he was finally going to deal with the angry controlling woman. Instead, the team was completely dumbfounded and confused by what happened next. The Ahab leader completely lost his temper at the team and reprimanded them for daring to question the Jezebel-led person's authority, thus, setting the stage for even more angry outbursts and abusive behavior by the Jezebel-led staff member in the future. My friend told me that it was at that very moment in the meeting that he made his decision to leave the organization. He said that he felt completely unprotected and uncared for by the Ahab leader and a sense of hopelessness enveloped him and the others on the team. Over the next year he and several of the others on the team left to work for other companies.

As Ahab strives to please the person with Jezebel, something interesting begins to happen. Over the course of time, the Ahab leader becomes so dependent upon the person with Jezebel for help in making important decisions that they lose their confidence to make any kind of a decision on their own. Their need for Jezebel's input on nearly everything causes great insecurity in them and gives Jezebel greater and greater amounts of control over the Ahab leader. The more insecure the Ahab leader feels, the greater the need for Ahab to do whatever is necessary to protect Jezebel from any and all criticism coming from the team or staff. This subtle dependency upon Jezebel that slowly creeps in is what creates near panic in Ahab when someone tries to point out Jezebel's abusive ways. Ahab becomes so dependent upon Jezebel for nearly everything that the Ahab leader truly doesn't think they or the organization can survive without the Jezebel leader. Not only does the Ahab leader lose confidence in himself, but Jezebel causes him to lose confidence in his whole team. Again, Jezebel's criticality extends to the whole team. As the Jezebel-led leader dumps criticism on the whole team surrounding the Ahab leader, Ahab begins to doubt the whole team and places complete trust in the Jezebel-led leader. Pretty soon, no one can decide anything without Jezebel's approval. This only amplifies Jezebel's worth in the eyes of the Ahab leader, creating even greater fear and panic over the idea of Jezebel leaving. This drives the need to protect Jezebel to even higher levels. It is truly a cycle of destruction.

Even if the Ahab-led person begins to see the Jezebel-influenced destruction going on around them, their fear of confronting Jezebel prevents them from doing anything about it. Included in this tangled mess of Jezebel control is the self-proclaimed notion that the Jezebel-led person is a prophet. The spirit of Jezebel deceives the host they use to accomplish their mission. They convince the Jezebel-led person into believing they have supernatural prophetic gifts. If we can understand that God created all the gifts of the Spirit, that Satan and his demonic army cannot create anything, we can begin to see how this unfolds. Because Satan has no creative ability whatsoever, his only option is to attempt to pervert the things created by God. Second Corinthians 11:14 reveals to us that Satan masquerades as an angel of light. He is not an angel of light, but attempts to pervert his image in order to deceive. Often, the Jezebel spirit will project thoughts into the mind of the person they host to make them believe they have extraordinary gifts of prophecy. The person may even have a gift of prophecy that has been warped or perverted by demonic influence and lies.

I don't believe demons have prophetic gifts or the ability to see the future. However, we dare not underestimate their intelligence and knowledge. We cannot know the exact age of angels, but we can see from Job 38:4-7 that they were around to watch the world as it was being created: *"Where were you when I laid the earth's foundation? Tell me, if you understand. Who marked off its dimensions? Surely you know! Who stretched the measuring line across it? On what were its footings set, or who laid its cornerstone—while the morning stars sang together and all the angels shouted for joy?"*

Angels have been around for a long time. They have thousands of years of gathered information and wisdom. So even the fallen angels have a level of knowledge that could be used to deceive a human being into believing they have special gifts. During my years on staff at Wellsprings of Freedom, I observed on multiple occasions Jezebel-led individuals who thought they had high level gifts of prophecy. They use this as a way to intimidate anyone who dares to disagree with them. One of the manipulative phrases they use to control people is: *"The Lord told me that we are supposed to_____!"* You fill in the blank. It is typically whatever they feel or want to happen. They attempt to use their perceived ability to hear the voice of God to shut down the opposition. If you disagree with them, they want to shut down your argument with the false narrative that you are really disagreeing with God. Most of the time, this silences those who dare to challenge them. Who wants to be seen as disagreeing with God? There is a level of pride associated with this, pride that usually follows most Jezebel-led people. When a Jezebel-led person is convinced they have high-level prophetic gifts, and they also do not believe they are ever wrong, that provides extra momentum to intimidate and deceive the people around them. Unfortunately, people with the Ahab spirit are very susceptible to Jezebel's declaration of being a prophet.

In one instance at Wellsprings of Freedom, a Jezebel-led individual declared to a group of team members that God told her that Wellsprings of Freedom had stopped listening to the Holy Spirit. This person went on to declare that God had taken his hand of blessing off of our ministry. Never mind the fact that she said this when we were in the middle of one of our biggest expansion periods. The truth that we later uncovered was that she was upset because God had purportedly told her we were supposed to change our model of ministry. According to her, we were supposed to change it so that she was in control of ministry sessions. What she meant by her accusation was that we were no longer listening to the Holy Spirit because we didn't listen to her. In her mind she was able to hear the voice of God at a higher level than anyone else, so she should be in charge. To her confused way of thinking, because we didn't listen to her, we weren't listening to the Holy Spirit. When we didn't allow her to have her way, she left. Sadly, she was able to convince a team of people to follow her into starting their own freedom ministry. They met together for about a month, and then, in typical Jezebel fashion, they broke up as they fought over who was going to be in charge.

Fear - Imagine your greatest fear. How often are you forced to deal with that fear? Most of us are able to avoid facing our deepest fears. If we are afraid of heights, we avoid heights. If we are afraid of snakes, we seldom go where snakes prominently exist. When we consider our fears and how well we might do if we were forced to deal with them publicly, it can give us compassion to pray differently for a person controlled by Ahab. Ahab-led people live in fear every day. Their greatest fear is typically the fear of rejection. Jezebel-led people manipulate or dominate others to obey or else they are punished. For family members, the punishment is usually in the form of being emotionally cut off from the Jezebel-led person. It's not until the Ahab-led person conforms to Jezebel's wishes that the Jezebel person will restore an emotional connection. If you are a person whose greatest fear is rejection, this emotional manipulation is devastating.

Sadly, for most Jezebel-led people, emotionally withdrawing from another person has no emotional downside for them. They are coldhearted and numb and feel no remorse for doing so. It's an emotionless chess game using any means necessary to manipulate people into obedience. This is proven out when an Ahab-led person chooses to stand up to the Jezebel-led person. Most often, the Jezebel-led person walks away from the relationship. They will choose to leave a relationship rather than not be in control. "If you want my love you will obey me. If you don't obey me, you don't get my love." This is how they stay in control. Ahab-led people know they will leave. It's their fear of rejection that causes them to do whatever is necessary to please the Jezebel-led person.

This is very true in the business world as well. Jezebel has to be in charge. Typically, if leadership doesn't give in to a Jezebel-led person's demands and temper tantrums, they will leave. It's just that their exaggerated ability to intimidate and control people can lead to messy situations. Too often, the Ahab-led individuals' unwillingness to deal with messy situations allows Jezebel to remain in power, which leads to even bigger problems. When Jezebel-led people don't get their way, they have no fear in making a big scene and taking on anyone who stands in their path. Jezebel will make sure there are very unpleasant consequences for anyone who dares to stand against it. Supernatural fear will often grip the Ahab-led person and cause them to wilt and hide. The Ahab leader will run away from an immediate confrontation and let Jezebel dominate the situation. In Christian organizations, the need to be seen as gentle and compassionate can be used to Jezebel's advantage. Jezebel will walk all over an Ahab person who doesn't want to deal with a tough and challenging situation. Jezebel-led individuals instinctively know that Ahab-led people will avoid confrontation, especially to those who are aggressively belligerent in how they react to authority.

If organizations can remember that Jezebel will not submit to authority, that will go a long way toward helping them defeat this spirit. When a Jezebel-led person is not allowed to bully and be in control, and they discover the organization will not give in to their manipulating ways, most Jezebels will leave. Once they realize they aren't going to be able to take control, there is no reason for them to stay. Being in control is everything. Once they know they can't control your organization, they will usually move on to the next location hoping to find a place they can control. Because of Jezebel's intimidating dominance over Ahab-led individuals, not giving into their obsession for control may be difficult. But being rigidly firm in not allowing them to control, intimidate, or manipulate you and your team will often have them leaving on their own in search of a place they can control.

The paralyzing grip that a Jezebel spirit can hold over a person with the Ahab spirit can be very frustrating for the team watching it happen. As the Ahab-led leader seemingly endorses the controlling and manipulating person with the Jezebel spirit, anger and resentment begin to build toward the leader. This is a natural response. I have experienced this personally in my own life and in the lives of those I have worked with. The longer the situation is allowed to continue, the greater the resentment builds toward the leader. Aside from leaving the organization, which unfortunately may be necessary, I would like to offer an alternative for those who are trapped for a season and cannot leave.

During a freedom session, I received a vison of a person who was consumed by an Ahab spirit and dominated by a Jezebel-led person. The Lord showed me a picture in my mind of what the Ahab-controlled person really looks like in the spiritual realm. In the vision, He showed me the core of the man, and what I saw brought tears to my eyes and helped me to be able to pray more effectively for him. He showed me a little boy sitting in the corner of a room paralyzed in fear. He had his hands covering his face as he cowered in the corner shaking and trembling uncontrollably. The fear touched the deepest part of his soul and convinced him there was no way out. His hopelessness and fear were rooted in the absolute terror of trying to confront Jezebel—a terror that was demonically magnified in his mind to frightening levels, causing him torturous agony. Plus, the Jezebel-led person had trained him that there were unimaginable consequences if he didn't obey. Yes, he was paralyzed, but he also hated himself for not being strong enough to deal with his fear and stand up to Jezebel. He resolved in his heart to let Jezebel lead. It was less frightening that way.

It was this vision that allowed me to help a client to pray differently. Rather than being consumed by resentment which only destroys us, the client began to pray differently for the Ahab-led person. He asked God to give him compassion for the Ahab-led person. He asked God to give the Ahab-led person wisdom and courage. He asked God to give this person the strength to stand up to his fear. He prayed for God to remove the demonic blinders that kept this person in bondage to paralyzing lies.

This prayer may or may not fix the situation, but it can't hurt. Yes, it ultimately boils down to a freewill decision on the part of the Ahab leader to dismiss the Jezebel-led person. But, praying this prayer is much better than boiling over with resentment. If the situation does not improve, then you can move on to another job. No one should have to put up with abusive leaders. But when you do leave, you will be able to leave knowing that you left operating in mercy rather than judgement.

Chapter 8

How Jezebel Destroys the Organization

The Jezebel spirit has an elusive way of slowly infecting everything within an organization. But one of the subtler things most ministries don't see until it has caused great damage is how it affects the organization long-term. This is partially because Jezebel is slow-moving and doesn't attempt to accomplish its mission overnight. It has no problem slowly injecting its virus into the organization over the course of months and years. It is capable of striking fast, but usually waits until it has first established itself deeply into the structure of the organization. Once it has imbedded itself and feels secure, it will then become more intentional about taking control.

As a Jezebel-led person is able to win over the trust of a supervisor, organizational leader, or a board member, it establishes deeper levels of control. The consequences of that control will begin to trickle down throughout the department or organization. There will also be long-term consequences that will affect the organization for months and years to come. Every decision Jezebel either influences or makes today will have a direct impact on the future. It bears repeating, Jezebel is a demonic spirit!

When it finds a staff member it can control, and that staff person is controlling significant parts of your organization, a demon is deciding your future. This is what many Christian organizations fail to see. When I suggest we should terminate and remove the Jezebel-led person, or at least downgrade them from positions of power, it is hard to separate ourselves from the humanitarian side of things. But when you hear about the same destructive patterns emerging over and over again, thousands of times across the world, we need to take notice. It's not easy, but making tough decisions for the sake of the congregation or institution will strengthen the organization as a whole.

Along with several other organizations today, churches are especially being held captive by this spirit and it is causing great harm. It wounds staff members (sometimes even causing pastors to leave the ministry), it keeps churches from growing, it stifles creativity and leadership, and can eventually shut a church down. If it doesn't shut the church down, it will keep it powerless and frail for ten or twenty years with one Jezebel leader and a handful of weak and incapable followers.

Jezebel-controlled churches typically become so dysfunctional that the occasional guests who visit seldom return. Because Jezebel works slowly over the course of time, wounding and damage is meted out in all directions. Congregants, staff, volunteers, programs, outreach, financial giving, attitudes, and future hope for the organization are all affected. How much of the damage is strategically intentional, or merely the consequences of poor leadership, is hard to know. I do not believe the Jezebel-led person ever sets out with the intent to destroy the organization; rather, they are puppets blinded by their own wounding and used by Jezebel to wreak havoc. The dysfunction caused by their wounding is what Jezebel uses to accomplish its mission. Because of the nature of Jezebel's lies, most hosts actually see themselves as agents of good. Jezebel's ability to convince them that they are the only one truly capable of leading sets them up to take control.

Remembering that Jezebel spirits often gain access into our lives through wounds, many wounded Jezebel hosts find the position they hold in the church is the only place they feel important. At home or at work they may feel meaningless and insignificant, but the position they hold on the board of their church gives them a title. That title may give them a measure of self-esteem they don't get anywhere else in their lives. A long-term controlling board member may chase away a successful new pastor for fear they might lose their position on the board. If the church grows, there will be new members, and new members equal competition. In this scenario with an insecure board member controlling the church, the long-term prognosis will be weak-to-mediocre leadership at best, with no growth, and probable losses.

So, as we begin to step into how organizations are affected long-term, I'd like to suggest this hypothesis: *Jezebel strategically uses the hosts' wounding and dysfunction for its purposes. It will use the hosts' addictive need for control for destructive causes, while falsely convincing them their ideas and actions are altruistic in nature.* Their pride convinces them they are always right, or they believe their false prophetic voice is always right. Both locks them into believing everything they do is justified and correct. This is what makes them dangerous. They cannot see their actions from any other perspective. Therefore, it is difficult to get them to change. They are causing great harm but can't see it. They see most corrective discipline placed upon them as a spiritual attack meant to stop the purposes of God. This can be very frustrating to the leadership team who are alerted to their controlling ways and desire to help the Jezebel-led person to be free. Sadly, it is not uncommon for attempts to help a Jezebel-led person to be met with resistance and an unwillingness to change.

Typically, Jezebel-led people can manage projects fairly well, but people follow them only because they have to, not because they want to. A project may get done with excellence, but the people dominated and controlled by the Jezebel-led person will pay a very high emotional cost. Jezebel will be seen as a champion, and will be more than willing to accept any and all credit. Meanwhile, the people who helped will be wondering if the emotional torment they experienced is worth staying with the organization. Top leaders can be deceived by a project well done, not realizing the deep emotional hit that was taken by the people in their organization. When this pattern is repeated over the course of time, good, hard-working people will begin to leave your organization.

Recognize the Subtle Ways Jezebel Effects the Organization

The leadership vacuum –

Destroy the leadership team and you severely cripple the organization. Because Jezebel-led people must dominate and control others, they will drive good leaders away from your organization. They will also attempt to remove strong leaders and replace them with people who are more geared to follow than lead. Jezebel-led people are threatened by strong leaders who speak truth and do not need Jezebel's help to be successful. Jezebel will attempt to undermine and control them. Strong leaders will not put up with Jezebel's excessive control. As the giftings of good leaders go unused and unappreciated, they will eventually leave. Because of the Jezebel host's ability to flatter and win over the trust of the most senior leader, as other strong leaders leave, Jezebel-led people will maneuver themselves into positions where they have a strong voice in who is hired to replace them. They will attempt to influence the hiring or promotion of weaker leaders whom they know they will be able to control. Jezebel will eventually create a structure where the newly hired or newly promoted weak leaders will rely on Jezebel for everything. This causes Jezebel to have greater control and appear more needed and irreplaceable. Jezebel-led individuals also stifle the progress of good leaders by not letting them lead their department or making sure they are not promoted. This will create a leadership vacuum.

Little by little those confident and gifted leaders who are truly anointed of God will exit the organization, either on their own or at the request of the leader who is being influenced by the Jezebel-led person. The people remaining, and those hired to replace the ones who leave, will fully submit to Jezebel. The organization will eventually suffer as those remaining can't lead, but are only allowed to follow directions. Without strong leaders, organizations will begin to stagnate and ultimately fail. A great question for an organization to ask is this: If the leader of the organization left today, is there anyone on staff who could successfully replace them? A better question: Are there multiple people who could replace them? Good organizations should be grooming multiple leaders to be ready to take higher levels of leadership, but Jezebel will see to it that this doesn't happen. Strong leaders are threats to Jezebel's control. The whole environment within the organization begins to shift. Only those who blindly follow are allowed to advance. Because Jezebel-led people are operating out of their woundedness, any doubt or resistance to their ideas are seen as rejection. Strong leaders who naturally offer their wisdom to fix problems intensify the Jezebel hosts' insecurity. The prideful Jezebel may not appear to be insecure, but they are, and it controls them way more than they know.

When highly educated leaders are treated like high school students working at their first job, eventually those leaders are going to move on to better things. Of course, this is what Jezebel wants. Organizational structures created by Jezebel-led leaders will try to direct every important decision from every department to come to them for final approval. Because no one can make any decision apart from Jezebel, the organization is tied up with delays, poor communication, and indecision. When the Jezebel-led person has to make every decision for every department, you can expect there to be a lot of meetings. Jezebel will have to have its hands in everything, thus it will meet with everyone to make sure they are doing it the way Jezebel wants. The Jezebel-led person will at first appear to be listening to all the ideas presented in meetings but will definitely make sure that by the time the meeting is over, its ideas are the ones being used. If it can't get group consensus, Jezebel will increasingly become more argumentative and angrier, and will eventually just take control and declare it will be done the way Jezebel wants. The more a person speaks against Jezebel's ideas in meetings, the more likely they will begin to be slowly ostracized and moved off of the leadership team. If Jezebel doesn't use pure domination to get its way, it will use emotional manipulation to coerce everyone to its way of thinking. Or the Jezebel-led person will manipulate and influence the top leader to remove an upward-moving, strong leader who is a threat to Jezebel's control.

As gifted leaders are slowly replaced or leave on their own, the overall leadership quotient of the organization begins to drop. If at the beginning of Jezebel's tenure, the average level of overall leadership was measured on a scale of 1 to 10 with 10 being the highest, it might have averaged somewhere between 6 to 8. But after a period of time under the direct influence of a Jezebel-led person, it is not uncommon to see the leadership quotient drop to an average of 2 to 4 or lower. This in itself is damaging to the organization, but it doesn't stop there. Each of those level 2 to 4 supervisors will hire people underneath them, and we seldom hire people who are equal or better than ourselves. It is frightening to consider that this is who remains to build the organization. They can sometimes maintain things for a little while, but seldom does the remaining leadership team have the firepower to grow an organization. In time, the organization begins to suffer losses.

Most Jezebel-led people are not leaders; they are domineering managers who demand obedience. They lack the ability to inspire others to be better, or even the ability to inspire others to want to follow them. Because of their title they demand obedience and respect. People follow them because they have to, not because they want to. John Maxwell calls this positional leadership. In his book, *"Developing the Leader Within You,"* Maxwell writes,

> *Positional leaders have more difficulty working with volunteers, white collar workers, and younger people. Volunteers don't have to work in the organization so there is no monetary leverage that a positional leader can use to make them respond. White collar workers are used to participating in decision making and resent dictatorial leadership. Baby boomers in particular are unimpressed with symbols of authority. Most of us have been taught that leadership is a position. Frustration rises within us when we get out into the world and find that few people follow us because of our titles (p. 6).*

When we consider how much nonprofits and churches work with volunteers, and how many of our pastoral staffs are filled with college-educated white-collar workers, we can begin to see where the trouble lies. Consider everything you have read up to this point about the characteristics of a Jezebel-led person. They are typically not collaborative or inspirational leaders who attract other leaders or volunteers. Who they do attract and promote are people who they can control, and they often like having the authority of a title. They like bossing people around. They typically can't get people to naturally follow them, so when they get a title handed to them, they are often corrupted by that power. This only further diminishes the leadership quotient of the entire organization. As these power-hungry managers begin to take charge of one department after another, good staff members leave along with good volunteers. High levels of employee and volunteer turnover will become the norm, creating even more chaos.

John Maxwell goes on to describe this in his book:

> *Leaders on the positional level often lead by intimidation. They are like the chickens that Norwegian psychologist T. Schjelderup-Ebbe studied in developing the "pecking order" principal that today is used to describe all types of social gatherings. Schjelderup-Ebbe found that in any flock one hen usually dominates all the others. She can peck any other without being pecked in return. Second comes a hen that pecks all but the top hen, and the rest are arranged in a descending hierarchy, ending in one hapless hen that is pecked by all and can peck no one (p. 7).*

Leading through intimidation will go only so far, and eventually good people will leave your organization.

As Jezebel-led people step higher and higher into positions of authority, their ability to deceive or manipulate the leader allows them to acquire more and more power and control. They begin to have greater influence over hiring and firing decisions. Good leadership is relationship based. Jezebel-led people struggle having relationships with anyone they cannot control or manipulate. They may start out well interacting with a new person, but their need to always be right, and their capacity to hurt other people without any feelings of remorse, will drive good leaders away. Jezebel-led people are very selfish and self-focused and usually are not empathetic caregivers. When a church or a non-profit is mostly led by people incapable of empathy and compassion toward others, people will begin to sense it and leave. The leadership vacuum will begin a slow process of destruction and will be like playing the game of "Jenga" where you never know which move will finally bring the whole structure down.

Confusion

Jezebel likes to spread confusion among the rank and file because it takes the focus off of what it is doing and infuses doubt and uncertainty into the organization. More often than not, Jezebel will strive to create a complicated leadership structure that will pit one person, department, division, or even one campus against another. Confusion unfolds when team members struggle to know who they are really supposed to follow—their supervisor, or the Jezebel-led person. Because Jezebel-led people demand obedience and usually have the backing of the organizational leader, they have no problem usurping control from a supervisor. Employees find themselves in the precarious position of trying to decide which one they should obey. Over the course of time, this dismantles the entire leadership organizational structure, and sets Jezebel up to control. Mid-level supervisors and their employees are in a constant state of confusion.

One of a Jezebel-led person's strategies is to set up a leadership structure where staff members have more than one supervisor, which causes a lot of confusion. Sometimes two supervisors are separately told they are in charge of the same project. It's the "relational triangle" we discussed in Chapter 2. The Jezebel-led person will tell one supervisor one thing and tell another supervisor something quite different in order to confuse and cause division in the ranks. This is where things can get really crazy for staff members. Two supervisors will often give one staff member two different answers as to what they are supposed to do. This totally causes such anxiety that staff members are afraid to even complete a task. Then, when the staff member goes to the Jezebel-led person, they might get an entirely different answer. This level of confusion can completely paralyze a team.

Jezebel's tactics are difficult to see as it will sometimes use its team of loyal followers to give out the inconsistent directives. As these Jezebel-led allies (who may also be supervisors) give out mixed and contradictory orders, team members will eventually become afraid to make any decision. They can't win. If they follow one supervisor's instruction, the other supervisor will reprimand them for not following their instructions. Eventually this will cause everyone to go to the Jezebel-led person for directions. That will help them escape from getting into trouble. This fits perfectly into Jezebel's plans, as it subtly trains everyone to come to the Jezebel-led person for guidance. Because the staff members don't see what is happening behind the scenes with the supervisors getting misleading information, the supervisors are blamed for being incompetent. Unfortunately, Jezebel can use this strategy as a way to take out any supervisors it doesn't want on the team.

Projects and programs will seemingly take forever to get started because everything to the finest detail must be approved by Jezebel. However, the team members will be the ones who are blamed for slow results. Unwanted team members will be given big projects with little to no guidance and then reprimanded and criticized for failing to complete the task. Jezebel is a critical, pushy, and demanding leader who forces people to submit. If they do not submit, there are consequences and the team members are trained to obey or else. The staff is led by fear and intimidation, not by influence and trust that allows the team to excel and grow their leadership skills. When only one person can make any kind of decision for an organization, everything slows down and strong leaders eventually leave. Jezebel delights in strong leaders leaving the organization. This allows them to be replaced with weaker leaders whom the Jezebel-led person can control. As Jezebel replaces stronger leaders with people who will fully submit to its authority, the strength of the entire team begins to diminish. Little by little the whole organization becomes a chaotic mess. Order, momentum, creativity, dollars, team health, and trust all disappear. As time goes by, the organization develops a bad reputation for how they treat staff and volunteers. This only perpetuates the problem of not being able to hire strong leaders and continues the cycle of confusion.

Selfishness

Jezebel-led people are selfish and see the world as revolving around them and their passions and gifts. Because Jezebel-led people are rarely compassionate, as they move up in the organization many of the programs that encourage fellowship, discipleship, or deep level interaction will slowly disappear. Jezebel-led people will often expect everyone to just follow them into their areas of passion. The Jezebel host will slowly replace programs that many in the church have loved or cherished because it doesn't align with the Jezebel host's vision. The higher the Jezebel host climbs up the leadership ladder, the more influence they have over the organizational programs. Jezebel wants to look good because it helps them to appear to be vital to the organization and untouchable. By steering or influencing the senior leader into directions that allow the Jezebel host to play to their strengths, the Jezebel host is able to look good to the organizational leader. They can appear to be a rock star in their area of expertise, while the majority of the church loses interest in serving. The senior leader is excited and focused on the strengths of the Jezebel-led person and is oblivious as to why people are leaving the church. People will leave because their gifts and passions are not able to be used or expressed.

It is important for the Jezebel-led individual to be seen as the most important and irreplaceable person on staff. Slowly shutting down areas where others can excel eliminates competition. If there is a ministry in the church that competes with Jezebel's preferred ministry for volunteers and loyalty, it is most likely in danger. Unless Jezebel can somehow gain control over that ministry in order to receive the accolades of its success, Jezebel will strive to shut it down. This can be extended to other staff members who are deeply loved and followed by large numbers of the congregation. They too may soon be targeted for firing, demotion, or reassignment to a position away from the mainstream. Jezebel must remove all competition for loyal followers.

Discernment

The word discernment means to know something through the senses. Discernment is a spiritual gift found in 1 Corinthians 12:10. This is an interesting spiritual gift as it allows certain believers in the church to know things or sense things they could not possibly see or know. This is a spiritual gift we rely on heavily in our freedom ministry. People with this gift have the ability to sense when evil spirits are present. As we have traveled around the world, what has been fascinating is how many people have the gift of discernment. Because it is usually not taught in our churches, most believers do not know they have this gift. It is when they step into the context of spiritual warfare ministry that they begin to understand how this gift functions and can be used to help people be set free. It's not that this gift hasn't been functioning. It has been; they just haven't been taught what it is. Until they learn what it is and how it can be used, they don't realize they are sensing things in the spirit realm. It's just that they knew things they shouldn't know but didn't understand why.

It has been a joy for me to watch hundreds of people through the years finally discover what discernment is and that they aren't crazy. In a booklet I wrote called, *"Understanding the Gift of Discernment in Children,"* one of our team members wrote a testimony about her discerning gifts. Here is a small portion of what she wrote:

> *I remember from a young age being able to know things I shouldn't have known. See things I was told I wasn't seeing. Feel things I was told I couldn't be feeling. This common message was given to me from people of authority as a child and continued into my college years. Because of my discerning gifts, I often encountered disbelief, condemnation, shame, and embarrassment. Throughout my adult years, I kept seeing and experiencing the unseen realm in various ways. I was always careful to not share what I felt, saw, or sensed because I never knew how it would be received. Every time prior in my life, it was met with resistance. It was not until being trained and ministered to by Wellsprings of Freedom International, that I ever heard a message that I was NOT crazy. They BELIEVED me, and affirmed my discerning gifts are of God, and for his glory. Now I am able to use those gifts to help others be set free.*

In our ministry we have discovered that there are many people in all of our churches that have these amazing gifts. However, because most people do not understand what they are, many in the church see them as being evil. This causes most people to remain silent. They are afraid of being condemned for something God intended to be a blessing to his people. Across our Wellsprings Network, we have hundreds of people who have been trained to use their gift of discernment to help people be set free from spiritual bondage.

As I was researching and studying to prepare for the writing of this book, I discovered a common theme. In John Paul Jackson's book, *"Unmasking the Jezebel Spirit,"* he writes, *"A Jezebel spirit defiles everything it touches. That which is holy becomes vile. People will begin to leave a church, not knowing why, simply feeling compelled to go as if they could feel the impending darkness"* (p. 14). This is not the only research material where I found this phenomenon occurring. As I began to contemplate this recurring pattern, it occurred to me what is happening. Those people in the church who have discerning gifts, but just don't know it, are indeed discerning what they sense in the spirit realm. They are discerning the Jezebel spirit. Their spiritual gifts are warning them of the impending danger to the organization, but their lack of awareness and understanding about discerning gifts causes them to run without knowing why. Over the course of time, many of those discerning the Jezebel spirit within the organization will eventually leave. They won't know it is a Jezebel spirit. In fact, they won't even know what a Jezebel spirit is. They will not necessarily see a Jezebel spirit, but will only sense an impending doom. This means they will not be able to give a solid account as to why they are leaving. This will cause confusion among the leadership team as they lose church members, but can't solidly identify why it is happening. This usually means that everything except the Jezebel spirit's presence will be blamed for the losses in attendance.

Busyness

There may be multiple reasons for this, but it is not unusual to find a common denominator in Jezebel-controlled churches. Often, a Jezebel-driven organization is overworked and overwhelmed with busyness. This is partially due to Jezebel's absolute need to dominate people and their lack of feelings or concern for the people who work under them. A Jezebel-led person's selfish determination to get their favored projects done in an unreasonable time frame will drive people crazy. And, it's not just crazy time frames. Jezebel-led people are notorious for creating one new project after another. While handing out projects to people, there is little to no thought from the Jezebel-led person as to how it will affect your overall schedule or how many other projects you have on your plate. If Jezebel wants it done, then it must be done. Certainly, there are times in any organization where there are seasons of high intensity in order to get a big project done. But, in a Jezebel-driven environment, the seasons of high intensity never seem to end. It is one season of crazy busyness right after another, usually turning into year upon year of busyness. It is hard enough to keep good employees, but when they are regularly driven to the point of burnout, many employees will eventually move on. As those employees leave, those submissive to Jezebel will be rewarded with promotions, which causes more loyalty to Jezebel.

In addition to Jezebel's propensity to drive people to burn out, Jezebel is also known to be highly critical. Nothing is good enough, there is always something to correct or change. Think of working in an environment where you are working crazy hours and nothing you do measures up to Jezebel's insane and impossible standards. Coming to work is not rewarding; it is absolute drudgery.

The next component to add to the busy environment is Jezebel's need to have absolute control over every decision. When Jezebel must be a part of every decision, there are many meetings. Meetings are important, and this is not a rant against meetings. However, when decisions are being made that should and could have been made at a lower level, even the meetings feel like a slap in the face. Meetings become reminders that you are not good enough or qualified to decide something on your own. The meetings themselves become like an iron weight around your neck as you are overwhelmed with projects with crazy timelines. But instead of getting the project done, you are sitting in a worthless meeting. Frustration sets in as you feel like you are wasting time being told what you should do by the ultra-controlling Jezebel-led person. Things that you already knew to do. And if by chance you do get to decide something on your own, look out, Jezebel will make sure that it was wrong. There will be multiple reasons why your decision didn't measure up to Jezebel's standards, even though all of your colleagues will think it was a brilliant idea.

As the organizational leadership quotient diminishes, the number of highly trained and competent people will diminish as well. This means more work for those left behind who are trying to do a job they were never trained to do. Because Jezebel-led individuals are afraid of hiring people who are capable of leading others, or who may point out Jezebel's dysfunction, they often will not hire anyone new. Work will just get added onto the plate of those remaining as Jezebel-led people believe they will be able to control them into success, regardless of hours needed to do the task. The longer the organization refuses to hire qualified workers and instead places more and more responsibilities on those remaining, the more people will leave the organization. Good luck to those who decide to stay. Jezebel will run them ragged with little to no thought for their well-being.

When the Jezebel spirit is able to influence a person at high enough levels, it can begin to drive an organization toward madness. Jezebel-led people use good causes, projects, and ideas to get the team running at an unbelievable pace. It is hard to push back against something that is blessing others. Never mind that the team is running ragged. Push back will be seen as opposing something good. Jezebel uses this as a defense mechanism to silence people when they complain. As soon as one project is completed, five more are added to the schedule. Jezebel doesn't always wait for a project to be completed before adding more things to the agenda to get done. The faster the team runs, the happier Jezebel becomes. When people are overwhelmed with projects to get done or else face the judgment of Jezebel, this spirit keeps the team too weary to fight against it. Plus, as this pace is impossible to continue long term, it allows the Jezebel-led person to have plenty of opportunities to criticize the team with the leader. The faster the team runs, the more discouraged and frustrated they become, which leads to anger, arguments, and team burnout.

Jezebel is masterful at getting an entire organization spinning way too many plates on sticks and watching for the plates to fall in order to criticize the individual's failure to perform. This will get them to run even faster as they try to reach the impossible perfection expected of them by Jezebel. Because no decisions can be made by anyone but the Jezebel-led person, team members can't run or lead their areas effectively. They are hindered by the shackles put around them by Jezebel's crazy demands to control everything. All of this craziness keeps the leader's eyes off of the Jezebel-led person who is supposedly trying to keep the ship running, while the Jezebel-led person blames the team for not measuring up. The leader's displeasure is kept on the team, and off of the Jezebel-led individual. The long-term effects of this kind of pace saps the joy out of the organization and leads to sour attitudes from the staff.

Wrong/Selfish Motives

When a Jezebel-led person steps into power, whether they are the boss or the one controlling the boss, as you break everything down, you begin to see there are hidden agendas. Is the Jezebel-led person striving to build the kingdom of God or a kingdom for their own glory? Is there a genuine desire to seek

God's plan or a plan that elevates the Jezebel-led person to greater power and control? Is more attention given to acquiring buildings and property than pouring into people's lives? Can the Jezebel-led person ever admit to being wrong? Does the leader demand that people blindly follow, or does the leader influence people to want to follow? How does the Jezebel leader respond to voices of caution and disagreement? Is there a wholehearted desire to see all of God's kingdom grow, or are other churches seen as competitors? When issues of bullying and control are brought to the forefront, is there an honest attempt to investigate, or are issues swept under the rug in a smug and dismissive way? Are well-meaning whistleblowers treated with respect, or are they punished for daring to speak the truth? Are well-meaning people from within the organization dismissed when they bring true godly correction to the leader? In Proverbs 9:7-9 we read these words: *"Whoever corrects a mocker invites insult; whoever corrects a wicked man incurs abuse. Do not rebuke a mocker or he will hate you; rebuke a wise man and he will love you. Instruct a wise man and he will be wiser still; teach a righteous man and he will add to his learning."*

Are there political power structures elevating a few to elite status which harbor them from serious accusations of misbehavior? Is there more effort placed on the Jezebel host's selfish projects rather than the needs of the people? In the midst of people choosing to leave the organization, is there an effort to discover why? Does the Jezebel leader attempt to divert attention away from failures and focus high emphasis on minor wins in an attempt to look good? Is it important for the leader to always be right, even when everyone knows they are wrong? Is there a need for the leader to lie and deceive others in order to always look good? Can the leader confront, reprimand, or correct the Jezebel-led person? Are there attempts by the leaders to hide hard data evidence that something is broken? Is the leader's need to look good more important than facing the real issues at hand? Can the Jezebel-led leader submit to any kind of authority?

Eventually people will begin to see the brokenness of an organization ruled by Jezebel, and they will leave. False excuses for why people are leaving will be invented by the Jezebel-led leaders to deflect any blame off of themselves. Usually, innocent people will be blamed for the organization's demise, rather than the controlling and manipulating ways of the leadership team. Jezebel cannot be wrong, so failure must be placed on others. Control is an enemy of growth. At a recent leadership conference, Craig Groeschel said this: *"You can have control or growth. But you can't have them both."* The need to control an organization, not take responsibility for failure, and ignore sound wisdom either leads to—or is the result of—pride. In Proverbs 11:2, we find this advice: *"When pride comes, then comes disgrace, but with humility comes wisdom."*

In the next chapter, we will discuss the importance of humility and how it can be the key to unlocking the chains of bondage Jezebel has placed upon its host.

Chapter 9

Hope for the Jezebel Host

This chapter is meant to be a blessing for anyone who might be the Jezebel host. I truly want to give you an opportunity to escape Jezebel's grasp. Perhaps what I have written so far has angered you. Maybe there has been a sobering realization that you are not who you want to be. It is my desire to help you find freedom. I'm sure what I have written so far has been unsettling, I'm sorry for that. I just don't know how to help people whose organizations are being wounded by this spirit without explaining how this spirit operates. I realize that all of us become a bit defensive when we are confronted with our own failures. I can only imagine how the Jezebel spirit must be taunting you to reject this writing and dismiss it as a hateful attack on you. I want to thank you for sticking with the book up to this point.

When I was a child and my parents disciplined me for bad behavior, I thought they were just being mean. I don't know that I fully understood the love my parents were providing to me through discipline until I became a parent. I then saw everything from a totally different perspective. I didn't discipline my kids out of hatred or revenge. I was trying to help them to be the best they could be. It was tough receiving discipline as a child, but I think it is even harder to receive discipline as an adult. Our pride steps in and steers us away from receiving correction. It is sometimes hard to receive correction. We become offended and filled with resentment. God knows this is how we often respond to correction and warns us of the dangers of doing so. In Proverbs 3:11-15 we find this instruction:

> *My son, do not despise the* LORD's *discipline and do not resent his rebuke, because the* LORD *disciplines those he loves, as a father the son he delights in. Blessed is the man who finds wisdom, the man who gains understanding, for she is more profitable than silver and yields better returns than gold. She is more precious than rubies; nothing you desire can compare with her.*

When we find ourselves resenting wise counsel, being offended by healthy suggestions, and resorting to victimization, we need to examine our heart. What are the underlying emotions and lies that cry out for our attention? What is it that snatches away our deep desire to be humble before the Lord? Why is it so hard to step out from under our addiction to control?

Jezebel is a spirit of control and it wants to amass as much control over humans as it possibly can. It is not just interested in controlling you. It wants to control other people through you. It manipulates you to manipulate others for the purpose of control. This is why it seeks to align with leaders. By controlling leaders, it can control greater numbers of people. What it never wants you to know is that you are just a pawn it uses to accomplish its mission. When you take steps toward freedom, it has to try to stop you. It doesn't want to lose its ability to control others through you.

It will try to prevent your freedom through intellectual mind games. By filling your mind with fraudulent excuses and/or reasons for controlling people, it strives to justify your right to control others. In addition to the mind games, it will seek to influence your emotions. The spirit wants to fully control you, so it does not want anyone else speaking into your life. In order to cement you under its control, it will trigger different emotions to block you from being able to receive corrective advice. Part of its defensive emotional shield includes the spirits of offense, anger, mistrust, resentment, rejection, denial, shame, embarrassment, insecurity, and doubt. All of which Jezebel can call into the battle against you, like a baseball coach bringing players in from off the bench.

When you read a book shedding light on how Jezebel manipulates you to control others, a wall of emotional defense begins to be erected in order to block you from the truth. A faucet is turned on and high levels of emotions begin to rise up within you, emotions that lead you into the mindset of a victim. This is partially why it is hard for you to receive correction and accept personal responsibility for controlling others. You fall for the false notion that you are the victim, not those who suffer under your unrelenting control.

The very first step is recognizing you have a problem with control. I know how the spirit of Jezebel blinds us and makes excuses for our controlling behavior, and that can be very confusing. But if you sincerely want to be free, there is a way out. Let's start with a heartfelt prayer, asking Jesus to help you open your heart to the truth and give you a willingness to change:

> *Dear Jesus, please help me be willing to see the truth. Push aside all my excuses and reasons for why I do what I do. Tear down my defensive walls and examine my heart. Please remove the blinding fog that covers my eyes and prevents me from seeing the truth. Help me to step beyond my first inclination that I'm perfectly fine and that there is nothing wrong with me. Force the Jezebel spirit to stand*

aside and stop invading my mind with lies that prevent me from accepting responsibility for my actions. Forgive me for my controlling ways. Holy Spirit, I give you permission to break through the hard-defensive shield that Jezebel uses to keep me in bondage. Give me the courage to face my flaws and walk toward repentance and change. Help me to let go of my need to control others. Give me a Christ-like mind and a willingness to submit to those who are in authority over me. Thank you, Jesus. Amen

There is definitely hope for those who are in bondage to Jezebel, but only if they can truly recognize and admit they have a problem. Letting go of the need to be in control is very difficult. Once we have mastered the art of manipulating people, it is hard to let go of that kind of power. For those who tend to be a bit controlling, but do not have a Jezebel spirit, letting go of your controlling ways will be much easier for you. But for those who are caught up in the bondage of a Jezebel spirit, this will be a battle. Everything inside of you will resist, which is a pretty good indication that you might be in trouble. If while reading the prayer above, you sensed any of the following, you may want to pray the prayer over again, only this time with even more determination.

- You felt anger rising up suddenly from nowhere.
- You sensed your mind laughing at the prayer.
- After a sentence or two you became indifferent and just skipped over it.
- You felt an intensifying defensive attitude.
- Your thoughts told you that you have a right to be this way.
- A haughty dismissive voice in your mind said, "This is ridiculous."

- Fear or panic set in, and you began to feel unsafe or unprotected if you move forward.
- You felt offended and the words "How dare you?" came to your mind.
- You felt extraordinarily numb and uncaring.
- You got a sudden headache while reading the prayer.

These are very common ways the Jezebel spirit will attempt to subvert you and keep you from finding wholeness and freedom. The more intense the feelings, usually the stronger the spirit has a hold on you. The Jezebel spirit does not want to let go of you. It has very likely enveloped you under the false disguise of protection. It may feel like it is your friend and stepping out from under it might make you feel vulnerable and unsafe. A subconscious sense of security is often how this spirit is able to invade a person's life. It is all a sham, but it works. The spirit of Jezebel lies to us in ways that are very specific to our situation. Deep emotional wounds are what most often opens the door to let a Jezebel spirit into our lives. The lies we hear that give them control over us are matched to the wounds we have experienced. So, when Jezebel presents a lie to us, it makes sense, appears to protect us, and seems like the right thing to do.

Think about this for a moment. Do you really want a demon protecting you? Do you want to trust a demon that wants to destroy your life and destroy the lives of others through you? Their lies lead us to do things that are harmful to ourselves and to the people around us. When you control people, it drives wedges between you and others. Many of those you control are people you love. Your control and domineering ways cause your loved ones to hold bitterness toward you. But they are afraid of the consequences of telling you the truth so they will stay silent and never tell you. Depending on the Jezebel host, they may be afraid of your temper, or they are afraid of the manipulating guilt and shame you place on them for confronting you. They will seldom speak out; they just hold it in and withdraw from you emotionally. Or, you emotionally disengage from them because they resist all your efforts to control them. Jezebel causes the host to have little to do with people who refuse to be controlled. It's as if there is a mental switch—disagree with a Jezebel-led person and they can flip the switch and you are meaningless to them. Examine your life for a moment. Do you mentally and emotionally shut people out of your life based on whether they obey you or not? Have you emotionally cut people off from you because they don't choose to follow you? If you have surrounded yourself with people who are loyal followers, who you know you can manipulate and control, you might need freedom from a Jezebel spirit.

Here is the hard reality statement that must be said. I do not say this to be mean, I am not saying this in order to try and control you. It's just a true statement. How you decide to receive the following truth will determine if you are going to find freedom or not:

> *The only way you are going to find true freedom is to admit that you have a control problem and be willing to humble yourself and commit to change.*

The Jezebel spirit has created a defensive shield around you to keep you locked in a state of bondage. It really is quite astonishing when it is unveiled to see how it works against you. It starts with an absolute disgust toward authority. The spirit of Jezebel refuses to submit to anyone! So, anyone who tries to correct you is seen as the enemy. Because of deep wounds you incurred at the hands of others, Jezebel is able to twist any godly instruction or correction and spin it into your mind as rejection. Another wall of the defensive shield comes from a distorted prophetic voice convincing you that you hear from God far more accurately than anyone else. So, when someone tries to help you see you are hurting other people, the distorted prophetic voice overrides the correction. The false prophetic voice in your mind gives you perfectly good reasons why you have the right to control them. It is for their own good. So, the reasoning behind controlling them seems to make sense, but when you add in the false prophetic voice, it further seals your perceived right to control other people. A demon, masquerading as the Holy Spirit, confirms in your mind your right to control others. When you accept the premise that it is the voice of God speaking to you, that overrides any human voice. This leads to spiritual pride. Even now, the idea that your prophetic gift may sometimes be distorted has probably ruffled your feathers. Please understand, I have been working with highly prophetic individuals for twenty years, and even some of the most gifted can be deceived and not have a clue it is happening.

If you have to be in control, you are going against the very nature of God who has given us free will. He has given us the right to make our own choices even though we sometimes make bad ones. God doesn't step in and control our right to choose. If God doesn't control us, then what makes us think it is okay for us to control people. In 2 Corinthians 3:17, we read, *"Now the Lord is the Spirit, and where the Spirit of the Lord is, there is freedom."* God is all about freedom, releasing us from our bondage to sin and shame. Satan, on the other hand, is all about holding us in bondage. Bondage controls us. When we choose to partner with Satan, whether it is through drugs, alcohol, pornography, secret sins, guilt and shame, or lies, we are held in bondage by our addictions and sin. Other words to describe bondage are slavery, captivity, oppression, and suppression—all words that describe control. When we control and manipulate people, we are striving to keep them in bondage to us. They must do what we say, or there is a nasty consequence unleashed upon them that ensures future obedience.

Before we leave this section, I have one more thought for those of you who control others. Take a moment for self-reflection. You know that you hate submitting to anyone, you refuse to let anyone tell you what to do. Since you hate it so much, can you try to put yourself in the shoes of the people you control? You are not motivated by someone trying to control you, so why do you think others would be motivated by you controlling them? They're not! They most likely resent you and are looking forward to the day they can get out from under your control. Control is never a positive thing. Ask God to help you become more like Him.

I think we sometimes justify our control over people because we believe we know what is best for them. We believe we can make better decisions for them. But the truth is, we are not God. Of course, when our children are small we need to make decisions for them until they grow up, but then, we must let go of controlling them. Not even God Himself controls our decisions, even when we decide to sin against Him. He teaches us in His Word how we should live, and then releases us to decide for ourselves. God could control us, but He declines and refrains from doing so. Jimmy Evans, in his message called "Reversing the Jezebel Curse," says this: *"We are the image bearers of God, what image are we projecting God to be?"* When we are controlling others, we are projecting God to be a domineering and manipulative God and, of course, He is not. When Jesus lived on the earth with us, He came as a humble servant. Philippians 2:5-8 helps us to see the model Christ has set for us to follow: *"Your attitude should be the same as that of Christ Jesus: Who, being in very nature God, did not consider equality with God something to be grasped, but made himself nothing, taking the very nature of a servant, being made in human likeness. And being found in appearance as a man, he humbled himself and became obedient to death—even death on a cross!"*

He could have come in power and authority and demanded we obey, but He didn't. He came as a humble servant. Since we are the image bearers of God, would you be willing to ask God to help you put aside your need to be in control and replace it with a gentle and humble servant's heart?

I know the enemy will want you to see this chapter as a rejection of you, or as an attack on you. Please know it is not intended to be hurtful. It is my hope that it will help you to see yourself from a different perspective and that there is a way out. If you can lower your defensive shield and look for truth, the truth will set you free. If you want to be well, you really do have a choice. If you can humble yourself and seek God's help, there is hope. The rest of this chapter is a suggested pathway out from under Jezebel's control of you. My prayer for you is that your eyes have been opened to how the enemy has kept you in bondage, and that God will give you a desire to be free. The only one who can help you be free is you. You have to want it, and be willing to do whatever it takes. You see, it's your choice. No one is forcing you. It's between you and God. And even He won't force you. He graciously leaves the decision up to you. Will you choose to be free?

Steps Toward Freedom

Recognize your need to be free - Perhaps the first step for a Jezebel-led person to find respite and freedom from Jezebel is to recognize they have a need to change and be set free. The first chapter of this book gives a list of common characteristics often found to be significant indicators that a person is being controlled by a Jezebel spirit. This is not for people who are being dominated or manipulated by a Jezebel-led person; this is for the person directly being controlled by the spirit. I recommend that you go back to this chapter and review the list. How many characteristics on the list describe you? In order for this to work you have to be ruggedly honest with yourself. Don't allow yourself to make excuses, or rationalize your controlling behavior. Ignore the voice in your mind that is trying to talk you out of doing this. That voice is not your friend. You can't fix what you don't know is broken. As you review the list, don't try to analyze why you act the way you do, just put a check mark by each one that somewhat describes you. The more check marks, the more likely you are being used by a Jezebel spirit. Don't beat yourself up, don't give up hope, just be honest.

Resist the lies – If your evaluation indicates you might have Jezebel tendencies, you can expect the negative thought voice in your mind to begin to convince you otherwise. The Jezebel spirit does not want you to believe that it is there. It has imbedded itself in your mind and has disguised itself as your thoughts. If you have done the evaluation, the Jezebel spirit is in a panic. Damage control will now become its number one priority. It must stop you from going any further or it will lose its control over you. It will project every lie it can invent into your mind, hoping it can shut down your ability to see the truth. It knows that if you see and accept the truth about how it controls you, it is finished. It will begin to lose its ability to manipulate and control you.

Its lies will go in all directions. Thoughts will come saying that you can't survive without it. You will hear the thought you can't have a demon if you're a believer. It will mock the list of Jezebel characteristics and get you to doubt they are even real. It will tell you that it protects you from being hurt again. Anger and defensive emotions will rise up to high levels as it causes you to feel rejected and criticized. Jezebel will try to get you to be offended by the list. Fear of looking like a failure will taunt you not to move forward. Control will tell you that you have to control others so they don't control you. Self-pity will try to convince you it's everyone else's fault and it's okay to feel sorry for yourself. Pride will convince you it's your job to control others because they couldn't survive without you. If you don't fix them, who will? A false prophetic voice will tell you that God has created you to be this way, and you have the right to control others. Fear will tell you that if you stop controlling others, they will die; it's your job to protect them. Sometimes there is a fear of being weak or being perceived as weak, and the lie is you have to prove you're not weak by dominating others. Control is an illusion, it projects a false sense of safety if you control everything. This is totally a lie. You can't stop bad things from happening. Fear will project into your mind all the worst-case scenarios and convince you that you must remain in control at all times to be safe.

Pride tells you that you can't be flawed, so you can't be the problem. It must be the environment around you. It creates an unwillingness to accept any responsibility for your controlling ways. Blame is cast in all directions except toward you. Jezebel must blame everyone and everything else so the focus is never placed upon itself. Another deceitful lie is that if you humble yourself and admit to failure, you will be rejected, judged, and criticized. Fear creates walls that isolate you from deep relationships; it causes you to reject others before they can reject you. Fear creates such a deep distrust of others that you have to do everything yourself. Jezebel tells you that you can't trust other people's ideas. The pride that works with Jezebel convinces you that you know better than anyone else. It causes you to not value the input of other people.

These are only a few of the lies that might begin to bombard your mind. Everyone is different and there are hundreds of different lies. Don't be fooled by the thought that since your lies weren't listed you must be okay. If you sense in your mind a strong resistance to contemplating the list of Jezebel's characteristics, you must resist the urge to ignore what is happening. Know that the resistance is coming from a demon who wants to continue to control you. The overwhelming resistance itself is a huge indicator that Jezebel is present and fighting to keep you in bondage. You may not hear any lies, but feel an overwhelming urge to run away from what is being exposed in your mind. Don't run, don't panic, accept that you are being influenced by an evil spirit and choose to take your next step toward freedom. Also, know that if your mind is usually full of negative chatter and it just went quiet, the demons are trying to deceive you by making you believe they really aren't there.

Renounce your actions – If you can remember that Satan is the father of all lies and the demons that have pledged allegiance to him are also liars and deceivers, it will help you take your next step. Most likely the thought voice in your mind has been projecting excuses into your mind for your bad behavior. It wants to control others through you and must make you believe that controlling other people is for their own good. It may be that you have been controlling things for a long time and it defines who you are. The Jezebel voice in your mind may be telling you that God created you this way and you can never change. That is a lie. Why would God assign a right to you that He doesn't even give to Himself? The voice may try to tell you that you are entitled to control people. Step back for a moment and examine all the places in history where one people group dominated and controlled another people group. Slavery comes to mind; also how Nazi Germany dominated and destroyed the Jewish people. God wants to lead and guide people with truth, and then gives them the right to choose. Satan wants to trap and bind people through dominating lies. Every temptation is bait laid out by the enemy in hopes of trapping you into the bondage of sin and guilt.

Controlling and manipulating other people does not produce freedom for them, it only shackles them to you. You may get away with it because of your title, or because you are a family member, but coercively forcing people to obey you is abuse. I'm not talking about normal employer-to-employee guidelines and protocol, as there are rules we must all live by. This controlling behavior is being compelled by force, intimidation, manipulation, and the exertion of strength to force someone to yield. This could be a wealthy Jezebel-led board member forcing a pastor to obey his demands or lose his significant financial assistance. This could be a female staff member using her sexual prowess to gain control over a pastor. It could be a dominating male leader who intimidates his staff through yelling and screaming and threats of firing. It might be a female leader who uses tears and emotional outbursts to manipulate the leader to get what she wants. Or, perhaps it is a parent who uses guilt and shame to manipulate their grown children in order to get them to comply to their demands. If you manipulate, dominate, or control the people around you to ensure they obey you, you need to renounce your abusive behavior.

The Merriam-Webster dictionary gives this definition for "renounce": *to give up a position with no possibility of resuming it.* Renouncing your control means you are abdicating your right to control others. Renounce also means: *to officially give up or turn away from.* By renouncing your control over others, you are committing to God that you will give up and turn away from your controlling ways. Nothing can or will change without your solemn decision to let go of the need to be in control. It is reaching the point in your life where you say to the Jezebel spirit: *"No more! You will not control me anymore."* It's where you desperately want Jezebel gone. With your whole heart you reject all of Jezebel's destructive influence: *"Jezebel, I am sick of you. I am ashamed of who you have influenced me to become. I renounce you and your controlling ways. I do not want you influencing my life any longer. You are not my friend, I want you out of my life."*

After you have fully renounced the Jezebel spirit, ask for God's help in showing you all those you have controlled, wounded, or mistreated through the years. Ask God to let you see through their woundedness how you have hurt them. Look for common patterns as to how you have wounded others, what specifically you did to hurt them, and what actions you need to take to stop that behavior. Usually just being willing to identify you hurt them and how you wounded them will help you to stop the bad behavior. But you have to want to stop. It won't happen if you do not recognize your mistreatment of others and purposely change. You cannot fall back into the old ways of life by ignoring your controlling behavior and making excuses for it.

As you walk through this process, don't be surprised if you discover your controlling ways are far more numerous and predominant than you could have ever imagined. Don't become overwhelmed, and don't fall for the temptation to give up and quit. Make a list, and keep bringing what has been hidden into the light along with a relentless commitment to change.

Repent – In Acts 3:19, we find these words: *"Repent, then, and turn to God, so that your sins may be wiped out, that times of refreshing may come from the Lord."* Most people think repent means to be sorry for your sins. However, that is only a partial definition. Repent means to review your sins with deep contrition and regret, and to be so sorry for what you have done, that you commit to change. Renouncing is agreeing and deciding you need to change, but repentance goes deeper. It is the realization of what you have done that leads to sorrow and regret. It is a deep understanding that takes place in your mind and heart that you need to change, and, therefore, results in a change of your behavior.

The challenge for Jezebel-led individuals is how the Jezebel spirit numbs your heart and blocks you from feeling regret or remorse for your actions. Jezebel knows the importance of repentance and must try to keep you from doing so. Ask Jesus to help you push beyond this barrier. Allow yourself to be transparent before God. Let the words of the psalmist be your prayer: *"Search me, O God, and know my heart; test me and know my anxious thoughts. See if there is any offensive way in me, and lead me in the way everlasting"* (Psalm 139:22-23).

Don't let pride stand in your way. In Romans 3:23, we learn the truth about ourselves: *"For all have sinned and fall short of the glory of God."* The prideful side of Jezebel blocks your ability to see your mistakes. The fear of being seen as a failure is also a barrier. Place your pride at the feet of Jesus. He loves you unconditionally; your sins are not going to change that fact. Humbly admit you are controlling others. Repent, and ask Him to forgive you. Let the sorrow for your sins rise up within you and in the midst of your regret, confess your sins before God and ask for His forgiveness. Then, trust in God's merciful care and in His promise to forgive you. (See 1 John 1:9.)

Freedom Sessions – If you have reached this point and have followed the steps toward freedom, I want to take a moment to encourage you. Well done! Standing up to a Jezebel spirit is one of the more difficult challenges you may ever have to face. Spiritual battle is hard work. The spirit that led you to control other people is itself a spirit of control that wants to dominate you. The work you have done up to this point has weakened its grip. But it is not entirely done with you yet. I'm sorry to reveal that to you, but I don't want to mislead you. Everything you have done to this point are necessary first steps on your journey toward freedom from Jezebel. Without those steps, nothing from this point on would be possible. Until we admit we have a problem, there is not much anyone can do to help us. You can only help people to the level they will allow.

Thank you for your obedience thus far. Now we have to discuss getting the Jezebel spirit and its helpers cut off of you. This is done through freedom sessions. All throughout the New

Testament, we find Jesus and his disciples helping people to be set free from demonic spirits. The Jezebel spirit is simply a demon that needs to be removed. Our ministry, Wellsprings of Freedom International, has been setting people free for over eighteen years, and we do it with absolute gentleness and care. We know there are other ministries who do things in very extreme ways, but that is not who we are. Hollywood movies have created a very distorted and frightening image of spiritual warfare that is not real. The model of ministry we use is centered around gentle and loving prayer sessions. These sessions are filled with a time of worship, biblical advice, and the application of God's authority and Word using a tender and loving inner healing model. It is through inner healing that we help our clients find freedom by guiding them through a very specific process of forgiveness. Demons take advantage of our deep emotional wounds to establish strongholds in our lives. By dealing with our emotional wounds, we can remove the root causes the demons have used to torment us. Dr. Charles Kraft, who has been a pioneer in the modern freedom ministry movement, has coined a phrase we like to use: "*Rats love garbage. If you remove the garbage, the rats will go away!*" By bringing forgiveness to our deep emotional wounds, the demonic strongholds must leave. In other words, the Jezebel spirit will be forced to let go of you.

I recommend that you don't try to do this on your own. It is important to find a trained freedom team who can help you be free. Wellsprings of Freedom has a growing network of trained teams stationed across the United States and around the world. (For more information on where to find a Wellsprings team near you, please check our website: Wellspringsoffreedom.com for contact information.)

Humility and surrender – For multitudes of reasons, Jezebel is like a piece of gum that is stuck to your shoe; it just doesn't want to let go. Jezebel will attempt to gain access back into your life through a secret hidden entrance. This one is so sneaky that it happens when you think your eyes are wide open and your guard is up. It sneaks its way back in through what I will call *behavioral default*. We've all heard of athletes who practice precise moves over and over again until it becomes automatic. Through sheer repetitiveness, we learn to react or respond to different events in specific ways. As we live our lives, we develop habits, some good and some bad. Many of these behaviors become our default position. We just naturally fall back into familiar patterns. Satan knows this and will try to use it to his advantage.

Through freedom sessions Jesus will remove the Jezebel spirit from you, and we praise God for that! Those demons will leave you and you will be free of them. But other spirits of Jezebel will be sent to hang out around the secret entrance into your life. They will be looking for old behavioral patterns that they can use to quietly slip back in. I don't share this with you to cause fear. You do not need to be afraid. I share this in order to expose their secret entrance. For example, in your Jezebel-led past, when things became chaotic in your life, the old pattern would be to become more controlling of your environment. In the old order of things, if you didn't get your way, your automatic behavioral response would be to demand or manipulate people to comply to your wishes. The more years Jezebel had control of you, the more difficult it will be to not fall back into the old behavior patterns. Without this warning, you might automatically fall back into patterns of behavior that Jezebel would latch onto in order to take control of you again. So, for your long-term freedom, behavior changes will need to be practiced until new patterns become automatic.

Two important keys can help you in this process—humility and surrender. One of the more difficult challenges for a Jezebel-led person is letting go of their pride. Many Bible scholars believe it was pride that caused Satan's downfall. In Ezekiel 28:11-17, there is a prophecy written against the King of Tyre that many believe is also a description of the fall of Satan because of the reference to being in the garden of Eden and that he was ordained as a guardian cherub:

> *The word of the* LORD *came to me: "Son of Man, take up a lament concerning the king of Tyre and say to him: 'This is what the Sovereign* LORD *says: "'You were the model of perfection, full of wisdom and perfect in beauty. You were in Eden, the garden of God; every precious stone adorned you: ruby, topaz, and emerald, chrysolite, onyx and jasper, sapphire, turquoise, and beryl. Your settings and mountings were made of gold; on the day you were created they were prepared. You were anointed as a guardian cherub, for so I ordained you. You were on the holy mount of God; you walked among the fiery stones. You were blameless in your ways from the day you were created till wickedness was found in you. Through your widespread trade you were filled with violence and you sinned. So I drove you in disgrace from the mount of God, and I expelled you, O guardian cherub, from among the fiery stones. Your heart became proud on account of your beauty, and you corrupted your wisdom because of your splendor. So I threw you to the earth; I made a spectacle of you before kings.*

Pride means: "to have an excessively favorable idea of one's own appearance, advantages, and achievements." It also describes someone who carries an arrogant right of superiority over others.

It's pretty clear that Satan lost his position in the heavenly realm because of pride. He was created by God and placed in a high position of favor. At some point in his existence, he succumbed to pride. This is more clearly described in Isaiah 14:11-15:

> *All your pomp has been brought down to the grave, along with the noise of your harps; maggots are spread out beneath you and worms cover you. How you have fallen from heaven, O morning star, son of the dawn! You have been cast down to the earth, you who once laid low the nations! You said in your heart, 'I will ascend to heaven; I will raise my throne above the stars of God; I will sit enthroned on the mount of assembly, on the utmost heights of the sacred mountain. I will ascend above the tops of the clouds; I will make myself like the Most High.' But you are brought down to the grave, to the depths of the pit.*

Imagine one of God's created angels becoming so full of pride that he believed in his own heart he had a right to be superior to God. He said, "I will raise my throne above the stars of God." We shouldn't be surprised, then, that the spirit of Jezebel would follow in the footsteps of Lucifer himself. Jezebel believes it has a right to be superior as well. Because Jezebel sees itself as better than others, and superior to others, it believes it has a right to control others.

As we bring healing and freedom to those who come to us for help, we must often confront the lies of enemy spirits. One of my favorite aspects of freedom ministry is overcoming lies with truth. The Bible is clear that the truth will set you free. In the midst of freedom sessions, we will interrogate a spirit of evil and demand it reveal its lies through the power and name of Jesus Christ. We will often replace the lies with Scripture verses that declare the opposite of what the enemy spirit is saying. In fact, I will often explain to the person seeking freedom that when the lies come, if you just think of the exact opposite of the lie, that is most likely the truth you need to replace the lie. If you have been struggling with a spirit of Jezebel, pride is one of the traits it wants to offload onto you. The opposite of pride is humility.

Humility means "lack of pride. To not be arrogant or assertive, to reflect a spirit of deference and submission." Jezebel is pretty much the opposite of all of these things. Philippians 2:3 gives us a great word picture of what humility looks like: *"Do nothing out of selfish ambition or vain conceit, but in humility consider others better than yourselves."* In order for you to step into long-term freedom you must reverse the broken patterns that have led you to where you are today. By repenting, you choose to turn away from your selfish ambitions and walk in a new direction. It means going from being superior to others to becoming a servant to others, just as our Lord and Savior Jesus Christ did for us. Think about how twisted and distorted things may have become for you. A demon is tempting and persuading you to control others while Jesus is teaching you to serve others. And like most temptations, the temptation to control others appears to be the better way.

If that is the case for you, it might be because you haven't surrendered your selfishness. If you think about it, controlling others is all about you. It's a one-person show that steals joy from everyone around you. People don't follow you because they want to, they follow because they are afraid of you. When you control people, you are not just stealing their joy, you're stealing so much more. You are robbing them of self-esteem, confidence, decision making, leadership development, the ability to think for themselves, freedom, the satisfaction of succeeding on their own, and the ability to step into the fullness of all God has created them to be.

Ask yourself why. Why must you dominate and control? Why must you always be right? Why are you unwilling to submit to authority? Why is your way the only way? Why must everyone bow to your demands? Why will you never accept blame for your failures? If you are honest with yourself, the answer will be clear. Much of what I have described is based on selfishness. It may be that everyone around you knows you are selfish except you. Please do not go around asking people if you are selfish. You will scare the daylights out of them for fear of having to answer, and they most likely won't give you an honest answer anyway. If you must control people, you are acting selfish. It simply means you must have your way above everyone else's.

Please do not be angry, and don't start the old behavioral process of making excuses for selfish control. Rather, put aside the demonic lies fed to you by the controlling spirit of Jezebel. Consider this. Up to this point, it has been difficult for you to submit to any authority except Jezebel! Will you surrender your need to control over to Jesus? Surrender means "to yield, concede, or submit to authority." Will you submit daily to the authority of Christ, and will you daily seek to follow His pattern for servant leadership? This will be a daily surrender to Christ-like servanthood until you can create all new behavioral default settings.

In many ways it is doing the exact opposite of what you are used to doing. The following is a chart of old patterns of behavior compared to what the exact opposite behavior will look like. This is to help you track your progress in creating the new default settings for your life.

Jezebel-led actions	Christ-like actions
Controlling	Empowering
Dictatorial	Influential
Critical	Encouraging
Prideful	Humble
Defensive	Vulnerable
Intimidating	Gentle
Manipulating	Leadership
Selfish	Benevolent
Unremorseful	Sorrowful
Emotional outbursts	Self-control
Refusing to submit to authority	Submissive
Unapologetic	Repentant

I'd like to close this chapter by sharing a testimony from a brave young woman who experienced her own battle with the spirit of Jezebel. I believe her story will be a source of hope to those who are currently controlled by a Jezebel spirit and are searching for a way out. My prayer is that her willingness to share her experience will give insight and direction for others who want to follow in her footsteps. As you will see, it is not an easy journey, it takes courage and determination, but it can be done.

Testimony

Honestly, I don't want to write this. Because as I dig into this, I don't want this to be me. I don't want to confess that I had the Jezebel spirit. Sharing this testimony leaves me vulnerable, and vulnerable is not a place where I necessarily want to be. This spirit caused me to feel like I needed to be in control of EVERYTHING, and it filled me with fear over the thought of what other people would think of me. But there is one truth I have to stay focused on: God is the only one that I truly have to please. This doesn't mean that I don't care about other people, but by focusing on God, I can truly care for others instead of worrying about what they think of me. I realize I am no more able to control what others think of me than I can control the weather. It's actually comical to me that I once thought I could.

So why am I writing this? I am sharing this to let you know about the HOPE that comes when you are finally free from the stranglehold of Jezebel, and why it is worth it to be set free. This is God's story and it is a miraculous story of redemption. Redemption from all the broken relationships in my life, and the need to be in absolute control.

Because I have been set free from Jezebel's grasp, I am able to look into the face of someone new and really see them the way God sees them, and not try to manipulate how they see me. I am now able to see the joy on my middle son's face as I allow him to ride his bike to school with his friends. Before, I couldn't allow him to ride his bike to school for fear he would get hurt. I can now allow my oldest daughter to go to the mall with her friends and not let my fear hold her hostage. I can take my youngest child to the park and not hover around him making sure I know where he is at all times. It is now actually fun to do a remodeling project with my husband and not get mad about his opinion, thinking that I won't be in control of every little detail. My children can actually stay up at night with their daddy to watch a fun movie, even though it is past the bedtime I had "given" to them. At work, I am able to honor the decisions my boss makes that I don't agree with, and try not to manipulate everything to be my way. I am learning to be real and vulnerable, and can even admit to being wrong in a relationship, something I could seldom do before. This allows me to find resolution with my friends instead of conflict. It is truly a blessing to not feel compelled to "make" someone in my family always see things my way. As you can see, control greatly defined who I was.

These may seem like small things to you, but my life was an accumulation of a million different moments of trying to be in control. This only led to being exhausted, frustrated, and never being able to enjoy or feel the peace of God. The truth is, as hard as I tried, I could not really control anything, but I was under the illusion that I could. And, of course, the enemy wanted me exhausted from trying to control everything, because this would prevent me from living out my purpose in the kingdom. In fact, I believe the need to be in control is the source of my greatest anger toward the Jezebel spirit. I can't believe that I let this spirit keep me in bondage for so long. It kept me from being what God wanted me to be and do. I have actually grieved this as a loss, because for a long time, I felt robbed and cheated of who I could have been and what I could have done. God has been so faithful in this, reminding me that everything is in His timing and my redemption from Jezebel was in His perfect timing.

I have served on a Wellsprings of Freedom team for a number of years, and have become very familiar with the spirit of Jezebel. In the midst of freedom sessions, I have observed person after person who has fallen under the spell of Jezebel's deceitful compulsion to control others. And sadly, we also ministered to those who were being controlled by Jezebel-led people. It is heart wrenching to see the wounds that can be inflicted upon an individual who is being abusively controlled by another human being. When we would minister to the person who was a domineering or manipulating bully, I would become very frustrated. All I wanted was for them to be able to surrender their need for control over to God, but Jezebel usually had so much control, that it rarely would happen.

I personally had gone through several freedom sessions for myself before the one where Jezebel was finally uncovered and removed. God's timing is perfect, so He knew that my heart was finally ready. Before this, I could not even dream of knowing about God's perfect timing because Jezebel convinced me to do everything in my timing. This made me feel like I could be in control of time. Isn't it crazy when you say that out loud? I thought I could manipulate time! It is laughable to me now.

The day my life really changed was on a Friday. The Wellsprings team I serve on was supposed to have a client *come in for a freedom session. As usual our team had gotten there early and was preparing and waiting for the session to start. During this time, for whatever reason I do not know, I opened up and shared some of my struggles. I remember being instantly frustrated that as I shared, the group did not seem to agree with me about the situations I was describing. This was such a common experience for me in my life. I wanted and needed everyone to always agree with me, and if they didn't, I would exhaust them until they did.*

The conversation moved to Pastor Tim Howard sharing about a new book he was writing on the Jezebel spirit. When I look back on this, I know this was the Holy Spirit working through Tim to share with me exactly what I needed to hear. As Tim was talking, I started to feel like I could not breathe. The Jezebel characteristics he was describing from his book made me feel like I was looking in a mirror, and that he was perfectly describing me. I was in complete shock and disbelief. Surely, this could not be me! Amazingly, or should I say miraculously, our client didn't show up that day for their freedom session. God knew that even though I was supposed to serve that morning, He had reserved that session for me. There is no doubt in my mind that this was a divine appointment from God the Father. Because our client didn't show up, Pastor Tim asked the team if anyone felt like they needed a freedom session. I told him that I felt like God had reserved the session for me, if I would be obedient.

I am so thankful for what took place that day, but I must confess, I was truly afraid. Tim led the session and my team served as discerners and intercessors for me. I don't remember much of the session, which I know was protection from God. I do know the Jezebel spirit had been affecting me pretty much my whole life. I suspect it was generational, which means I was born with it. When I was around four-years-old, I experienced a deep emotional wound that allowed the spirit of Jezebel to increase its hold upon me. Over the course of time, the Jezebel spirit began to dominate me and convince me to dominate other people. Through lies projected into my mind, I thought controlling people was how I was supposed to protect them from harm. Somehow it convinced me it was a friend.

Although I don't remember much about that day, there is one very important thing that God won't let me forget, and I am sure it is because I am supposed to share it with you. The only way to get rid of Jezebel is to get ANGRY at the damage it has done. It has such an ability to control and manipulate all of your feelings, emotions, and thoughts, that it deceives you into thinking it helps you. I discovered in order for me to finally get rid of it, I had to get mad at all the wreckage it had caused in my life. It was looking at all the wreckage that allowed me to see Jezebel for what it really was, a spirit of destruction. My experience with Jezebel was that it was so deceptive that it hid behind other spirits to keep me from knowing it was there. The discerning team members in my session discerned it was hiding in my life behind the spirit of Fear.

Jezebel had me convinced that it was okay to be fearful, and it was through my fear that Jezebel was able to manipulate me. It did this by convincing me that controlling others would protect everyone around me. By using fear as a shield, Jezebel was able to hide my sin of having to be in complete control. When this was discovered, I was able to see through Jezebel's schemes. I found that the spirit of Fear dangles the carrot, and Jezebel tempts me into taking the bait. The spirit of Fear would ask me questions. For example: "What if you can't pay the bills?" or "What if you aren't *watching your kids and something happens to them?" Fear would stir up my emotions around all the what-ifs or unknowns in life. And we have lots of those, don't we? Then, Jezebel would convince me that by controlling everything, I was able to protect myself, and others, from all the things I was afraid were going to happen—which were all the things Jezebel told me were going to happen if I didn't stay in control. Sadly, over the course of time this became a vicious cycle in my life.*

I have kept a journal since my "divine appointment" so I would remember why I hate Jezebel so much, and write down all the ways it worked in my life. Jezebel tricked me into trying to control and manipulate how people saw me. Right after the session, I journaled this concern: "The hardest thing for me right now is trying to resist manipulating how others see me." This had become such a familiar way of life for me. Almost everything I did and said was for my own purpose instead of for God's. Jezebel led me to scheme and always have an ulterior motive. I was extremely frustrated if people did not see me how I wanted them to see me. And, it drove me crazy when people didn't see situations the same way I saw them. This was so overwhelming. I felt like I could never rest, because if I did, something might fall out of my control.

In my marriage, I tried to control everything. My husband felt like he could never do anything right. He told me he always felt like I was on a mountain looking down at him. The problem was that I hated anything that was not done on "my terms." I despised any differing ideas or opinions that he might have that were different from mine. Jezebel messed with the hierarchy of our home, and this prevented my husband from his godly role as head of the home.

Jezebel affected my relationship with my children. I limited things that my kids could do if I didn't feel like I was in control, even normal everyday activities that most children are allowed to do. I had to know where they were at all times. This included denying them from doing things they were created to do. God created my kids in His image and for His purpose, and I can see how I was preventing His will from being fulfilled in their lives. This was centered around my need to control their every move. I controlled what they would wear and what they could say. I was trying to control everything so my kids would be "seen" in a certain way. I blamed this on my fear, but underneath the fear, Jezebel was there trying to control their every move.

At work, you can probably imagine how the Jezebel spirit drove me to control others, especially as a sales professional. It drove me completely crazy when my customers didn't see things the same way I did, or my potential customers would decide not to do business with me. This actually would spur an anger inside of me that they were not "seeing things my way" and I had to manipulate them until they did. I also struggled with the hierarchy at my job because I didn't want to submit to any authority. I struggled big time with any control my bosses had over me.

Even my friendships were affected. Keeping friendships was very hard for me. I actually felt like I needed to control their lives as well. If I could not control them, I would try to manipulate them until they conformed. If they didn't conform to my way of thinking, I would let the friendship dissolve. I was not willing to keep the relationship if I could not control them. You can imagine what this meant for me, I always felt alone and isolated—which I have come to learn is exactly where the enemy wanted me to be. One *of my spiritual gifts is the ability to encourage people, and when I isolated myself from others, I was not able to use my spiritual gift. Jezebel tried to pervert some of my other spiritual gifts as well—my gifts of discernment, prophecy, and knowledge. Sadly, I found myself using those amazing gifts of the Spirit to try and gain more power and control.*

Finances was another problem area for me. I felt like I had to be completely in control of how financially sound we were and how "secure" our future was. My security rested on what our bank account numbers looked like, and we all know what a roller-coaster ride that can be. The lie I always heard was "If you don't do something about the finances, who will?" I now realize that I loved money because it gave me a false sense of power and control. As you can tell, I was addicted to power and control. Unfortunately, it was the need for control, that was actually controlling me.

Stepping Toward Freedom

God did something wonderful during that unplanned freedom session. The Jezebel spirit was forced to leave that day. My eyes were opened to Jezebel's manipulating control over me and how it used me to control others. When I saw the truth, an angry determination rose up within me to be free. For the first time, I saw my controlling behavior as a sin, and I was overcome with remorse. God was simply waiting for me to join Him in the battle. Once I was willing to release my need to be in control, Jezebel was removed from my life through the power of Jesus Christ.

I would be lying if I told you that everything has been easy since that day. Truthfully, I have to wake up every morning and surrender control to God. I have to ask myself the question hundreds of times a day, "Are you trying to control that?" And if I discover I am trying to take back control, I have to immediately relinquish control back to God.

Pastor Tim asked the Lord that day for me to have "supernatural vision" to be able to see if Jezebel was ever trying to work itself back into my life. I am so thankful God granted this to me. Sometimes I may not see it right away, but eventually, I can see and sense the small subtle ways Jezebel uses to try to "sneak" back into my life. In addition to this, God has given me heightened discernment to see Jezebel in lives of other people. This has been critical to me, so I don't get sucked back into having a power struggle with another Jezebel-controlled person. This is where I believe Jezebel is able to cause the most destruction.

God and I have spent a lot of time together (and we still do) to work through all the brokenness that Jezebel brought into my life. I have had to repent from the sin of being "mad" at God for letting Jezebel into my life. God didn't let Jezebel into my life. I did. I have heard God say, "You can be sad or disappointed, but only mad at the things that are not of me." In other words, like I stated above, I can be mad at the enemy for all they were able to steal, kill, and destroy. But I can't be mad at God. I have learned that God is a gentleman, and He was waiting for me to let go of my need to be in control. Although it was extremely unfortunate that Jezebel was able to trick me into letting it come into my life at an early age, I exercised my God-given free will to let it stay. It was a choice that I made every day and in every decision. I did it in order to stay in control. I gave Jezebel more and more power and the legal right to stay. I share this with you so you know you are not a victim. You do have a choice, and you can make it right now. A freewill choice to surrender your need to be in control. Only God can make all things new. Please trust me, this will be the hardest, but most rewarding, decision you will ever make.

So, if you are reading this book, and any of this sounds familiar, please be encouraged! I want to encourage you. There is so much more for you. Don't believe the lie that "this is just how God made me." If you can surrender to God and give up the need to be in control, God can do things with your life that you could never imagine. I am living proof that Jezebel can be defeated. You just have to want it, and be willing to submit your control over to God.

Since that day, I have asked the Holy Spirit to give me ways to continuously resist allowing Jezebel back into my life, and this is what I sense He has taught me.

1. Choose God and His gentle ways every day.
2. Remember, God gave us free will. He does not control His children. So, what makes us think it is okay if we do?
3. Ask yourself this question: "Do I really need to have control over that?" I have asked myself this question so many times since my session, and I can tell you that the answer is always no. God is truly in control of every little detail in my life, and He does such a better job with them than I do.
4. Submit to order and authority. Do not try to manipulate how you want things to be.
5. When you feel out of control (and this is a scary place for us who struggle with Jezebel tendencies), say out loud, "Jesus, I am releasing my need to be in control over to you." Say this out loud and as often as is necessary for you to feel at peace.

6. Choose to love, not hate. Jezebel wants to destroy, but you must choose to encourage. Jesus was a servant leader, Jezebel is a selfish controlling leader.
7. Do not look too far ahead. Pay attention only to today. You and God will do today what you can, and that will lead to tomorrow. Put your future in the hands of God, and don't try to manipulate His plan.
8. Learn to laugh about the things Jezebel did and tried to do in your life. Let go of all guilt and shame. You are forgiven, so do not let Jezebel continue to oppress you with shame from the past.
9. Keep your eyes open for Jezebel and its sneaky ways. Don't let the familiar behaviors of the past come creeping back in. Call it out, and repent of it as soon as you see it happening again.
10. Humbly pray with deep sincerity. I'm not talking about prayers that make you look good. These are prayers asking for God to examine your heart. Don't hide any secret desire to control or ignore controlling tendencies trying to make their way back in. Confess and repent of any Jezebel-like behavior. Stop it in its tracks before it gets a hold on you again.

Chapter 10

Protection Against the Jezebel Virus

One of the saddest comments I have often heard from people who leave their secular jobs to work for a Christian organization is this: "I was shocked to discover that the working environment was more toxic in my new Christian environment than in my old secular job." This is not always the case, but it does happen more often than we think. Typically, in the business world we work our way to the top, learning as we move our way upward. Sometimes we learn good leadership from good supervisors, and on occasion, we learn how not to lead from bad ones. Frequently, in the church world, a young pastor right out of college is thrust into a leadership role with very little leadership experience. All too often they are isolated and alone and left to figure things out on their own. Sometimes they are trying to deal with a toxic church board, and become wounded and bitter. Other times they are handed the reins of power with little-to-no accountability or direction. Both scenarios can lead to Jezebel-like tendencies.

Another problem I see happening is young leaders not being given enough training in organizational management. They often lack the training and the experience to know how to lead and manage effectively. This can cause feelings of inadequacy, worthlessness, and a sense of not being good enough. As you can imagine, this can open the door for a confident and controlling Jezebel-led person to sweep in and begin to take over. They will flatter, offer their assistance, fill in the leadership gaps, work hard, accomplish much, and cause even greater feelings of inadequacy in the young leader. Soon the Jezebel-led person will be doing so much to help the young leader that the young leader becomes totally dependent upon the Jezebel-led person. The leader places high levels of trust in the Jezebel-led person and feels a deep sense of indebtedness to them. Slowly at first, but soon the tables get turned and the Jezebel-led person is actually controlling the leader. Nothing happens in the organization without the Jezebel-led person's blessing and approval. A demon, using an individual, just took over the oversight of the organization or church.

It is easy to think that what happens in the demonic realm is just a random coincidence. That demons don't plot strategies or plan attacks against us. I continue to be amazed at how many Christians don't believe in evil spirits or that Satan is a real entity at war with God. When we have this mindset, the enemy can do whatever they want. We give them free rein to wreak havoc upon our religious institutions and our lives. Most churches don't offer any classes on spiritual warfare and how the enemy works to destroy us. As Wellsprings of Freedom has traveled across the world training and equipping churches on how to set people free, we have discovered a deep appreciation for our teaching on spiritual warfare. Most pastors have expressed to us how little is being taught about this in our colleges and seminaries. Many are being told that demons do not exist anymore.

Demons do exist, and they have thousands of years of practice at waging war against God and the human race. Revelation 12:7-9 states,

And there was war in heaven. Michael and his angels fought against the dragon, and the dragon and his angels fought back. But he was not strong enough, and they lost their place in heaven. The great dragon was hurled down—that ancient serpent called the devil, or Satan, who leads the whole world astray. He was hurled to the earth and his angels with him.

Then in verse 17,

Then the dragon was enraged at the women and went off to make war against the rest of her offspring—those who obey God's commandments and hold to the testimony of Jesus.

Notice who they are waging war against: those who obey God's commandments and hold to the testimony of Jesus. One of the ways they wage war is by using human beings whom they have deceived and are able to control through carefully planted lies placed into their minds. Both God and Satan work through human beings to accomplish much of their work on the earth. Because of the lies demons tell, the believer being used by Satan doesn't even know they are being manipulated for enemy purposes. The lies projected into our minds by the enemy will seem like our own thought voice, or we are made to believe it is the voice of God. So, as they project lying or deceptive thoughts into our minds, and we think it is our thought voice or God's voice, we will often listen and act accordingly.

To a Jezebel-led board member, the deceptive lie might be that the pastor doesn't know what he is doing and it is your job to protect the church from his foolish ideas. To a sharp businessman, the voice in your head might tell you that without your expertise, the new young pastor will fail, so you must control him to success. To a pastor, the lie might be, "You are the one trained in ministry, don't listen to anyone else for advice." For many Jezebel-led individuals, their control starts by stepping in and fixing things that are not being done or things that are broken. This is all good, until spirits of pride and control begin to consume them with their lies. "Nobody can do anything right, you have to do everything." Slowly their thoughts lead them into higher and higher levels of needing to be in control.

As the need to control increases, the spirit of Jezebel will subconsciously step in and persuade a person to "take charge." All for the good, of course! So, a demon slips in and begins to offer suggestions into a person's mind on how things can and should be better. Then, little by little the demon begins to convince a person that they know best and that everyone else just needs to get out of the way and let them lead. Demons are highly experienced at what they do. They won't take control right away, but will slowly create an indebtedness from the leader toward the Jezebel-led person and slowly take over. Their initial intentions always seem to be good, it is part of their strategy, but at some point, things begin to fall apart.

The reality is that demons are always looking for and plotting ways to destroy our ministries. We should not be surprised, as the Bible warns us about this in John 10:10: *"The thief comes only to steal and kill and destroy."* At Wellsprings of Freedom, we are continually amazed at how this happens. We travel around the world training and equipping churches and ministries how to do freedom ministry. Usually within a month or so after the training, the leader of the newly trained ministry team will call us with a problem. And the problem is often the same problem from church to church. Someone who has signed up to serve on their new ministry team begins to take charge and dictate how the ministry is going to be done. Amazingly, they want to remove some of the most effective key elements that make our ministry successful. In addition to trying to dictate how the ministry will be done, they also create all kinds of chaos, anger, and division amongst the new team members. Anything to destroy the new team.

This is not just happening in our ministry; the pattern is prevalent wherever there is anointed ministry taking place. We have discovered that Jezebel hates effective ministry and has people staged to step in and try to create chaos and division for the purpose of destruction. Jezebel knows that by stealing control away from a ministry or a church, it can cause the greatest amount of damage. Because Jezebel is a spirit of control, it makes sense that this is the spirit that Satan uses to attempt a takeover. And wherever Jezebel is able to take control, destruction will soon follow. One more thing. To the ministry leader, rarely is the person with the spirit of Jezebel seen as the problem. Because they often put in more hours than anyone else, they are seen as the only one trying to fix the problems. It is for this reason that we need to implement safeguards for our organizations.

Ways to Protect Your Church and Staff from Jezebel Tendencies

I know every organization is different; they are different-sized and have differing missions. So, as we look into safeguards, I understand that it's not a one-size-fits-all-kind of thing. The suggestions for protecting your ministry listed below may not all be feasible for your particular ministry. There may only be enough staff or organizational structure to do a few, while other organizations may be able to implement several of the ideas.

- **Whistleblower system** – There must always be a way for team members to report abusive and controlling team members without fear of reprisal. This may at first appear easy to do. However, Jezebel-led people work hard to control as much of the organization as they can. This includes having all information and complaints funnel through their position. All too often, the complaints about over-the-top controlling behavior are about the Jezebel-led person who has been assigned to receive the complaints! It can be a deeply frustrating and hopeless situation. Everyone knows who is doing the abusing, and everyone knows they cannot report the abuse.

If the Jezebel-led person is the senior leader, where can the team go to file a complaint? If the Jezebel-led person is the best friend or right-hand person to the senior leader, fear will keep team members from saying anything. If the Jezebel-influenced person is a family member of the senior leader, where can team members go to file a report? This is especially difficult when the highest-ranking leader is influenced by the Ahab spirit discussed in Chapter 7 of this book. The Ahab-led leader is highly influenced to protect the Jezebel-led person at all cost. As a case in point, do you remember the story I shared earlier about the controlling and manipulating supervisor who took one of her teenage employee's car without permission? When everyone in the department heard the story of how she was protected by the vice president, everyone in the department knew that it was hopeless to even bother to try to submit a complaint about her abusive ways.

In many church settings, it is difficult to create a system where complaints will truly be heard by a neutral source. The complaint will almost always go to a loyal board member or a fellow staff member who is friends with the person accused. What does an employee do when they need to file a complaint against his/her boss? There always seems to be an unhealthy protective connection from the leadership team toward the alleged abusive individual. Jezebel's ability to flatter, intimidate, or use emotional manipulation stymies most complaints. It is not uncommon for a complaint that is supposed to go to a neutral panel to be buried or lost before it can be delivered. Jezebel knows all the tricks to defend itself from being removed.

Even outside mediating firms paid to deal with complaints in an unbiased way are subject to being controlled. Quite likely, it's the controlling leader who may be the one who approves the future hiring of their firm. It just makes sense that the firm would strive to please the one who hires and pays the bills.

An idea might be to initiate the board of directors to create a strategy for handling complaints. One that is safe for the employees and cannot be corrupted or manipulated by a controlling staff member who has high levels of authority. It could be as simple as recruiting two designees outside of the organization where complaints could safely be brought forward. If this were to be decided, it should consist of both a male and a female, as there may be times when a female employee would only feel safe sharing with another woman. The individuals chosen to be the two designees should not have any attachments to the staff. Those chosen as designees should have a representative of the board of directors available to them for the purpose of bringing forth any grievances they have received. The person chosen from the board of directors to receive the complaints should not be a staff member or have close attachments to a staff member. The next steps could be determined by the members of the board of directors who are not staff members. Once the two designees have been determined, this should be communicated to the staff along with contact information on how they can file a complaint if the need should arise.

- **Protect the pastor** - Surround the pastor with people who are anointed leaders, who are shepherds and not controlling managers. Those who are in close proximity to the lead pastor should be the best leaders you can find to reflect the lead pastor's heart and mission. They must have a servant's heart that goes in both directions. They are not only able to serve the lead pastor, but they also have a heart to serve those who are equal to, or who are under their leadership level on the team. When a Jezebel-led person gets next to a pastor, they are able to produce at a high capacity, taking a lot of responsibility away from the pastor. This will eventually cause the pastor to rely heavily upon them to oversee the day-to-day operation of the organization. When a pastor is confronted with the fact that this high capacity leader is controlling and abusing other people, they panic. They become very narrow focused, believing the lie that they can't survive without the productive Jezebel-led person.

    In addition, anointed and called staff pastors who are supervised by controlling managers will lose their joy in doing ministry, and we need to protect them too. All too often, the controlling supervisor who does not have the training or experience to effectively run a specialized department is making all the decisions for that department. Pastors who are equipped and experienced in specialized ministry will be overruled time and again as they watch their ministry ideas be replaced by a controlling supervisor who is inexperienced in ministry. Before long, frustration will set in and the anointed pastors will leave the organization.

The truth is that there are many highly productive leaders who are capable of having a shepherd's heart and who know how to lead a team successfully. This kind of leader can actually produce more because they know how to build and inspire a highly productive team. They are relational team builders who desire to collaborate and bring out the best in the team around them. They are not controllers; they are uplifters who develop teams, not personal domains. They are empowering leaders who seek to pour into others to help them be the best they can be. Gifted and anointed leaders trust in their team and give them permission to lead their departments. Strong leaders openly celebrate the successes of their team members without taking any of the credit.

Jezebel-led people simply cannot allow others to think for themselves, which stifles teamwork, creativity, and anointed ministry. Any compliments handed out by Jezebel are given to those who follow Jezebel's directions and make Jezebel look good. But seldom is encouragement handed out to a person operating outside of Jezebel's control. In fact, they are usually targeted for criticism.

The board of directors must do their best to protect the pastors by surrounding them with persons who are not seeking all the accolades and limelight. In the book, *Hero Maker,* the authors Dave Ferguson and Warren Bird talk about how everybody wants to be a hero, but few understand the power of being a hero maker. There is something special about a leader who seeks to develop those who are under their authority and raise them up to be heroic leaders. This is not developing a team of robots who do whatever you say, but instead, it is raising up team members who are allowed to create, make decisions, and excel in all that God created them to be. Find shepherds who are gifted in leading and encouraging people to greatness, not just staff, but volunteers as well.

If you are the lead pastor and are fortunate enough to have dynamic leaders on your team, ask God to help you examine your heart. Are you controlling? Do you need the praise for things going well? Are you critical of your staff members because they sometimes look better than you? Can you give credit to others when they do a good job? Do you allow them to create and plan events for their departments? Can your team members do an event without you changing everything just because your ego needs to have the final say? Do you encourage or discourage your team? Are you excited when one of your team members succeeds or do you get nervous? Can you publicly promote big events being done by your staff that have little to do with you? Is it okay for a couple of your staff members to have more success than you? What are some of the secret ways you keep your thumb on a more successful team member so they don't look better than you?

- **Monitor for cliques and favoritism** – Jezebel does create alliances and works to get those friends promoted to leadership positions. Team leaders and department heads should always be looking for Jezebel tendencies within their departments and sounding alarm bells when they see it in other departments. Because of Jezebel's ability to blind the leader above them, a church might want to consider creating a committee of three to four people who have been trained to spot Jezebel tendencies, and who have shepherd's hearts and the gifts of wisdom and discernment. This committee should be authorized to monitor your staff at all levels, looking for any signs of Jezebel-like tendencies or control. They might also be chosen to hear the complaints brought forward by employees who feel bullied or abused, or implement employee satisfaction surveys at the committee's discretion.

The committee should be made up of a combination of staff pastors, board members, outside professionals, and people within the organization who are highly trusted. Their findings should carry significant weight as they are presented directly to the board of directors, not to a pastor on staff. It might be established that their recommendations can override any leadership team member who might be blinded by a person with Jezebel or who is a Jezebel-led person. Great care should be given to make sure a controlling Jezebel-led person is not placed on the committee. This committee is exactly where a Jezebel-led person will strive to volunteer in hopes of running and controlling the committee. Try to choose strong, tenderhearted people who are humble and courageous.

- **Safe environment for new ideas** – Institute brainstorming rules for meetings where new ideas are being sought. Create a safe place for all new ideas to be heard without criticism. Not all ideas will be used, but they should at least be heard. Watch for people who strive to dominate the conversation or belittle other people's ideas. People who repeatedly get upset when their ideas are not adopted by the whole group should be carefully observed. They may be demonstrating Jezebel tendencies. When Jezebel must always be right, they don't play well in these types of meetings.

One of the major differences between a free society and a dictatorial led nation is the way in which they allow for new ideas to emerge. In a nation led by a dictator, new ideas are squelched, and strict guidelines are enforced based on how the dictator believes things should be. New ideas that are different from theirs are seen as threats to their leadership. No ideas that are counter to their own are allowed. This is why all dictatorships will eventually crumble as there is no place for new ideas to even be considered, let alone implemented. Societies where new ideas and inventions are rejected are doomed to failure.

Our God is a creative God, and ideas are like sparks of wisdom originating in the mind of God and passed on to His children who are willing to listen. Then, when those ideas are blended with other people's ideas, the original concept becomes stronger and stronger. All of us see things from different perspectives, and when we are in an environment that allows for the exchange of ideas, amazing things are possible.

When Jezebel-led leaders become so filled with pride that they are the only ones capable of having good ideas, their organizations are in trouble. They become like miniature dictators who have preconceived guidelines for how things are going to be. New ideas that don't fit into those guidelines are extinguished. Ideas and thoughts presented by others that indicate the organization is broken are seen as rejection, and are vigorously dismissed. Great ideas are lost, synergy is lost, creativity is lost, and without creativity, the organization will eventually die.

- **Avoid conflicts of interest** – A conflict of interest is favoritism given to an individual because of a relationship. When a person who is related to the leader is put in a position of great authority, it sets the leader up for Jezebel to establish itself within the organization. By avoiding this situation altogether, the leader can often save the organization from much damage, and the leader is removed from the awkward position of having to choose to side with the team or with a controlling family member. Even if the family member isn't controlled by Jezebel, the scenario where a leader will have to choose between an idea presented by a family member or a staff member will eventually occur. This can lead to great frustration for everyone involved. The leader, the close family member, and the staff member will be unnecessarily placed in a difficult position. A long time ago, when I worked for a printing firm, I wanted to hire a family member. The owner of the company gave me some very sound advice. He said, "Never hire anybody that you cannot fire." Too many organizations fall into this trap. When we hire family members that are close to high level management team members, the accountability structure for reporting possible abuse from this family member is compromised. This happens especially when the employees watch the organization or department leader defend or excuse their family member at every turn. This shuts down the ability of the team to file complaints against controlling family members for fear of personal repercussions. Organizations must be careful to avoid putting their employees in this very difficult position.

When an employee cannot safely file a complaint without fear of repercussions because their supervisor is related to the boss, you have an unfair accountability structure. When the employee sees that the boss repeatedly protects the family member no matter what the family member has done, you have an unbalanced and awkward situation. This is not fair to the team and creates an atmosphere of fear and intimidation inside the organization.

- **Leadership training** – It's way too easy for leaders to have a twisted view of what it means to lead others. Giving orders, dominating people, demanding respect, and verbally whipping people into shape are not qualities of a good leader. Too many leaders think that their title gives them the right to expect people to serve them no matter the personal cost to the employee or volunteer. You can certainly lead that way, but you won't create a healthy work environment that can sustain long-term success. Ego, and stereotypes of what a boss is, can get people into a world of trouble. That's why there is a need for training. In John Maxwell's book, *The Right to Lead,* he quotes Robert Townsend: *"A leader is not an administrator who loves to run others, but someone who carries water for his people so they can get on with their jobs."* Often, a troubled leader isn't a bad person; they just haven't received good leadership training.

    For churches or organizations hiring employees directly out of college, find a trusted mentor outside of the organization to work with your new employee who will coach them in leadership and business etiquette. If there are funds available, look for leadership training opportunities that a staff member can physically attend or participate in online. Perhaps another highly respected pastor in your community would be willing to invest in the future of a new young pastor. This shouldn't be limited to new or young employees. If you have a dynamic pastor doing a good job, but lacking in leadership skills, be proactive and help that pastor get the training they need to be a great leader.
- **Additional safeguards** – Those people in your organization who tend to be controlling need to be placed under strong leaders who can monitor their actions and

behaviors. These strong leaders need to be educated on Jezebel characteristics, so they are not manipulated, bullied, or blinded by interactions with the controlling employee. Because Jezebel is capable of high levels of intimidation, both in temperament and in the spirit realm, the leader must be able to stand strong. They need to be able to confront and discipline a highly controlling individual with courage, gentleness, and steadfastness.

Make sure to keep those who are overly controlling out of high levels of leadership. The temptation will always exist for them to control others. Help them stay balanced. Monitor mid-level supervisors and employees for controlling tendencies. Just one bully or controlling person can destroy the morale of an entire department.

If you do not already have one, create an Employee Handbook. Include in the handbook sections on: Unacceptable Conduct, Workplace Violence, Sexual/Workplace Harassment, Bullying, Separation of Work Policies to ensure good financial practices, and Whistleblower Policies. Meet with your employees to explain and discuss the policies and procedures written in the manual. Take time to discuss the definition of abuse, what abusive behavior looks like, and how to report bad behavior. Just as a reminder, retaliation against an employee who submits a complaint is a federal offense.

Chapter 11

Answering the "Why" Questions

"Why" questions are often the hardest to answer. Several years ago, as I was watching Chuck Kraft lead a freedom session, the person seeking freedom asked a "why" question: *"Why did God allow that to happen?"* I so appreciated Chuck's response. He said, *"Well, I have discovered over the course of my life and ministry that God seldom answers the 'why' questions."* This is so true.

When there is a tragic accident, or when we lose a loved one, "why" questions seem to come to the forefront of our mind. These kinds of questions can lead to bitterness toward God and even cause us to doubt God's love for us. The same is true as we contemplate why the Jezebel virus is able to remain entrenched in our beloved organizations. As I have talked with ministry leaders who have been blindsided, or team members who have been wounded by this spirit, the "why" questions eventually come to the surface. We have all asked those same "why" questions more times than we can count. I don't want to pretend to have all the answers because I don't. But I do believe God has given me some possible insights that may help us as we wrestle through our own "why" questions.

The mystery – How do we explain why Jezebel-led people are seemingly allowed by God to continue in their role of hurting people and destroying the church? Why does God allow them to stay in positions of power so long that the organization is often destroyed? One explanation could be the reality of free will. God simply doesn't interrupt a human's freewill decision, even when their decision causes great harm to others. Or, could it be the grace of God? A grace that lets dysfunctional leaders remain in power giving them opportunity to repent and change. Perhaps it's because of fear. Anxiety that rises up and paralyzes those around the person with Jezebel and enables them to remain in power. Every situation is different, and there is no way to assign the same answer to each individual setting. For those who have been forced to endure the frustration of working in a Jezebel-controlled environment, you have most likely asked your own version of the "why" question.

I am reminded of a pastor friend who had a controlling board member going behind his back to all the adult Sunday school classes trying to turn them against him. I can remember a controlling pastor who was so dominating that he chased 80 percent of his congregation away within just a couple of years. Then, for ten years, he and his faithful thirty people chased every new person away from the church because of their dysfunction. I recently talked with the president of a nonprofit who was doing really good work until a business leader in the community came into the organization and tried to take it over.

I have been amazed at the number of people who discover I am writing a book on the Jezebel spirit, who feel compelled to tell me their own story of suffering and abuse. In almost every case, they are confused, frustrated, and wounded. Time after time, they express deep appreciation to me for being willing to write a book on this issue. Their confusion as to why it is allowed to happen continues to haunt their mind.

What if we can't answer the "why" questions? What do we do then? I find that God's Word is the best place to go for those seeking comfort, solutions, and promises. Truthfully, there are many questions that will never be answered this side of eternity. Can we learn to live with that? I think we can. But it all hinges on our ability to trust in the goodness and omniscience of God. In Genesis 50:20, Joseph speaks astonishing wisdom over his brothers who had sold him into slavery. He said, *"You intended to harm me, but God intended it for good to accomplish what is now being done, the saving of many lives."* What a staggering revelation into God's character! When everything seemed hopeless for Joseph and it appeared God had abandoned him to slavery, God was there and He had a plan. When Joseph was falsely accused of a crime and it seemed he was forgotten and left to rot in prison, God was there, and He had a plan. God never abandoned Joseph, and He will not abandon you! If you find yourself in the midst of despair, and it feels like you are all alone, God is there, and He has a plan.

How many years did Joseph suffer not having any remote idea of what God was up to? When you are in a Jezebel-led environment, and it appears that no one in leadership is willing to confront the controlling abuse, don't lose hope. Instead of letting the enemy convince you that God has abandoned you, stand on the promises of His Word. One of those promises was given to us through Paul when he said, *"And we know that in all things God works for the good of those who love him, who have been called according to his purpose"* (Romans 8:28).

I am convinced that this is exactly what God is doing when we are mired in what appears to be a seemingly hopeless situation. We may not always know what God is up to, but we can trust Him. We may not have an answer for the "why" questions, but He is there working everything out for our good.

Things to consider - Where is God in the abusive and controlling environment? This is one of the questions many ask when they are caught up in the middle of an abusive situation. Part of the answer can be attributed to free will. Free will is one of God's laws that cannot be broken. He will not interrupt a man's right to choose, but He is always by our side. He never leaves us or abandons us, but He cannot make the decision for a Jezebel-led person to stop controlling. He influences them to stop, but they have the free will to listen or ignore His desire for them to change. We all know this as we have all been tempted. How many of us have heard His voice telling us to walk away from a sin, but instead, we choose to ignore the tug on our heart to do the right thing?

It's easy for us to fall into the trap that everything is God's fault. It is definitely one of the lies demons use to drive a wedge between us and God. But can we blame God when a human being chooses to sin? Certainly not. It might be easy to put all the blame on the Jezebel-led person for the controlling environment, and they are part of the problem. But what if *your* freewill decisions are just as much to blame for your grim situation, especially if you are part of the leadership team? Fear can be a dominating spirit that can paralyze us. Just as a controlling spirit can dominate the Jezebel-led person, so can a spirit of fear dominate a leader. When fear incapacitates a leader or leaders from confronting the Jezebel-led person, that leader or leadership team contributes to the problem as well.

Overcoming fear is a choice. I remember the first time I shared Christ with another person. I was so afraid, I wanted to run and hide. I didn't want to step outside of my comfort zone. I could have chosen to keep my mouth shut, but I didn't and I'm glad as that person prayed to receive Christ. My choice that day led to many other occasions where I shared Christ with others. Just a little bit of courage changed my life and the lives of many others.

Over and over again, I have seen and heard stories of how a Jezebel-led person was confronted and forbidden from controlling others, and soon after, they left the organization. I wonder sometimes how one hour of courage might possibly be all it takes to stop years of abuse. While we are frustrated with God for not fixing the problem, He might be waiting for us to step into a little bit of courage. While we are asking Him why He's not protecting our organization, He may be asking us why we are choosing to be paralyzed by fear.

Unfortunately, not everyone in a Jezebel-controlled environment is in a position to stop the problem, courage or no courage. If your supervisor or organizational leader is the Jezebel, or is being controlled by a Jezebel-led person, it will be almost impossible for you to do anything about it. You are truly in a difficult position. I want you to know that I am sorry for your pain. Without a leadership team who is willing to confront the Jezebel environment, you must figure out if you are to stay and survive, or if you are to leave. And if you do sense God asking you to stay, why?

Reasons to Stay

On-the-job leadership training – After ten years with one organization, a friend of mine shared with me how much of that time was spent in a department controlled by a Jezebel-led person. He told me that unless you were one of the Jezebel-led person's allies, it was a fairly tough place to work. Being an ally meant you basically never crossed the Jezebel-led person, and that included the supervisor. It was in that ten-year setting that he observed and watched the kind of damage a Jezebel-led person could have over an entire department. He watched how production was severely impacted, and how much different the environment was when the Jezebel-led person was on vacation. He also watched how the supervisor was controlled by a Jezebel-led person through emotional manipulation or by outbursts of rage.

He realized that by controlling the supervisor you controlled the department. It was in this setting that he saw the hopelessness of many of the employees. They knew that saying anything to the supervisor would only put a target on them, as they repeatedly watched the supervisor run to the Jezebel-led person out of fear. The fear that the Jezebel-led person might find out about people talking to the supervisor drove the supervisor into a panic. He would go to the Jezebel-led person as soon as he could find a way to do so secretly and share with them the name of the individual who had come to him with a complaint. He lived in fear as he thought the Jezebel-led person would think he was betraying them. Within a day or so of the supervisor talking to the Jezebel-led person, the Jezebel-led person would circle back to the person who complained and let them know not to do it again. Amazingly, my friend learned a great deal about leadership from a broken and dysfunctional environment. He also learned a great deal about the power of courage.

After ten years of enduring this Jezebel-led environment, he was promoted to become the supervisor of the department. In his first week as supervisor, he learned that by gently, yet firmly, confronting the Jezebel-led person, all the nonsense would come to an end. He said it wasn't easy enduring a rage-filled rant when he confronted the Jezebel-led person for the first time. But refusing to be manipulated by control and expecting behavior changes was necessary to bring order back to a broken department. He learned how much respect a supervisor can receive by protecting the whole team. Much of what he learned in the midst of those stormy years influenced his leadership style. He told me how much he actually learned from the mistakes of his former supervisor, and how he was determined to be different.

If you are stuck in a Jezebel-led environment and don't see an easy or quick way out, ask God what He wants you to learn.

Ask God to show you the things He wants you to know that will make you a stronger and better leader, and a more balanced and relational person.

God is refining you – I, too, have worked in very broken work environments. I can't even begin to tell you how much I learned about perseverance, patience, humility, and self-control in the middle of very abusive work settings. It wasn't always fun, but I learned a lot. I remember when I came to Christ in the midst of working in a Jezebel-led department. I was very rough around the edges, and I believe God used those difficult days to sand and refine my life for what was yet to come. I had no idea then that God was going to call me into ministry. There were times when I didn't want to go to work, but I went anyway. There were days when I didn't want to be Christ-like, but I was Christ-like anyway. I remember days when I totally blew it and had to go back and ask people to forgive me, and humility was planted in my heart. I learned to be kind when I didn't want to be kind, and I learned how to relate to difficult people. In Romans 5:3-5, Paul writes, *"Not only so, but we also rejoice in our sufferings, because we know that suffering produces perseverance; perseverance, character; and character hope. And hope does not disappoint us, because God has poured out his love into our hearts by the Holy Spirit, whom he has given us."*

It's easy to get angry with God when you are in the midst of suffering. It's easy to focus on the now and forget that God is prepping you for the future. Living in a Jezebel-led environment is very hard. It isn't fair. It causes emotional wounds that Satan wants us to blame God for. But remember, it isn't God hurting you; it's the freewill choice of another broken human being. In the midst of the struggle, thank God for His refining fire. Thank Him for how He is developing your character.

You are a source of strength to other team members – What if God has called you to be a source of strength and encouragement to others on the team who are being demoralized? What if your understanding of the Jezebel-led environment allows you to fearlessly come alongside of a great young leader and help them to see the problem isn't them? What if it is your encouragement that keeps them in ministry? Being in a Jezebel-led environment is a lonely place. Nothing done by those working under the control of the Jezebel leader, or those outside the Jezebel leader's circle of allies, ever seems to be good enough. The Jezebel-led person and their team of allies will never take responsibility for mistakes. They will make sure to pass the blame onto others. It will be made clear to lower-level employees that they are nothing more than expendable pawns. Jezebel-led environments are filled with confusion, chaos, and out-of-control schedules. In the midst of all the confusion and chaos, when lower-level employees are blamed for things they didn't do, it is quite natural for those employees to feel like they are losing their minds. Everything seems upside down and backwards, and those trapped in the middle will at times question their own sanity and competence.

Strong and anointed leaders are especially targeted by Jezebel-led individuals. They are threats to the Jezebel-led person because they are strong leaders. Whenever a leader joins the team who could possibly draw loyalty away from the Jezebel-led person, something must be done. If a new leader will not conform to the Jezebel-led person's control, that leader must be demoralized and delegitimized. The truth is, even though Jezebel-led people demonstrate over-the-top boldness, deep inside they are very insecure. That insecurity cannot allow for other leaders to appear better than they are. In addition, the Jezebel spirit itself cannot allow an anointed leader to succeed. Anointed leaders who will potentially do great things for God are absolute threats to Satan's opposition forces. The Jezebel spirit will attempt to drive them out of ministry using every demonic trick and lie possible to discourage them and defeat them. We must not forget the force behind everything is a demon. Taking out young leaders in the process of destroying an organization is an even greater demonic victory.

God may ask you to stay at a broken organization for the very purpose of protecting a young leader or even a group of young leaders. You may be the only voice of sanity helping them to see things more clearly, and giving them encouragement when they feel defeated. Your words of affirmation and inspiration may be the very words that keep them from leaving ministry altogether. You may also be a catalyst in helping them move on to find another organization where they can grow to be everything God created them to be. Living in a Jezebel-led environment can suck the life and confidence right out of a person. So much so, that they begin to believe the lie that they don't belong in ministry, and are unqualified to be in leadership. You may be the one chosen to keep them believing that they are truly gifted and called to ministry.

God has something remaining for you to accomplish before He releases you – I've learned in my life that God has impeccable timing and plans for each one of us. You may be called to stay in a broken environment to help pick up the pieces when things finally crash. There might be one person who God knows you are going to lead to Christ in a few months and keeps you where you are until that happens. We have to trust in God's goodness and omniscience. If you are one of those called to stay behind and ride out the storm, it may be one of the most difficult tasks you will ever be given by God. Those called to stay behind will watch the organization go into a destructive spiral. It may start out slow at first, but as the controlling issues continue, more and more people will leave the organization. In a church setting, when finances take a downturn, the church may be forced to let staff members go. This will reduce the amount of ministry able to be offered, which can lead to more people leaving and more funds disappearing. As the damaging cycle unravels before your very eyes, it will break your heart, and prayer will become your best friend.

Asking God for patience, self-control, and wisdom will consume your prayer life. Jezebel-led leaders can never be wrong or release control, so any ideas you present to them to counter what is happening will be ignored. In Steve Sampsons's book, *"Discerning and Defeating the Ahab Spirit,"* he writes,

> *Jezebels, however, rarely have any intention of changing—and they usually do not. Typically, they are so wounded that they refuse to take responsibility for anything and are "content" to remain as they are. Between their low self-esteem and inflated ego, their pride keeps them from admitting just how wounded they are. They go through life manipulating people and situations and making everything everyone else's fault.*

As you attempt to share wisdom and common sense with the Jezebel-led leader, you will most likely be rejected, and you will hurt for others and your organization. Frustration will mount to very high levels and only prayer will keep you balanced. It may be that God has asked you to stay behind to be the prayer warrior He needs to stand in the gap. There will be some days where the anguish will be so overwhelming that you will feel inadequate to even pray. In those situations, ask the Holy Spirit to pray for you: *"In the same way, the Spirit helps us in our weakness. We do not know what we ought to pray for, but the Spirit himself intercedes for us with groans that words cannot express. And he who searches our hearts knows the mind of the Spirit, because the Spirit intercedes for the saints in accordance with God's will"* (Romans 8:26-27).

On many occasions you will have to sort through your own emotions and words and rely on God's words instead of your own. There can be great frustration in not knowing how to pray when things are falling apart around you. When you speak truth and it is ignored, it's too easy for your prayers to become tainted and filled with wrong motives. Continually ask God to purify your prayers and strive to bless and not curse. Don't let revenge slip into your prayer time and fervently ask for God to protect the organization. Focus on the health and well-being of the organization and for God to protect those being wounded. Pray for the leader and leadership team to not be blinded by the Jezebel-led person. Ask God for truth to be revealed and for the leaders to have the courage to do what needs to be done. If the leader is controlled by Jezebel, or is being controlled by the Jezebel-led person, ask for God to bring truth and courage to the board of directors or the governing body over the organization.

God is calling you to care for the flock – This pertains more to those who are on staff at a church that is being dominated by a Jezebel leader. Usually the Jezebel-led leader is more self-focused and doesn't have time to care for the people. God may be asking you to stay behind and endure the pain because of God's love for His people. Jezebel-led people are wounded and broken and often have hardened hearts that lack the ability to show compassion to other people. They can be very self-absorbed and simply do not have the time or the motivation to deal with hurting people. Because of His mercy for those who are wounded and broken in the flock, God may ask you to be a surrogate caregiver. Most likely, it will not be noticed by the Jezebel-led leader. If it is noticed, jealousy on the part of the Jezebel-led leader could put a target on your back. Love and care for people anyway.

God's timing – Part of our frustration in the middle of long and difficult situations is not being able to see the future. If we could just see down the road a few years, many of our questions and concerns would be answered. God is the eternal chess master. He has been making moves on our behalf years in advance of where we are today. Some of those moves don't seem to be for our benefit when they occur. I remember applying for a supervisory position many years ago. At the time it seemed like the position was a perfect fit for my knowledge and skill package. I did not get the position. However, I was told that I was the first choice and the most qualified. They went on to explain to me that a supervisor in another department was on the verge of being laid off. They chose to move that person into the position I was hoping for. I was devastated. I felt like God had let me down. Lies flooded into my mind that God didn't care about me. I knew the other person and I was glad they had another position to step into, but I couldn't help feeling disappointed.

I stewed about it for a while and then finally let it go. What I didn't know was that God was protecting me in a very big way. Several months later, I was promoted to an even better position. After serving in that new position for six months, I was then offered a job with a brand-new company and shortly after became a vice president. If I had been given the first position I applied for, I would have never gotten to know the person who offered me the job with the new company. But the story doesn't end there. Two years later, the company I originally worked for filed for bankruptcy and closed down. Had I received the job I was so desperately seeking, I would have been unemployed. One more thing. The new job that I stepped into gave me all the on-the-job training I needed to launch a nonprofit ministry years later. While I was brooding over a missed job opportunity, God was preparing the way for Wellsprings of Freedom International to be born.

Currently, people I met many years ago, long before Wellsprings of Freedom was even conceived, are part of the Wellsprings ministry today. God was introducing me to people years in advance, knowing they would be significant leaders in the ministry today. That may not seem significant to you, but many of those people were people I met in Russia while serving on short-term mission trips. Had God not sent me to Russia, our current president would most likely not be serving here. God was behind the scenes orchestrating events years in advance of Wellsprings of Freedom's existence. My first trip to Russia took place three weeks before I even knew spiritual warfare existed. And years before God led me to start a nonprofit ministry, He was introducing me to the future leaders of the ministry. God is always going before us preparing the way. With that said, when we are in the midst of really tough situations and it feels like God has abandoned us, He hasn't. He always has a plan. He is going to somehow redeem your situation. It may not be right away. It might take years for His plan to unfold. But do not lose hope. He is going to work for your good.

When we consider all the aspects of God's timing and how it might affect the reasons why God may allow a Jezebel leader to stay in a position of control, it can be very confusing. In our minds, the quick and easy answer is to remove the Jezebel leader. It seems appropriate to stop the abusive control that is causing wounds in other people and destroying the organization around you. But if and when that doesn't happen, could there be legitimate reasons for God to delay the process? I believe so. In order to understand, we need to look at things from an entirely different perspective: God's long-range perspective. What could He possibly be doing today that will affect a person or an organization ten or twenty years down the road? There are probably many answers to that question depending on each and every situation. But for the sake of helping us look at this differently, here are two possible considerations:

1. What if a person has become so complacent in their job that God is using their difficult circumstances to move them on to something that will profoundly impact the kingdom?

    I have a friend whose job situation became so unbearable due to a Jezebel environment, that when God called him out of the secular world and into full-time ministry, he jumped at the opportunity. When what was once the job of a lifetime became tarnished by a controlling Jezebel, the temptation to stay in a very lucrative job was removed. He followed God's call, and the results that he is having in his new position is definitely impacting thousands of lives for eternity.

2. What if God has something significant for the controlling leader to do before He moves them on to their next position?

    This one isn't as fun to think about. When we are living in the midst of a Jezebel-led environment, we just want the obsessive control to stop. But what if the controlling leader is the thorn under the saddle that pushes a fearful young leader out of their comfort zone and into what God created them to do? It might also be that there is a program to launch, a message to preach, a funeral to perform, or a soul to be saved before God moves the controlling leader out of the organization? What if a new campus is launched that will one day reach thousands of people?

I'm not suggesting that an abusive Jezebel-led leader who is wounding people and destroying the organization should not be removed. No one should be forced to live in an abusive environment. I know a Jezebel leader might say that if a frustrated employee doesn't like working there, they can go find another job. If it was just one dissatisfied employee, that might be true, but when much of a department or organization is being negatively affected, removing the Jezebel-led person makes more sense. The two considerations I shared above are not reasons why we should keep an abusive controlling person in a high-level position. Rather, it is meant to explain why God might choose to tarry for a while before removing a Jezebel-led leader. In my experience, if you have the backing and the approval of the proper authority to remove a controlling Jezebel-led person from power, do it as soon as possible. Choosing to delay could give Jezebel more time to figure out a plan for removing *you*.

Warning for those who stay – When you choose to stay, and are in the holding pattern of waiting for something to happen that will change the situation, don't be surprised if the unseen spirit of Jezebel doesn't try playing games with your mind. Games of taunting and hopelessness. Lies that it will always be like this, nothing is going to change. Lies that you are defeated and worthless. Lies that you are a loser and that you really aren't making a difference. When time passes and nothing seems to be changing, the enemy will tell you that God has abandoned you and is siding with the person who is manipulating and hurting the organization. Don't listen. Abusive control is not the heart of God. Sadly, you will be able to know this as you watch God slowly withdraw his blessing from the organization.

The purpose for giving you multiple reasons why God might ask you to stay on the job in a Jezebel environment is for hope. Many of us get discouraged and lose hope when we cannot see a purpose for our current sufferings. If we can see a reason to hang on, it makes it a little easier for us to endure our hard circumstances. If you are trying to decide what to do, knowing your purpose, or the reason why God is calling you to stay, might help in your decision. If you do not sense a strong calling or purpose for staying, it could be a release from God to move on.

For those who are living in a Jezebel-led environment, you may not be able to stop the controlling individual, but that doesn't mean they can always control you. You do have a choice. You can choose to leave, and there is no shame in leaving. In fact, there are times when you should leave.

Reasons to leave –
- You are being targeted because you spoke truth about the broken environment.
- Your spiritual gifts are being ignored and God's calling on your life is being squelched.
- The overwhelming busyness of a chaotic Jezebel environment is negatively impacting your family life.
- The constant critical atmosphere is destroying your self-confidence.
- You refuse to be manipulated and controlled by intimidation, guilt, and shame.
- The environment becomes so toxic that God withdraws His blessing from the organization.
- You refuse to watch others being regularly wounded by malicious control.
- The direction of the organization shifts to something different than you were hired for.
- You have no desire to be part of an abusive and controlling organization.
- You refuse to participate in a dysfunctional leadership style.
- You refuse to lie and pretend everything is great when it is actually falling apart.
- You can't continue to tell the deceiving stories that cover up what is really going on.
- You are being blamed for things you didn't do.

- The leader of the organization is controlled by a Jezebel-led person.
- You are overwhelmed by a heaviness that won't go away and steals your joy.
- Your integrity won't allow you to participate in an environment that doesn't model the character of Christ.
- When it stops being about God's Kingdom and starts being about the Jezebel-leader's kingdom.
- There is no other option to stand against the abuse going on in the organization other than to just walk away.

No one should feel guilty for leaving an abusive situation. That's easy to say, not as easy to do. Most likely you will experience some measure of guilt—partially because of the manipulating prowess of the Jezebel spirit, and partially because of your loyalty and love for the organization. Many, not all, controlling leaders will manipulate people through guilt and shame. This can be a form of religious or spiritual abuse. I once had an individual come to me and share that they wanted to leave their church but couldn't. I asked why they wanted to leave. The response I got was shocking. They explained how the pastor of the church they attended controlled their every move. They weren't allowed to purchase anything without his permission. They had to get his approval for any major decisions they were considering as a family. They even had to go to him for permission to take a family vacation. When I asked them why they couldn't leave, my heart broke for them. The pastor had taught his church that he was God's anointed and only he was qualified to make decisions for them, including asking him for his permission, and blessing to leave the church. If he didn't give them permission to leave, and they left, they were sinning against God.

In work environments, Jezebel-led leaders will try to maintain control over you in a slightly different way. If you share with them you are thinking of leaving for a better position, they will most likely try to talk you out of it. They will tell you that you aren't quite yet leadership material, and you need to stay under their watchful eye as they help develop you. The trouble with that is, they don't develop you. They keep you under their controlling thumb. You are never allowed to make decisions, only follow their orders, therefore, you will never be good enough in their mind to leave. It is fascinating to me that when a person does decide to leave, even after months and months of being criticized and told you don't measure up, the Jezebel leadership will get mad at your leaving. They are insulted at your perceived defiance of them, and the fact that they can no longer control you. Once you leave, they will have very little to do with you again.

Don't be surprised if the Jezebel-led leader in your organization doesn't try to manipulate you with guilt and shame. Not necessarily like the story above, but by accusing you or making you feel like a traitor. Or they deemed you as subversive because you tried to point out the dysfunction. Remember, the Jezebel-led person can't accept the idea that they could be broken. In their minds, they are God's chosen, so if you choose to leave the organization, you are stepping away from God. This is part of the pride that is interwoven into the Jezebel-led person and the loyal allies. Imagine the hubris, the unspoken idea that they are the truly called ones, and if you leave their organization on your own, you are a traitor to them and God. If you hadn't yet discovered that everything is about them, you most likely will when you leave.

Most Jezebel-led leaders demand loyalty. When you can't step under their dominant control like good little soldiers, they will dismiss you as disloyal to the cause. They may even consider you as disloyal to Christ. If you leave their little nest, they may brand you as a failure, enemy, traitor, or as someone trying to hurt them and God's Kingdom. When everything is about them, they take your actions to leave personally. Leaving is rejection of them and will be taken as a personal insult. Therefore, they will create their own story of why you left. Because of this, you need to leave well and have a measuring stick to gauge the quality and integrity of your exit. With the measuring stick in place, you will not fall prey to Jezebel's attempt to heap guilt and shame on you for leaving its control. Leaving in a healthy and godly way will protect you from the confusion and chaos that a Jezebel-led person spins to keep the blame off of themselves. They cannot allow your exit to reflect their failure. So, Jezebel-led people will try to spin stories about you that will cause even you to doubt yourself. This is magnified and projected into your mind by the Jezebel spirit as well. We dare not forget that an evil spirit is actively working with the Jezebel-led person, and against you. This is why you need to have a balanced way to measure your exit.

Leaving well – If we are called to leave…how do we do it well? What is the measuring stick to use when deciding to leave, or how can we leave without dividing or hurting the Kingdom of God? Too many leave under the control of their raw emotions. This is understandable considering the heartache and pain that is experienced in a controlling environment. But we must never let our anger and resentment become the motivational force to divide an organization, especially a church. When leaving, leave gently and quietly. You don't have to stay under the leadership of an abusive controlling leader, nor under a leader who is controlled by another person who abuses and controls. The following list is meant to be a guide you can follow to help you leave well, but it is more than that. It is a protective shield for you and the church. You don't want the weight of being responsible for dividing a work of God on your shoulder. The Jezebel spirit is already doing that. Can you see how the Jezebel spirit would thoroughly enjoy manipulating your emotions and enlisting your help to cause division? That way, when the organization is destroyed, you get the blame, and Jezebel gets off completely free.

It's easy to get impatient and want to take matters into your own hands, but we must trust that God has it all under control. We must trust in His timing, for He sees things we do not see. If Jezebel is truly in control, the organization will fail. Don't fall for the temptation to be an accomplice in that process. Don't give Jezebel the opportunity to make you the scapegoat for the damage it is creating. Following the list below will also protect you down the road, when the Jezebel spirit tries to blame you when things fall apart. It is not uncomon for the Jezebel-led person to try and smear you after you have left. In fact, I have heard stories of people who were afraid to leave for this very reason. They knew they would get smeared as soon as they walked out the door, and were afraid it would keep them from being hired by another organization. There is such confusion spun off in all directions by a Jezebel spirit. Even if you leave well, the spirit will try to make you feel guilty for leaving and cause you to believe the organizational decline was somehow your fault because you left. Allow the measuring list to give you peace of mind when the storm of confusion comes.

Measuring list:
- Leave without causing division.
- Leave trying to protect the church or organization from harm.
- Leave without trying to take people with you—they may follow, but not because you encouraged them to follow.
- Leave without openly trashing the remaining leadership team.
- Leave without seeking retaliation or revenge.
- Exit as quietly as possible, not making a public display or scene.

- Leave with the motive of bettering your personal circumstances, not getting even.
- Always examine your motives for leaving. You may leave angry after having witnessed many injustices and abusive control, but don't leave with the desire to inflict harm.
- You may leave as a silent protest against wrong and injustice if you have brought those injustices to the leadership's attention, and you have been ignored or rebuked for daring to speak truth to the situation.
- Carefully look into your own heart—are you leaving because of injustice or because you want control?
- Make sure you are leaving over broken principles, not because you didn't get your way.
- Be careful you are not the only one seeing the situation the way you see it; make sure there are others who see the same brokenness and dysfunction you see.

If you can leave following this list, you have left the organization without causing harm… however, you may not be able to leave spiritually or emotionally unharmed. Living in a Jezebel environment and trying to expose a Jezebel environment can lead to much pain and heartache. It is likely you will leave with wounds deeper than you can imagine. Wounds inflicted by other men and women of God are often the hardest to bear. It is important to understand that just because a Christian organization harmed you, it was not God doing the harm. Satan and his demonic following are masterful at misdirection and blaming God for not stopping the perpetrators of the pain from hurting you. Remember, this is about human free will. Humans hurt each other every day, not God.

Do not be surprised when you leave if many untruthful things are said about you. You may be branded as a traitor, or incompetent. Blame for the overall failure of the organization might be cast in your direction. You might hear it said that you are the controlling one, or be branded as an agitator or troublemaker. It is quite possible the entire situation will get turned around on you. For example, you have been deeply hurt and wounded, but the Jezebel leader may choose to spin the story so that they are the victim. They may speak of how your leaving has hurt them and wounded them. They will do everything they can to keep themselves from being blamed or looking bad. Jezebel-led people cannot look bad or appear to look bad, so they will spin stories to make themselves to be the wounded "victim." They put on an emotional show and get people to feel sorry for them. Then, in the midst of their emotionally staged act, they seek sympathy and support through their display of counterfeit sorrow. They do this and get away with it, and it will be painful to watch. The abusive controlling ones fool everyone into thinking they are the abused. Abusive spouses are especially adept at playing this game. It will cause you, the abused, to doubt yourself. This is why you want to use the measuring stick to help you know you have left well. When Jezebel tries to cover you with either guilt or blame, you will be protected by an honest evaluation of your motives and final actions. You will know why you left, and why it wasn't your fault.

Chapter 12

You're Not Crazy

I had lunch with a dear friend recently who had a bad experience with a Jezebel-led person in his church a number of years ago. As he reminisced about his experience, just talking about it brought tears to his eyes. He got choked up recalling the pain and loneliness he felt when he walked through his journey of torment. Seeing his pain reminded me of the number of times I have sat with countless other people who have been deeply wounded by the Jezebel spirit. Each of their stories are gut-wrenching and painful. It caused me to reflect back on how lonely it can be, and prompted me to write about it. It may appear to be out of place and discouraging, but the emotional torment is real. Discussing it may bring some clarity and understanding to those who are currently walking in the midst of their own Jezebel-induced pain. Just knowing that many others have walked this path before you may be a source of hope.

Trying to survive in a Jezebel-led environment can be maddening, partially because of the pervasive control, but also because you are dealing with a demonic spirit. If you are dealing with a person who is controlled by a Jezebel spirit, and that person steps into an organization that is influenced by a territorial-level Jezebel spirit, Jezebel's ability to control is greatly magnified. If the leader, leadership team, or authority structure have been seduced and are controlled by a Jezebel-led person, hopelessness will prevail. You will feel a weight of heaviness that can't be explained, and the oppressive control will steal your dreams and suffocate your joy. High levels of fear will permeate the whole environment and slowly drive you into submission. Eventually, you will feel like you have lost your mind as everything you have learned about integrity and leadership is turned upside down. The chaos, deception, false blame, and Jezebel's perceived ability to win, will indeed make you feel like you are going crazy. Your desire to call out and stop the injustices you see will dominate your mind. And the longer it is allowed to go on, the more you think you are going insane. Trust me, you are not.

Letting go – Jezebels are politicians; they have connections everywhere. They make a beeline for the highest-level leaders in an organization or even a denomination. They masquerade themselves as extreme agents of good to those above them, and hide their dysfunction and controlling ways from them. They are really skilled at this, and it provides them with an extra layer of protection if things begin to fall apart. By having the trust of the highest levels, when things fall apart, they can blame everyone else and the upper-level people will believe them and feel sorry for them. Long term, after everything crashes, this will help them to step into a better position where they can begin their destructive journey all over again. Jezebel's ability to win over the trust of significant leaders is alarming and will frustrate you as you watch them harming the organization and still be able to climb up the leadership ladder.

There will be days when you feel all alone with no one to go to, complain to, or get any kind of assistance from. You will be on your own. Everything inside will scream for justice, but none will be found. Jezebel will have gone before you and developed relationships with just about anyone who could be in a position to listen and offer help. You will feel trapped and hopeless. You will want to fight, you will want to get even, and you will want to tear the abusive structure down. But when you try, no one will listen, no one will believe, and you will feel abandoned.

One of Jezebel's strategies is to isolate the opposition. That's when the spirit of Jezebel begins to play in your mind. You are the problem, you are the dysfunctional one. Jezebel accuses people of the very things it is, and does. Jezebel will then begin the process of convincing you that God has abandoned you, that God is protecting the abuser, and that must mean you are the broken and crazy one. A hopeless despair will begin to overtake you and shake you to your core. Every attempt to expose Jezebel will be disbelieved and thrown back in your face. Jezebel will begin to play games with you, doing something very mean and abusive right in front of you, taunting you to step in and fight again. It is only toying with you to produce even deeper levels of fear and discouragement. It will try to get you to retreat from God by focusing your anger at Him for not removing Jezebel.

By getting you to separate yourself from God, it will get you to fight in your own strength. Jezebel is a fighter and wants to consume you in battle. If it can draw you into daily skirmishes and battles, it keeps you emotionally distraught and unbalanced. Before long, you're consumed with trying to win a battle you can't win, and it's likely you will lose sight of your God-given purpose. It will also keep you off of your God-ordained mission and you won't have the time or energy to do the things you are gifted and called to do.

I'm not saying Jezebel can't be defeated, because it can—but not if the leadership team is unwilling to confront the Jezebel-led person, or if the leader is the Jezebel-led person. You may have to surrender the whole situation over to God. You may have to surrender your need to win. You may have to surrender your need to be right. You may have to step back or even step out of the organization and wait for God to address the situation in His time. It may be so bad that the only way out is for the whole organization to collapse. Even then, there will be someone who is ready to give the Jezebel-led leader another chance to do it all over again at a new location.

Once Jezebel has drawn you into the battle, be careful. It will consume you with an insatiable desire to win. So much so, that even when you leave an organization, or a relationship, it still tries to draw you back into the fight. It is as if Jezebel has a fishing pole and throws out a baited hook in your direction just hoping you will reach out and take the bait to fight again. It may not be able to control you on a daily basis anymore, but it will certainly try to keep you off of your mission. Jezebel-led family members, ex-spouses, former controlling boyfriends or girlfriends, parents, or siblings are all capable of drawing you back into meaningless battles that Jezebel uses just to torment you and keep you in a crazy cycle of anger. You will think that everything with the old controlling person is behind you, and then, out of nowhere, an irresistible invitation to jump into the fray will land right in front of you. Learn to recognize where the invitation is truly coming from, and resist the urge to reengage.

I'm not trying to paint a picture of hopelessness, but an unchecked Jezebel environment is a bleak place to be. Jezebel-led people are so able to insulate and endear themselves to leaders that they are practically untouchable. Without a strong and courageous leader or leadership team, most Jezebel-led people will remain in a position of power. Trying to confront them, or remove them without the support of the leadership will usually only cause harm to you, and though it isn't fair, it is reality. As believers we want fair and equal justice for all, but we must realize we live in a broken world. Even inside Christian organizations, leaders can be deceived. This is where wisdom comes into play. There are some battles you can win, and some you cannot. Learning the difference is imperative to your survival in a Jezebel-led environment. Some situations will be completely untouchable until the Jezebel-led person makes a big mistake, or the organization falls into such disarray that the leadership is replaced. Know where you stand before you attempt to fight. Your situation may not be winnable. If you are a tank or a cannon trying to defeat an atomic bomb, you will lose. Try to stay hidden or move on as soon as you can. Get out from under Jezebel's control and live again in freedom.

Living in a Jezebel environment – I don't want you to be blindsided by what typically takes place in a Jezebel-led environment. Here are some things you can expect will happen to you.

- You will be criticized – nothing you do will be good enough. Even your best work will be torn apart and judged to be inadequate.
- You will be ignored – none of your ideas will be acceptable. Nothing you say that makes complete sense will be heard. Ideas you share in open meetings will be mocked and rejected as being ridiculous.
- You will be blamed – Jezebel-led environments cannot succeed for very long. When the organization begins to crumble, don't be surprised when Jezebel places the blame on you. It won't matter that you haven't been allowed to make any leadership decisions for a long time. You will be targeted as the reason for things falling apart.
- You will be excluded – Jezebel-led people and their allies consider themselves to be superior to you. If you are not 100 percent loyal to the Jezebel-led leader, you are meaningless, expendable, and unworthy to be in their circle or group.
- You will be isolated – if you legitimately question troubling issues in your organization, Jezebel-led leaders will see you as an enemy. The Jezebel-led leader and their

allies will declare war on you and you will become an outcast. They will ice you until you choose to leave the organization.
- You will be overlooked – only the loyal circle of allies will be considered for promotion, awards, and public recognition.
- You will feel like you are going crazy – even when it's obvious who is to blame for the organizational failure, they are never at fault. At times, you will be accused of the very things they are doing.

Let me assure you, you are not going crazy and you are not losing your sanity. It's just part of the Jezebel-induced atmosphere of confusion and accusation. There is usually such a chaotic and busy environment going on all around you, that there isn't time to reflect and analyze what is going on. In the midst of being given project after project with impossible deadlines, there is barely time to consider anything else but getting the jobs done—let alone the pressure of trying to get them done without being criticized. Remember, part of Jezebel's scheme to keep you under its control is to never allow you to succeed. It must always keep you chasing after a goal it will never let you attain.

Hopefully by reading this book you will begin to realize what is going on and that neither you or God are to blame. It is difficult enough trying to survive in this circus-like atmosphere. You don't need to carry unnecessary blame as well. I hope that by understanding what is happening to you, it will relieve some of the Jezebel-imposed weight you are carrying. It won't put an end to the oppressive and crazy environment, but it may help you to cope if you choose to stay, or until you can safely leave. Surviving in the midst of those two decisions may come down to surrender.

Surrender – Yes, the atmosphere around you is broken, and though you may be blamed, it is not your fault. Don't fall for that lie. When you work in a Jezebel-controlled environment, you know very well you are not allowed to make any decisions. All major decisions will be made by the Jezebel-led person and enforced by its allies. As the organization begins to fall into a slump, those in leadership will be looking to blame everyone but themselves for the downturn. If you are the targeted scapegoat, don't take on that lie. Surrender the lie to Jesus. He knows the truth about what is going on. There is no need for you to carry the weight and blame for the organizational dysfunction.

Every day will present a whole new set of trials and tribulations. Unfair accusations, being ignored, dismissed as being stupid, mocked, bullied, manipulated, and highly criticized are all possible daily occurrences for you. Anger, resentment, bitterness, and getting even will dominate your mind. This is all completely understandable. However, none of these are healthy reactions for you to dwell on. Hanging on to these things creates a poison that will begin to negatively transform you from the inside out. It is as if you are living in a wound.

"Living in a wound" means that you are living in an ongoing hurtful relationship or situation. It is very difficult to heal a wound that gets torn open again and again on a daily basis. Just when you offer up forgiveness toward the controlling bully, another round of abuse is hurled your way. Complete removal from the toxic situation is probably the most certain way to close the door on the enemy's abusive control. Unfortunately, sometimes you can't always get out of it right away. There will be times when you will be forced to walk through the humiliating abuse. You will find yourself in a place where you need to surrender your anger and bitterness over to God on a daily basis. Strive not to let the hurts build up. Instead, acknowledge the hurt—if only to Jesus—and forgive continuously. When we are living in a wound, it is easy to become discouraged and believe the lie that there is no way out. Seek help from people you can trust outside of the organization. Find people who can pray for you and offer sound advice for how to get out of your situation. There will be times when all you can do is pray—which may be your only link to sanity.

How to pray – This may appear to be a simple and unnecessary suggestion. But when you really begin to pray with integrity about your situation, it can get very confusing in a hurry. It is hard to pray for an organization that has abusive leaders. You want to pray for the church or nonprofit organization to succeed, but how do you do that when the organization is wounding people? If the organization succeeds, that means the abusive control will only be allowed to continue and spread to others. So how do we pray? How can we remain a blessing and not be a curse? Here are a few suggestions to help you pray more effectively. Of course, always let the Holy Spirit guide you as you seek direction during your prayer time.

1. Wisdom – When I'm confused about how I should pray, I always start by asking God for wisdom. In James 1: 5, we find these words: *"If any of you lacks wisdom, he should ask God, who gives generously to all without finding fault, and it will be given to him."* This passage gives me permission to approach God with all my crazy ideas of how to pray without feeling condemned for asking. I can pour out my heart, which includes the good and the bad and ask God to help sort through it all.

    In Richard Foster's book, *Prayer: Finding the Heart's True Home,* he writes these comforting words:

> *The truth of the matter is, we all come to prayer with a tangled mass of motives—altruistic and selfish, merciful and hateful, loving and bitter. Frankly, this side of eternity we will never unravel the good from the bad, the pure from the impure. But what I have come to see is that God is big enough to receive us with all our mixture. We do not have to be bright, or pure, or filled with faith, or anything. That is what grace means, and not only are we saved by grace, we live by it as well. And we pray by it. We will never have pure enough motives, or be good enough, or know enough in order to pray rightly. We simply must set all these things aside and begin praying. In fact, it is the very act of prayer itself—the intimate, ongoing interaction with God—that these matters are cared for in due time.*

Foster goes on to say,

> *What I am trying to say is that God receives us just as we are and accepts our prayers just as they are. In the same way that a small child cannot draw a bad picture, so a child of God cannot offer a bad prayer. In simple prayer we bring ourselves before God just as we are, warts and all.*

It was this book that nearly twenty-five years ago opened my heart to prayer. I continue to refer to it from time to time just to get a refresher on prayer. I believe this is what the book of James was teaching us two thousand years before. We can ask for wisdom without fearing that God will somehow try to judge us or find fault with our prayers. We can be open with him and pour out our hurts

and fears without shame. I have found that it is in the pouring out of my messy and confusing emotions that God reaches down and begins to adjust my attitudes and thoughts. He begins to do just what He says in His Word. We can ask for wisdom, and it will be given to us.
2. Forgiveness – In Chapter 6, I wrote about the need to forgive. However, when you are living in a wound, when you experience a form of abusive control nearly every day, the need to forgive becomes a daily necessity. By forgiving, you are not condoning the bad behavior. Abusive control is wrong. Much of the behavior of a Jezebel-led person will be hurtful to you. So, by forgiving them you are not saying it is okay to hurt other people. You are not going to them personally and offering to forgive them either. This is between you and God alone. Forgiveness is releasing your right to revenge and getting even. It is letting go of all the resentment and anger that is pent up inside of you. It is trusting in God's judgement and timing as to how and when the Jezebel-led person will be reprimanded and removed.
3. Protection for you and the organization – When a Jezebel-led person is allowed to wield high levels of control over an organization, that organization is headed for trouble. If they are allowed to go unchecked, the power-hungry Jezebel-led person will only increase in its controlling and destructive ways. Without an accountability structure, which most Jezebel-led people will ignore anyway, the boldness and brashness of the Jezebel-led person will intensify at an alarming pace. The destructive behaviors and decisions over the organization will begin slowly. They may not even be seen or felt in the early stages of the Jezebel virus spreading within the organization. Usually by the time the destructive patterns are

uncovered, Jezebel has entrenched itself into the leadership structure. Pray for God to protect and preserve your organization.

Ask God to hide you and protect you from the unthrottled wrath and judgement of the Jezebel-led person. Ask God to help you be as cunning as a fox in your interactions with the Jezebel-led person. Pray for God to help you stay off of Jezebel's radar and to do your job as unto Jesus, not to Jezebel. Working for Jesus will help you to continue to love your job, even if the atmosphere is broken. Also, ask Jesus to protect the organization and remove Jezebel before the organization is destroyed beyond repair.

4. Remove the blinders – Because the Jezebel-led person is controlled and empowered by a demonic spirit of Jezebel, the ability for this spirit to deceive is off the charts. It may supernaturally influence and win over the leadership team. The leader or leaders of the organization will either be intimidated or mesmerized into protecting the Jezebel-led person. They will believe the Jezebel-led person over an entire department full of people. It is difficult to believe until you see it happen. Pray for God to remove the blinders that prevent the leaders from seeing the truth. Pray also that the mesmerizing spell that covers the minds of the leadership team will be removed. Ask God to open up the eyes of the leadership team to what Jezebel is doing to them and the employees. In addition, forgive the leaders who are aligned with the Jezebel-led person and are being used to protect the Jezebel-led person. They are blind and do not know it. Ask God to open up their eyes so they can see the truth of what is happening within the organization.

5. Expose the Jezebel spirit - As the Jezebel-led person is allowed to continue to wound people and make destructive decisions for the organization, things will begin to fall apart. Unfortunately, the Jezebel-led person will be very adept at blaming everyone but themselves for the mess that is unfolding. This just exacerbates the situation as good people are blamed for the failures of the Jezebel-led person and its allies. As Jezebel gains in power and control, it usually becomes far bolder and is more susceptible to making huge mistakes. Ask God to expose the destructive patterns and behaviors of the Jezebel-led person to those who are in a position to do something about it. *"God resists the proud, but gives grace to the humble"* (James 4:6). Ask God to expose the pride and arrogance of the Jezebel-led person for all to see. As you pray for God to expose them, don't be surprised if the bad behavior doesn't intensify. In order for their spiritually abusive behaviors to be exposed, they will have to reach a level where they can be seen. This won't be a pleasant experience for those around the Jezebel-led person, but a necessary one if Jezebel is going to be uncovered.
6. Courage and grace – You will not be the only one feeling the oppression and being subjected to the controlling nonsense handed out by the Jezebel-led person. Others will feel exactly as you do, but are completely afraid to express it for fear of reprisal. Fear typically dominates a Jezebel environment. There is such confusion that no one really knows who they can trust. Many will have the desire to isolate from everyone out of a sense of fear. Ask God for the courage to watch for those who are also being belittled or mistreated and reach out to them with the grace of God's love. Help them to know they are not alone and that you will be praying for them. Caution: Satan

can use these vulnerable situations to develop unhealthy feelings for someone of the opposite sex. Guard your heart. Perhaps a whole band of you can work extra hard to encourage one another and help each other to know you are not alone nor are you going crazy.

7. Exit plan – You do not have to stay in an abusive controlling environment. Do not fall for the lie that you are trapped and there is no other place to go. Don't fall for the lie that this is just your lot in life, or that somehow you deserve this. If you are living with a controlling abusive partner, their lies to you will only be attempts to make you feel so worthless that you think no one else would want you. That is not true. It is only their effort to keep you isolated and in bondage to them. If you are in a controlling environment at work, don't be surprised if the criticism doesn't make you feel like you are such a poor employee that no one else would hire you. This is all part of the strategy to keep you under an abusive person's control. Ask God to begin to help you to see and/or devise an exit strategy to get out from under the controlling oppressive environment. Also ask God to open up doors and contacts that will lead you out of your abusive situation. Then, pray for the courage to take whatever steps God places before you to get out from under the oppressive control. Imagine what it would be like to work for someone who appreciates your hard work. Imagine what it would be like to work at a place that is open to hearing your suggestions and ideas. Those places exist, go find them, and don't settle for anything less. If you are in an abusive relationship, seek good counsel from an organization that is trained and equipped to help people find places of safety.

8. Ask God to check your motives – As humans, we can be easily deceived. We are most capable of convincing

ourselves we are right and everyone else is wrong. Tempting thoughts are more than able to allure us away from what is real and true. Our emotions can deceive us, and our desires can tantalize us to things that are not in line with God's will. Knowing this, we must be careful to make sure we are not the controlling one. If you are being deceived by a Jezebel spirit, it will cause you to refuse to submit to authority. Ask God to show you if you are really under the control of a Jezebel-led person, or if it is actually you trying to be in control. Look over the list of Jezebel traits found in Chapter 1. Ask God to show you if you have several of those characteristics and if you are the one in need of repentance and change. We must all submit to some authority. We all have bosses or boards that we are subject to. Being given work assignments and being held accountable to do a good job is not abusive control. The leadership structures in all organizations are for the good of the whole. Following rules is expected of all of us, and if you cannot step into alignment with a leadership structure that is fair, you may be the one needing freedom from a Jezebel spirit. Ask God to help you to see what you may not want to see. Be ruggedly honest with yourself. Let God shine the light of truth into your heart and reveal truth. Most likely you are not the Jezebel-led person, but you must be willing to allow God to examine your heart. If you are resistant to letting that happen, you may be the controlling one. You may be angry with your employer because you can't submit to authority. Ask God to help you sort through your motives.

While we are on the subject of prayer, it is easy for us to think that we can just pray the Jezebel spirit off of the person it is attached to. It is a good idea, but seldom works. The problem is that the person with the Jezebel spirit must want to be free.

Usually they are so addicted to the power they have developed that they can't let go of the spirit. We can only help people to the level they want to be helped. Demons take advantage of our free will and will leave only when the person with Jezebel repents and truly wants them to go.

We may not be able to pray off the Jezebel spirit from a person without their full cooperation, but I do believe we can ask God to remove the mesmerizing spell Jezebel places over the leader. We can pray for the leader to have supernatural wisdom in how to remove the Jezebel-led person from their staff. We can also ask God to determine if and where a person influenced by Jezebel can safely serve within the body of Christ. Pray for the demonic ties from the Jezebel spirit toward the staff to be cut off and removed. A leader who discovers they have been controlled by a Jezebel-led person may need to meet with the staff and ask for their forgiveness for not protecting them. This can go a long way toward helping to cut off the ties of the demonic alliances who have attached to some of the team members.

Prayer should be lifted up for the leader and leadership team who has to confront Jezebel. Jezebel has a way of causing great fear and anxiety for the person or team who is required to perform this unpleasant act. This fear and anxiety can be amplified to very high levels against the leadership team to shut them down or cause them to back down. It doesn't necessarily come from the person who has Jezebel; it comes in waves from unseen forces of evil leading up to the confrontation. We must pray for supernatural courage to be given to the leader and the leadership team trying to unmask and remove a person with Jezebel. Pray for God to give them supernatural wisdom in how to confront Jezebel, and the mental fortitude and strength to move forward.

Final thoughts – If you are in the midst of your own despair because of a Jezebel environment, my heart goes out to you. Writing about this spirit has been a real challenge. When you are under the control of this dominating force of evil, it truly does feel helpless. My goal has been to expose this spirit and hopefully open up the eyes of those serving in nonprofits and churches to what Jezebel is capable of doing, as well as trying to offer help and hope to those who are under its oppressive yoke.

I feel led to circle back around to a scripture verse I shared with you earlier found in Revelation 2:18-22:

> *To the angel of the church in Thyatira write: These are the words of the Son of God, whose eyes are like blazing fire and whose feet are like burnished bronze. I know your deeds, your love and faith, your service and perseverance, and that you are now doing more than you did at first. Nevertheless, I have this against you: You tolerate that woman Jezebel, who calls herself a prophetess. By her teaching she misleads my servants into sexual immorality and the eating of food sacrificed to idols. I have given her time to repent of her immorality, but she is unwilling. So I will cast her on a bed of suffering, and I will make those who commit adultery with her suffer intensely, unless they repent of her ways.*

As stated earlier, one of the most often asked questions is: Why does God allow Jezebel to stay in power as long as He does? In the passage above, God does give the Jezebel-led person time to repent. I am thankful for God's mercy, aren't you? Interestingly, the scripture tells us she was unwilling. That may not always be the case in your situation. But it is true that the addiction to power and control is hard to let go of. The next most often asked question is: Why are churches allowed to be decimated by this spirit? Often, it is the way things are structured. When the Jezebel-led person is the leader, or is controlling the leader, they are in charge. It is very difficult for subordinates to remove them from their position. Plus, there is another factor that is easily overlooked. When the Jezebel-led person and their allies are pastors, we trust them. When they tell us everything is going well, we believe them. The same holds true for nonprofit organizations run by Christians. We want to trust in them. If Jezebel has entwined itself into the fabric of a church or nonprofit leadership structure, this trust factor gives the Jezebel leader an extra layer of protection. When they are confronted, our disbelief that they could lie allows for them to continue on their path of spiritual abuse. That's partially why I have written this book. By exposing the characteristics of this spirit, hopefully churches and nonprofits will be better able to protect themselves from its devastating corruption.

Jezebel-led people are purveyors of spiritual abuse. If they can hide behind the title of pastor to enable their abusive ways, they will. It is similar to a police officer who goes bad and becomes corrupt. We expect higher standards of trust from these individuals and we typically give them the benefit of the doubt. Jezebel uses this to its advantage. That way Jezebel is able to cause destruction in a couple of ways—by taking down churches and nonprofits, and by soiling the overall image of clergy and nonprofit leaders worldwide. That's another reason why we need to be diligent in uncovering the Jezebel spirit from our churches and nonprofits. Just as one bad cop can harm the reputation of an entire occupation, so it is with Jezebel leaders in the church. When Jezebel-led pastors or staff members control and wound people, Satan distorts the facts. He is quick to tell people that if God's chosen leaders are abusive and don't care, then, surely God is abusive and doesn't care. When the very place we believe we should be able to trust is untrustworthy and abusive, the greater the depth of the wound. We expect bad guys to hurt us, we don't expect the church to hurt us. Often, this is the last straw for many people. Sadly, many of them leave the church and never return. This is just another reason why we need to uncover this spirit and strive to remove it before it hurts more people.

Not dealing with Jezebel allows it to have access and control over our organizations. Thus, suffering and destruction will follow. It is either our inability or unwillingness to contend with this spirit that brings forth devastation. Inability stems from not being in a high enough position to remove the controlling individual. Inability might also include those who are in a position to do something, but are genuinely deceived. In the midst of their deception they choose to believe the Jezebel-led person over those who are being abused and are complaining. In either case, it is not your fault. You are dealing with the spiritual realm, not flesh and blood. Don't blame yourself for the actions of others. Sometimes the level of deceit over those who could change things is unimaginable.

For those who are in a leadership position and have the means to do something but are unwilling, please reconsider. Look over the following list of possible next steps:

- Ask God to remove any blinders Jezebel has over your eyes.
- Strive to get information from those who are not on the elite team of followers. Because the elite team may feel controlled, they will never admit to it, so go to the non-elite team members for answers. Even they may be reluctant to give you information because of fear. Make sure you protect them.
- Reread the list of characteristics in Chapter 1, and look for those patterns in your organization.
- Pay attention to important data that may indicate problems: financials, attendance, inability to keep staff

members, inconsistent stories from leadership, fear or reluctance to hire new people, highly involved servant volunteers choosing to leave, lack of openness with information, controlling atmosphere, leaders are always right, tough questions are not welcome, diminished caregiving, problems are never the fault of the Jezebel-led person, blame is placed on others, fear in the rank and file. When the pressure is on, the Jezebel-led person turns themselves into a victim. Your fear to do something is off the charts.

- If you establish you have a problem, strive to identify who the Jezebel-led person is. Examine all the reasons you are reluctant to confront this person. Have they flattered you, or caused you to feel like you are indebted or obligated to them? Are they able to manipulate you with guilt or emotional outbursts? Have you used them to do things you are uncomfortable doing, like disciplining or firing people? Are they blackmailing you because of a sexual encounter?
- Once you are certain you know who the Jezebel-led person is, recruit a small team of trustworthy leaders who will walk and pray with you in this battle. Seek the counsel of someone you trust who holds a similar job title as you and works in a different organization.
- Create a plan for how you will confront the Jezebel-led person, and lay out the evidence in an easy-to-follow format. Decide who will join you in the confrontation, making sure that person is loyal to you. It will be helpful to have decided in advance the consequences for their abusive actions. In the midst of your confrontation, do not waver from those consequences, even if they try to manipulate you with guilt or shame.
- If you fire the Jezebel-led person, go after the best replacement you can find to replace their position.

My experiences and conversations with hundreds of leaders of churches and nonprofits have led me to this premise: When organizations simply tell a Jezebel-led person, "No, you cannot have control," they will generally leave the organization. And when leadership allows them to stay in positions of control, the whole organization will suffer and quite possibly cease to exist after a lengthy time of suffering and turmoil.

Caution – God has created men and women who have been gifted with leadership. We must understand that there are those who take charge, make decisions, and are quite capable of leading others. When these folks make a final decision that goes against what you had hoped for, it does not mean they are influenced by a Jezebel spirit. This book is not about chasing away good and strong leaders from our organizations. We need them. Somebody has to make the final decisions on very important matters. Many of God's chosen leaders have been given a godly vision for the future. This book is not intended to diminish their role as leader. It is not my intent to get people all fired up and on a mission to remove strong leaders who are doing a great job. But spiritually abusive leaders are an entirely different story. This book has attempted to lay out a clear case for the abusive patterns of Jezebel-led individuals. Look for those repeated patterns so you can remove the virus from your organization. Isolated incidents that very rarely occur do not constitute a pattern of abuse.

For those of you who have tried to point out the destructive patterns of control and abuse to the leadership team, and as a result, you have been rejected and ostracized, only time will tell the final story. By leaving quietly, or staying and silently letting the situation play out, you may be inappropriately blamed for Jezebel's failures. But leaving quietly and not causing any troubles will place the burden on the back of the Jezebel-led person.

They may cry out and call on people to feel sorry for them. They may take on the role of victim, and blame everyone else for their failures. But after a while, they will run out of people to blame, and they will continue in their downward trends. The controlling toxic environment will eventually catch up to them. At some point, people will begin to see the same patterns replaying over and over, and the dysfunctional Jezebel leader will be exposed.

For those who have been chased away by what you believed to be a Jezebel-led environment, there is always a chance that you were wrong and that you misjudged the situation. Time will reveal the truth. If you were wrong, the organization will flourish. If you were right, the truth will be exposed. The Jezebel environment will become increasingly toxic over the course of time and the organization will experience devastating losses. Please don't relish the destruction of an organization so you can be proven right. Place the whole matter into the hands of God and let Him be the final Arbiter and Judge.

Having experienced what it is like to work in a Jezebel-led environment multiple times in my life, I know the hopelessness that can invade your mind. I have been one of the helpless team members who didn't have the authority to do anything about it, and I have been the leader who was forced to remove the Jezebel-led person from the team. Both situations were difficult in different ways. Much of this book has been about tough situations that sometimes seem to have little-to-no hope. Writing about the Jezebel spirit has not been an easy task. It's hard to write a book that exposes the truth about the Jezebel spirit and stay positive, especially when it is devastating our churches and our lives.

When we are in the middle of a Jezebel-led environment it is very difficult to look beyond our own situation. We get overwhelmed with frustration, and covered by a hopelessness that blocks our ability to see life outside of our organization. Having lived in, and having talked with those who have lived in a Jezebel environment, I am very aware of the oppressive gloom that presses in from all sides. It is suffocating and dark. At times, the hopeless despair seems to invade every area of our lives. The heaviness presses in and casts a dark shadow on everything we do. Sometimes, when we are living in a Jezebel-led environment, we feel like our hope is gone. It's hard not to see everything in our life through that twisted lens of hopelessness, and we can become blind to the good that God is doing all around us.

We can get so focused on the Jezebel-led environment that we fall for the lie that God has abandoned us. He has not abandoned us. Nor is He pleased with the spiritual abuse that is occurring. In Psalm 94:20, (NLT) we find these words: *"Can unjust leaders claim that God is on their side—leaders whose decrees permit injustice?"* Be careful not to misread the heart of God. Jezebel-led people remaining in a position of power does not constitute God's blessing. If an organization that has a long history of success is suddenly declining under a Jezebel-led leadership team, it may be that God has already withdrawn His anointing. It's not much different than how He deals with us as individuals. If we want to live life doing things our way instead of His, He gives us the freedom to do so. When things fall apart, there are consequences. Just because Jezebel-led people are able to remain in charge, and are able to paint a rosy picture covering up their failures, doesn't mean that God is affirming their abuse and has abandoned you. He sees your pain, and He knows what you have endured.

Jezebel's attempt to convince you that God has abandoned you is to discourage you. It does this by getting you to focus on the false perception of success being proclaimed by the Jezebel-led leader. Even when the organization is crumbling, Jezebel-led leaders have a way of looking confident and rewriting history. When we fall for the lie that God has abandoned us and is pleased with those causing spiritual abuse, our remaining hope slips away. Don't fall for the demonic ruse. It's simply an attempt to drive you out of ministry and deeply undermine your faith. We must trust in the unchanging character of God. He is not a God of abuse. He is not a God of lies. He is not a God of pride. In Psalm 9:9-10 we read these words: *"The LORD is a refuge for the oppressed, a stronghold in times of trouble. Those who know your name will trust in you, for you, LORD, have never forsaken those who seek you."*

If you are living in this shortsighted place where there seems to be no hope, I want you to know there is life beyond the walls of your environment. I can tell you this because I have broken free from some of those situations. There is hope all around you even if it is not readily seen in your Jezebel-controlled situation. God has not turned His back on you! He is not angry with you. And, He is not blind to what is happening to you. The psalmist tells us that He does hear your cries for help: *"The righteous cry out, and the LORD hears them; He delivers them from all their troubles"* (Psalm 34:17). *"For the LORD will vindicate his people and have compassion on his servants"* (Psalm 135:14).

Vindicate means "to free from allegation or blame." In other words, God will exonerate you from all the blame you have endured at the hands of abusive leaders. All of Jezebel's destructive ways will eventually be revealed. Do not give up hope. Growth seldom happens in toxic environments. All the pretending that everything is good will be exposed. When good people continue to leave and funding dries up, a time will come when a reckoning takes place. All the hidden dysfunction will be uncovered, or the Jezebel-led leaders will leave before they can be blamed. Either way, the abusive leadership structure will come to an end and a new leadership team can be put in place. The timing of everything may very well be linked to the severity of the consequences and backlash brought forth by the Jezebel-led leader's bad decisions and behavior.

Our hope is in the Lord. He is way bigger than any person or demonic spirit. For eternal reasons we will never understand, He may delay removing a Jezebel-led person or team. In the meantime, He will give you the grace to stay, or He will bless your decision to leave. Either way, God is God and He doesn't change. Psalm 130:7-8 assures us that His great love for us shines like a beacon of hope: *"O Israel, put your hope in the Lord, for with the Lord is unfailing love and with him is full redemption. He himself will redeem Israel from all their sins."*

When hope seems lost, look around you. The sun will come up tomorrow morning. God's love for you is unfailing. There are people around you who love you and believe in you. If Christ is your Savior, your sins are forgiven and you have the promise of eternal life. Remember, God has given you free will. You have the right to make your own choices. Hope is knowing you do not have to stay in an oppressive environment. Hope dwells in the air of every breeze, every flower, and every tree. Hope can be found in God's Word and in the midst of heartfelt prayer. Hope is on the faces of children, and in beautiful sunsets. Hope is everywhere if we will just take the time to look. God has not abandoned you in your suffering.

In Psalm 56:8-11 (ESV) we read these words of God's infinite care for us:

> *You have kept count of my tossings; put my tears in your bottle. Are they not in your book? Then my enemies will turn back in the day when I call. This I know, that God is for me. In God, whose word I praise, in the Lord, whose word I praise, in God I trust; I shall not be afraid. What can man do to me?*

Our God records our tossings (sorrows) in the night, and captures our tears in a bottle. Nothing is hidden from His sight.

Our sufferings do not go unnoticed. You have not been abandoned. He cares deeply for you! You can trust in His goodness.

I want to leave you with these words of hope found in 1 Peter 4:19–5:1-6:

> *So then, those who suffer according to God's will should commit themselves to their faithful Creator and continue to do good. To the elders among you, I appeal as a fellow elder, a witness of Christ's sufferings and one who also will share in the glory to be revealed: Be shepherds of God's flock that is under your care, serving as overseers—not because you must, but because you are willing, as God wants you to be; not greedy for money, but eager to serve; not lording it over those entrusted to you, but being examples to the flock. And when the Chief Shepherd appears, you will receive a crown of glory that will never fade away. Young men, in the same way be submissive to those who are older. All of you, clothe yourselves with humility toward one another, because, "God opposes the proud but gives grace to the humble." Humble yourselves, therefore, under God's mighty hand, that he may lift you up in due time.*

Final prayer – Lord, may all who read this book, and find themselves in the midst of a Jezebel-led environment, know that they are loved. Give them wisdom and courage. The wisdom to know what to do, and the courage to do what they know. Give them strength and endurance to accomplish your calling in their lives. Renew their hope in a hopeless setting. Remind them daily that you have not abandoned them, but as they walk in humility, you will lift them up in due time. May your peace and strength abide upon them now and forever. Amen.

Bibliography

Deere, Jack. *Surprised by the Power of the Spirit.* Grand Rapids, MI: Zondervan, 1993.

Edwards, Gene. *A Tale of Three Kings.* Carol Stream, IL: Tyndale House, 1992.

Ferguson, Dave and Bird, Warren. *Hero Maker.* Grand Rapids, MI: Zondervan 2018.

Foster, Richard J. *Prayer: Finding the Heart's True Home.* New York, NY: HarperCollins Publishers, 1992.

Frangipane, Francis. *The Jezebel Spirit.* Cedar Rapids, IA: Arrow Publications, 1991.

Freed, Sandie. *The Jezebel Yoke.* Bloomington MN: Chosen Books, 2012.

Howard, Tim *Understanding the Gift of Discernment in Children.* Rock Island IL: Wellsprings of Freedom, 2017.

Jackson, John Paul. *Unmasking the Jezebel Spirit.* North Sutton, NH: Streams Publications, 2002.

Johnson, David and VanVonderen, Jeff. *The Subtle Power of Spiritual Abuse.* Minneapolis, MN: Bethany House Publishers, 1991

Jones, Alfred. *Jones' Dictionary of Old Testament Proper Names.* Grand Rapids MI: Kregel Publications, 1997.

Kraft, Charles and DeBord, David. *The Rules of Engagement.* Eugene, OR: Wipf and Stock Publishers, 2000.

Maxwell, John C. *Developing The Leader Within You.* Nashville TN: Thomas Nelson, Inc., 1993.

Maxwell, John C. *The Right to Lead.* Nashville TN: J. Countryman, a division of Thomas Nelson Inc., 2001.

Sampson, Steve. *Discerning and Defeating the Ahab Spirit.* Grand Rapids, MI: Chosen Books, 2010.